THE TROMBONE
Its History and Music, 1697–1811

MUSICOLOGY: A BOOK SERIES
Edited by F. Joseph Smith

Additional volumes in preparation

THE TROMBONE
Its History and Music, 1697–1811

David M. Guion

Gordon and Breach
New York London Paris Montreux Tokyo Melbourne

© 1988 by OPA (Amsterdam) B.V. All rights reserved. Published under license by Gordon and Breach Science Publishers S.A.

Gordon and Breach Science Publishers

Post Office Box 786
Cooper Station
New York, New York 10276
United States of America

Post Office Box 197
London WC2E 9PX
England

58, rue Lhomond
75005 Paris
France

Post Office Box 161
1820 Montreux 2
Switzerland

3-14-9, Okubo
Shinjuku-ku, Tokyo
Japan

Private Bag 8
Camberwell, Victoria 3124
Australia

Library of Congress Cataloging-in-Publication Data
Guion, David M., 1948–
   The trombone: its history and music, 1697–1811
   (Musicology series, ISSN 0275-5866; v. 6)
   Bibliography: p.
   1. Trombone. 2. Trombone music—History and
criticism. I. Title. II. Series.
   ML965.G84 1988   788'.2'09033   87-19678
   ISBN 2-88124-211-1

61,922

CONTENTS

v

CONTENTS

INTRODUCTION TO THE SERIES

The Gordon and Breach *Musicology* series, a companion to the *Journal of Musicological Research,* covers a creative range of musical topics, from historical and theoretical subjects to social and philosophical studies. Volumes thus far published show the extent of this broad spectrum, from *Music and Its Social Meanings* to *Late Renaissance Music at the Habsburg Court* to the present volume, *The Trombone: Its History and Music 1697–1811.* Forthcoming titles will include works on musical biography, the music of Stravinsky and Mendelssohn, and a musical *festschrift* honoring Gwynn S. McPeek. The editors also welcome interdisciplinary studies, ethnomusicological works and performance analyses. With this series, it is our aim to expand the field and definition of musical exploration and research.

ACKNOWLEDGMENTS AND NOTES
ABOUT THE PLATES

This volume is based on my doctoral work at the University of Iowa, although much new information has been added to it. I would like to thank Dr. Frederick Crane, my advisor, and the rest of my committee for their help. While at Iowa, it was my privilege to serve as Dr. Rita Benton's research assistant for more than three years. No young scholar could ask for a better introduction to the craft of musicological research. No other single individual has had more influence on the course of my research, even though she died when work on this project was barely started. Most of the research was done at the Newberry Library in Chicago, where I have always found the staff cheerful and helpful.

I am grateful to Miss Tineke Schouten, who translated the Dutch article for me, to Sister Baptist Stohrer of Rosary College for her help with some Latin passages, and especially to Mr. Matthew Heintzelman of the University of Chicago, who translated most of the German articles in Chapter 2. Dr. Bertil van Boer of Wichita State University wrote to me several times about Swedish trombone parts while he finished his own doctoral work. Dr. Henry Howey of Sam Houston State University has made numerous helpful comments in conversation and graciously allowed me to quote at length from his doctoral essay. And just when I thought I had finished writing, I learned of the recent work of Dr. Trevor Herbert of the Open University in Wales. I am grateful for his assistance in obtaining it.

The musical examples in Chapter 2 are from photographs of the original

xi

editions of the works they come from. These were made from books and microfilms from the libraries of the University of Chicago and the University of Iowa. Examples from Bach *Neue Ausgabe sämtlicher Werke*, Fux *Sämtliche Werke*, Gluck *Sämtliche Werke*, *Hallische-Händel Ausgabe*, and *Neue Mozart Ausgabe* are used with the permission of Bärenreiter Verlag. Examples from *Haydns Werke* and Salieri's *Tarare* are used with the permission of G. Henle Verlag. Henle's new collected edition of Beethoven's works does not yet include any of the music cited here, so for the oratorio, I used the old Breitkopf & Härtel set, and for the symphonies, Eulenberg pocket scores. Eggert's symphony is from *The Symphony, 1720–1840*, a series edited by Dr. Barry S. Brook and used with the kind permission of Garland Publishing, 136 Madison Avenue, New York, NY 10036. My thanks also to Dr. David Swanzy of Loyola University (New Orleans) and Dr. W. Sherwood Dudley of the University of California, Santa Cruz for their permission to use the examples in Chapter 8, which all come from their dissertations. All of the other examples are from scores owned by the Newberry Library, except for the Pleyel symphonies, which are from Dr. Rita Benton's microfilm.

Special thanks goes to Mr. Stephen Glover, editor of The Brass Press in Nashville, TN, and Dr. Tom L. Naylor, editor of The Brass Press's spectacular publication *The Trumpet & Trombone in Graphic Arts, 1500–1800*. More than half of the plates I have used come from this book, which is truly one of the treasures of my library.

Four of the last five plates have captions. Here are notes and Naylor's translations:

Plate 16: one of 36 copper engravings comprising Johann Christoph Weigel's *Musicalisches Theatrum* (ca. 1722)

Trombone

I am searching for glory in every place,
In antiquity, as well as in effect,
One can see what I can do in both Testaments,
I destroyed walls when spoken to in a proper manner,
No offering or feast could be properly conducted without me,
And nowadays I adorn a large instrumental choir.

Plate 17: An anonymous eighteenth-century Dutch etching.

I have to bend down, holding my instrument of pipes, so as
to direct it so it will give a sound.
Look how my club hangs from my body, as a result of my
movements.
Hear my bells ring. I blow the zink and make it sound dis-
tinguished.

With it I can easily cure the sick.
Though I can lower and raise the sound, my lungs remain
full of air, and my pocket remains empty.

Plate 18: "Thaleia—Muse of Comic Poetry," a seventeenth-century engraving, although the trombone looks more modern than the one in Plate 16.

Thaleia
If our story is great, or if it is a comedy of life,
Our story, even after it has been told does not satisfy God;
It does not create the eternal well-being which pleases us;
And expressed it does not include the praises of God.

Plate 19: "The Hearing," a copperplate engraving from Anton Joseph von Prenner's collection *Theatrum artis pictoriae* (1735), after an oil painting by Jan Breughel the Elder (1568–1625).

Plate 20: One of a series of five engravings of musical instruments by Martin Engelbrecht (1684–1756).

Trumpets, Kettledrums, and Trombones
Here one demonstrates music for devotion, pleasure and
*   dancing;*
For various types of musical instruments.
When one hears boom boom boom tra-ra-ra
and that tra-ra tan-ta-ra boom boom resounds,
then life begins to swell in one's body,
Joy penetrates to the heart through the ear.
Music about men and horses
can only be satisfied by fighting.
Trumpets, timpani, muskets, Barthaune!
They make the right sound together.
On the other hand, zinken and trombones
are needed always in peacetime,
as well as in sorrow and times of joy
whenever music is well presented.

Plates 1 and 15 come from *Encyclopedie de la musique et dictionnaire du Conservatoire,* which unfortunately does not identify the sources. The rest of the plates are from works cited in the text, and so require no comment.

LIST OF PLATES

LIST OF MUSICAL EXAMPLES

CHAPTER 1

THE TROMBONE AND ITS MUSIC IN THE SEVENTEENTH AND NINETEENTH CENTURIES: AN INTRODUCTION

Most standard reference works on musical instruments have little or nothing to say about the trombone in the eighteenth century. Perhaps the explanation for this neglect lies in the fact that the use of the trombone was at once less extensive and less conspicuous than in either the seventeenth or nineteenth centuries. Unfortunately, the omission gives two false impressions: that the trombone was not used in a musically important way in the eighteenth century, and that there were no important changes in its appearance, reputation, function, or repertoire. In fact, all of these aspects changed greatly by the end of the century, and nearly every important composer called for trombone at least occasionally.

Two treatises flank this period and serve to show how extensive the changes were. Daniel Speer's *Grund-richtiger ... Unterricht der musicalischen Kunst* (1687, revised 1697) represents the culmination of Baroque thought about the trombone. Joseph Frölich's *Vollständige theoretisch-pracktische Musikschule* (1811) includes the first modern description of the trombone. The pertinent sections of these two treatises, along with important documents in between, are reproduced, with translation, in Chapter 2.

1

THE SEVENTEENTH CENTURY

The Instrument

Speer describes a trombone with four diatonically numbered positions, rather than the seven chromatically numbered ones in modern descriptions. In the first, "near the mouthpiece," A_1, A, e, a, e', g', and a'' can be played. Speer also considers c' as a first-position note, but writes that the slide must be extended two *Querfinger*. See pp. 15–16 for an explanation of this term.

   In second position, Speer gives G, d, g, b, and d', b^b, being available with the slide extended as for c'. Speer gives only F, c, and f in third position; and E, B, and B^b in fourth. Once again the slide must be extended to play B^b. Speer's first position is in the same place as the modern first position. The extended position for c' matches the modern second. Therefore, Speer's second position corresponds to modern third, with an extension to modern fourth. His third position is modern fifth position. He gives no extension for this one because his fourth position is only a semitone lower, or modern sixth. The extended position for playing B^b, then, is the same as the modern seventh position. Therefore, Speer describes a tenor trombone in A, not in B^b like modern tenor trombones. Following the same reasoning, it can be seen that his alto and bass trombones are in d and D respectively. Speer's description matches earlier ones by Michael Praetorius and Aurelio Virgiliano.[1]

   Of the three standard sizes of trombones (alto, tenor, and bass), the tenor was the most important in the seventeenth century, as it is now. Physically, the trombone has changed less since the seventeenth century than any other instrument in continuous use, but there are some important differences. The bell was conical in shape, with very little terminal flare, and much smaller in diameter than the modern bell. The bore was also narrower than on most trombones used today. Baroque trombones had no tuning slide, stockings, or water key. Modern authors disagree about whether the metal used to make them was thicker or thinner than today's standard. Sibyl Marcuse exemplifies the confusion on this point by asserting on one page that early trombones were made with far *thinner* metal than

---

[1] David Guion, "The Pitch of Baroque Trombones." *Journal of the International Trombone Association* 8 (1980), 24–28.

modern ones, and later mentioning *thicker* metal as one reason for the mellower tone of the earlier instruments.[2]

Many modern musicians prefer to use the word "sackbut" when referring to the Baroque trombone. All other instruments in constant use since the Baroque have changed more. The other brass instruments now have valves. (Some trombones have one or two triggers, valves operated with the left thumb, but these are optional features, not a definitive attribute of the modern trombone.) Woodwind instruments have many more keys now, and different fingering systems. Stringed instruments have likewise changed. Even violins built in the seventeenth century have been modified with an angling neck and heavier bassboards and soundposts, among other changes. Furthermore, steel strings have replaced gut strings, and the bow has been completely redesigned.

But even though it is the other instruments, and not the trombone, that have changed so much, only the trombone is ever described with a different word for the earlier model. "Sackbut" is merely an old English name that passed out of use when the English stopped using trombones. When, in the late eighteenth century, the instrument returned to English musical life, it had hardly changed at all, but Italian musical terminology was so influential that it became known by its Italian name, trombone, rather than its English name. In response to the number of times people, including musicians, have asked if the sackbut is something like a trombone, I have stopped using this misleading word.

Most Baroque trombones were made in Germany, but in the early seventeenth century they were used all over Europe. Most of the surviving music is from Italy, England, and various German-speaking areas. Apart from a few operas, notably Claudio Monteverdi's *Orfeo* (1607) and Marc' Antonio Cesti's *Il pomo d'oro* (1660), most of the music played by trombones was either for church or some civic ceremony.

The Music

Italy

In Italy, large churches like San Marco in Venice often kept trombonists on their regular payroll. Composers who wrote music for

---

[2] Sibyl Marcuse, *A Survey of Musical Instruments* (New York: Harper & Row, 1975), 809, 811.

that church with trombone parts include Giovanni Gabrieli, Claudio Monteverdi, and Dario Castello. Smaller churches hired trombonists for special occasions. Claudio Sartori's bibliography of Italian instrumental music lists at least 102 pieces with trombone parts from at least 46 collections, most of which appeared before 1640.[3] Sartori shows the tables of contents, not all of which mention instruments. In some cases, I know the instrumentation only from another source. There are probably other pieces with trombone parts that Sartori does not identify as such.

In addition to the "orchestra" at San Marco, there were at least seven piffari bands in Venice, which consisted mostly of wind instruments, including trombones.[4] But while Venice seems to have had more trombonists and trombone music than other Italian cities, it was not alone. Among non-Venetian composers named in the title pages transcribed by Sartori are Giovanni Paolo Cima of Milan, Adriano Banchieri of Bologna, and Carlo Milanuzzi of Verona. (The piece with trombone in Milanuzzi's collection is by P. A. Mariani, of whom nothing else is known. Perhaps he was a student of Milanuzzi's who died young.)

The high point in the publication of trombone music was reached in the 1620s. By 1640, it had slowed to a trickle. San Marco kept a trombonist on its payroll until 1732,[5] but the trombone may well have disappeared from other churches even earlier.

Austria and Germany

Economic hard times in the middle and late seventeenth century forced many Italian composers to look outside of Italy for patronage. A significant number worked at the court of the Austrian Emperor Ferdinand III, who reigned from 1637 to 1657. Ferdinand was not only an enthusiastic supporter of Italian music, but also an amateur composer, who used trombones in his own compositions. Brass instruments never fell out of favor in Austria. Therefore, just as the

---

[3] Claudio Sartori. *Bibliografia della musica strumentale italiana stampata in Italia fino al 1700* (2 vols. Florence: Olschki, 1952, 1968).

[4] Eleanor Selfridge-Field. *Venetian Instrumental Music from Gabrieli to Vivaldi* (New York: Praeger, 1975), 14.

[5] Ibid., 21.

Plate 1. A 17th-Century Wind Band from the Low Countries.

trombone was beginning to disappear from Italian music, a remark-able series of pieces with trombone parts began to appear in Austria and continued into the nineteenth century.

As in Italy, most of this music was for the church. It included music for chorus and orchestra, solo voices and small instrumental ensemble, and instrumental ensemble without voices. The trombone was used both as a doubling instrument and as a soloist. Notable Italian composers who wrote trombone music for the Habsburg court include Antonio Bertali and Marc' Antonio Ziani. Among the composers native to the Austrian Empire were Heinrich Biber, Johann Schmeltzer, Pavel Vejvanowsky, and the emperors Ferdinand III, and Leopold I, and Joseph I.

The various German states also used the trombone extensively. Heinrich Schütz wrote much of the best trombone music of the seventeenth, or any, century. His contemporaries and followers who wrote for trombone include Andreas Hammerschmidt, Matthias

Weckmann, Johann Erasmus Kindermann, and Johann Rudolph
Ahle.

Cities, as well as churches, hired musicians to perform at civic
ceremonies. In fact, both church and court hired the town band for
their own special needs. Because of its association with official
pomp and splendor, as well as its religious connotations, brass music
had higher social standing than string music, which was associated
with dancing and secular celebration.[6] Although the town-band
movement has attracted considerable scholarly attention, we will
probably never know as much as we would like about it; bandsmen
jealously guarded the secrets of their craft. The best known of these
bands, in modern times anyway, was in Leipzig. Publications of two
of its members, Johann Pezel and Gottfried Reiche, constitute the
bulk of what we know about the band repertoire. These collections
call for one or two cornetts and three trombones.

Other countries

The English court maintained a similar band throughout most of the
seventeenth century. The most important music for it was written by
Matthew Locke and John Adson. But unlike the Germans, who
used the trombone throughout the eighteenth century, the English
stopped using it in favor of the bassoon during the reign of Charles
II (1660–1685).[7]

At least one composer in the Low Countries, Nicolas a Kempis
of Brussels, wrote music with trombone parts. Flemish cities had a
long tradition of town bands dating back to the Middle Ages.

I have found no reference to French music for trombone in the
seventeenth century. Marin Mersenne, however, mentions the instrument and expresses his preference of playing style in *Harmonie
universelle* (1636), and there was at least one trombone maker,
Pierre Colbert, in Rheims in the late sixteenth century. Pictorial
evidence from the time of Louis XIV clearly shows the trombone as

---

[6] James Albert Wattenbarger, *The Turmmusik of Johann Pezel* (Ph. D.
dissertation: Northwestern University, 1957), 56.

[7] Anthony Baines, "James Talbot's Manuscript (Christ Church Library
Music MS 1187). I. Wind Instruments," *The Galpin Society Journal* 1
(1948), 19.

a member of a wind ensemble.[8] (See Plate 15.) Apparently, the French used it only as a doubling instrument or bass instrument.

THE NINETEENTH CENTURY

Hardly any of the statements I have made about the trombone in the seventeenth century are also true of the instrument in the nineteenth century. Two important changes can be seen from a mere glance at Fröhlich's treatise. First, the trombone is described as having seven chromatic positions instead of four diatonic ones. Second, it is no longer in A, but in B^b.

Treatises continue to be an important source of information. Books that describe instruments in a general way continued to be written, but the nineteenth century saw the rise of a new kind of publication: orchestration manuals such as Hector Berlioz's *Grand traité d'instrumentation et d'orchestration modernes* (1843). Another important feature of nineteenth-century music that, as far as the trombone is concerned, has no parallel in the seventeenth or eighteenth centuries is the explosion of instructional material, including etudes by Edmond Vobaron, Antoine Dieppo, O. Blume, Friedrich Belcke, C. Kopprasch, and J. Friedheim, some of which are still in use today.

The Instrument

It is less easy to describe the physical appearance of the trombone in the nineteenth century than in the seventeenth century: and not because it had changed so much. Actually, it had changed less than any other instrument that was still in use. Various experiments with valves and the shape and direction of the bell need not concern us here. Except for the trigger, none has found permanent acceptance. The difficulty of describing the nineteenth-century trombone results

---

[8] M.A. Soyer. "De l'orchestration militaire et de son histoire," *Encyclopédie de la musique et dictionnaire du Conservatoire.* pt. 2: *Technique--Esthétique--Practique* vol. 4: *Orchestration--Musique liturgique des différents cults,* ed. Albert Lavignac and Lionel de Laurencie. (Paris: Delagrave, 1929), 2143.

from the fact that it was no longer so nearly an exclusively German product. Trombones were made all over the Western world, and each nation had its own ideal; about the only universally adopted innovation was the flaring bell, a change that took place in the middle of the eighteenth century.[9]

In Germany, the traditional trio of alto, tenor, and bass trombones (in e^b, B^b, and E^b or F respectively) persisted at least nominally throughout most of the century. The bores of German trombones became larger than was customary elsewhere. When fitted with a large mouthpiece, the tenor trombone often replaced the bass trombone. When such an instrument was fitted with a trigger, it was called a tenor-bass trombone. The alto trombone was largely abandoned by the end of the century, although it persisted in Germany longer than elsewhere.

The tenor trombone quickly supplanted both the alto and the bass trombones in France. The bore of French trombones remained narrow, but started to widen at the tuning slide, ending, as everywhere else, in a flaring bell. According to Anthony Baines, this earlier widening of the bore enabled these instruments to produce adequate low notes.[10]

In England, French-style narrow-bone tenor trombones were used for the upper two parts in bands and orchestras, but the lower part was played on a bass trombone in G. While having a wider bore than the tenors, this instrument was very narrow for a bass trombone. It was so difficult to achieve a good blending tone quality on it that Anthony Baines felt it necessary to single out one twentieth-century player, William Coleman, who could do it.[11] These bass trombones were sometimes equipped with a trigger in D, which enabled them to produce notes in the contrabass trombone register.

The Music

Trombones were still used in church music in the nineteenth century, but they were not nearly so restricted to it as they had been in the

---

[9] Philip Bate, *The Trumpet and Trombone: An Outline of Their History, Development and Construction*, 2nd ed. (London: Benn; New York: Norton 1978), 147.

[10] Anthony Baines, *Brass Instruments: Their History and Development* (New York: Scribner, 1978), 243.

[11] Ibid., 245.

seventeenth century. They took part in high culture (symphonic music and opera), middle culture (dance orchestras and military bands), and low culture (oom-pah bands). They even served as virtuoso display instruments. Many flashy trombone solos were written in the nineteenth century. In short, trombones were used in every kind of instrumental music except chamber music. But no nineteenth-century piece that is performable on a trombone recital is worthy of comparison with the music of Gabrieli, Schütz, or even many minor composers of the Baroque. Except as an orchestral instrument, the trombone no longer attracted the attention of the best composers.

Clearly, many changes in the trombone's role took place during the eighteenth century. Therefore, it is a mistake to ignore this period in histories of the trombone. The pages that follow will account for many of the changes. Alas, this book cannot be what I initially intended. Too many reference tools essential to my original conception are either inadequate or simply do not exist. For example, descriptions of trombones in catalogs of musical instrument collections are not sufficiently detailed to allow adequate documentation of the trombone's structural changes over the course of the eighteenth century. Many thematic catalogs and other lists of music do not give instrumentation. Those that do so for smaller works often omit the instrumentation of larger works like operas and oratorios. Many make no attempt to date the works.

In addition to the deficiencies of existing reference materials, much of the music remains unpublished, and therefore unavailable for perusal without extensive European travel. There are, therefore, serious but unavoidable gaps in what follows. Besides music made available in the various historical sets and collected works, nearly everything available to me was published in France. For this reason, I may give French music relatively more emphasis than it deserves. Nevertheless, it seems worthwhile to offer a broad overview rather than a more specialized study. In this way, the gaps at least become more obvious than they would otherwise be.

CHAPTER 2

WRITINGS ABOUT THE TROMBONE IN EIGHTEENTH-CENTURY TREATISES, ENCYCLOPEDIAS, AND DICTIONARIES

Throughout the eighteenth century, musicians wrote descriptions of the trombone. None wrote in sufficient detail that a history of the trombone in the eighteenth century could be written on the basis of these writings alone, but they are nonetheless an invaluable source of information. Every work cited by later writers, including later eighteenth-century writers, has been sought for inclusion in this chapter. Inevitably, some important documents are lacking.

Two authors, Haider and Braun, are cited in two of the articles given here, those of Christian Schubart and Joseph Fröhlich, respectively. (See pages 83 and 92.) I have found no other reference to anyone named Haider (or Hayder or Heider or Heyder). Robert MacDonald mentions a trombone method by Andre Braun[1], which is probably the same one cited by Fröhlich. Ottmar Schreiber cites *Beschreibung einer Reise durch Deutschland und die Schweiz* by Christoph Friedrich Nicolai.[2] This important travel diary was published in 12 volumes. Unfortunately Schreiber's documentation is

---

[1] Robert James MacDonald, *François-Joseph Gossec and French Instrumental Music in the Second Half of the Eighteenth Century*, 3 vols. (Ph.D. dissertation: University of Michigan, 1968), vol. 1, 345, n. 505.
[2] Ottmar Schreiber, *Orchester und Orchesterpraxis in Deutschland zwischen 1780 und 1850* (Berlin: Junker und Dünnhaupt, 1938), 139.

11

not sufficiently detailed for me to locate the passage he refers to.

Most, if not all, of the articles given here are based at least to some degree on earlier writings. Often these are cited in sufficient detail that no comment is necessary. In some cases, no citation is given at all, but a word-for-word copying of an earlier article betrays the source. Such instances are noted in the commentary about each article. Sometimes a citation is given in such a way that it is not possible to identify the source.

Of the articles given here, those of Daniel Speer, Sébastien de Brossard, and Friedrich Erhard Niedt are cited by later articles in this chapter. Those of Brossard, Johann Mattheson, Niedt, Filippo Bonanni, Ephraim Chambers, Giovanni Battista Martini, and Jean-Benjamin de la Borde are copied by later authors, in whole or in part, without attribution.

With one exception, the following articles are presented in order of publication. In the case of multivolume works that appeared over several years, the date given is that of whatever volume includes the article(s) on the trombone. In this way, a progression from the earliest-written (Speer) to the latest (Fröhlich) can be shown. Three of these articles were published posthumously: those of Niedt, Schubart, and Charles Burney. Burney's article, written about 1805, did not appear until 1819, eight years after the publication of Fröhlich's treatise. I have reversed the order of these two treatises in this chapter.

All capitalization, spelling, and punctuation are given exactly as printed, except that in some of the earlier German works I have substituted the comma for the virgule (/). I have had to supply paragraph breaks, especially in Zedler's *Universal-Lexicon*. I have not been able to duplicate the German method of indicating different octaves, printing one or two straight lines above the note names. Instead, I have used the apostrophe or quotation mark. This substitution should cause no confusion as it results in exactly the same designation of octaves that I have used throughout the dissertation. In cases where the author does not specify different octaves, I have not attempted to straighten it out. Most of the time, the author's intentions are fairly obvious. In other cases, it seems best to leave the ambiguity in the translation. As some of the spelling and capitalization in the originals are strange to modern eyes, and in some cases wrong even by eighteenth-century standards, this paragraph can be taken as a general-purpose "sic."

DANIEL SPEER

Grund-richtiger ... Unterricht der musicalischen Kunst[3]

(1697)

Daniel Speer was a prolific composer and author whose political tracts attracted enough attention to earn him a year and a half in prison. His writings on music provide a gold mine of information about middle Baroque theory and practice. His article on the trombone summarizes and expands important earlier writings on the instrument, and thus serves as the culmination of early and middle Baroque writing about it. It also exerted tremendous influence, directly or indirectly, on nearly all German writers about the trombone for more than a hundred years.

Speer first issued his musical treatise in 1687 with the title *Grundrichtiger kurtz- leicht- und nöthiger Unterricht der musicalischen Kunst (A Fundamental, Short, Easy, and Necessary Introduction to the Art of Music)*. Ten years later, he brought out a second, greatly expanded edition. The major changes in content were the increase in the coverage of keyboard instruments from a brief article of 10 pages *in octavo* to a major section of 150 pages *in quarto*, and the inclusion of musical examples to illustrate the correct way to compose for the various stringed and wind instruments. Speer also substituted fingering charts for the verbal descriptions in the first edition.[4]

The middle Baroque was an age of wordy and pompous treatises. Although Speer himself claimed to despise the fancy, high-flown style of his contemporaries,[5] he provided a title for his second edition even more pretensious than that of the first: *Grund-richtiger*

---

[3] Daniel Speer, *Grund-richtiger, kurtz- leicht- und nöthiger, jetzt wolvermehrter Unterricht der musicalischen Kunst* (Ulm: Georg Wilhelm Kühnen, 1697), 221-24.

[4] Henry Eugene Howey, *A Comprehensive Performance Project in Trombone Literature with an Essay Consisting of a Translation of Daniel Speer's "Vierfaches musikalisches Kleeblatt" (Ulm 1697)* (D.M.A. Essay: University of Iowa, 1971), xiii, xiv; Rosemary Roberts, "Speer, Daniel," *The New Grove*, vol. 17, 822.

[5] Ibid., xvii–xviii, 248–49.

kurtz- leicht- und nöthiger jetzt wol-vermehrte Unterricht der Musi-calischen kunst oder Vierfaches musicalisches Kleeblatt (*A Funda-mental, Short, Easy, Necessary, Now Greatly Enlarged Introduction to the Art of Music, or, A Fourfold Musical Cloverleaf.*) Speer must have either loved extravagant titles or enjoyed poking fun at them. He subtitled one of his musical collections *Neue gebacken Tafel-schnitz*, or, *Newly Baked Table Scraps*. The cloverleaf imagery in the title of Speer's second edition continues throughout the treatise. Each major section (on rudiments, keyboard instruments, wind and string instruments, and composition) is called a cloverleaf.

Although Speer, as a literary man, must have read widely and known the writings of such illustrious predecessors as Praetorius, his own work is based on his wide and varied experience as a musician. Especially early in his career, Speer was restless and moved fre-quently. He served as a *Stadtpfeifer* in Stuttgart for a while in the 1660s. At the time of publication of both editions of his *Grundrich-tiger ... Unterricht*, he was a school teacher and cantor at Göppingen, although he spent five of the intervening years first in prison and then more or less in exile.

One reason that the trombone was not described more frequently in the Baroque era is that the local musicians' guilds attempted to keep the playing of wind and stringed instruments a trade secret. Apparently, a significant number of professional musicians feared that if books offered instruction in playing technique, too many people would begin to play instruments and guild members would lose their livelihood.

Therefore, Speer found it necessary to open his third cloverleaf with a defense for his decision to write and publish. He claims that having such a book would save the *Stadtpfeifer* and their students considerable trouble, pointed out that not everyone who would read it would have the aptitude to play the instruments, and that, in any case, no one could learn to play from a book without the guidance of a teacher.[6]

Speer's treatise, therefore, unlike any other work given in this chapter until Fröhlich's, was written largely for students and teachers, not primarily for scholars, composers, interested amateurs, or curious lay people. For this reason, Speer's description is more detailed than any other until Fröhlich's.

---

[6] Ibid., 139–40.

It has already been explained in Chapter 1 how Speer's explanation of the slide positions points to a tenor trombone in A. One typographical error needs to be pointed out. Speer gives the seventh note from the bottom in first position as *g#'*, which is impossible. the note could possibly be *f#'*, which is the seventh partial in what modern trombonists consider a very sharp second position. Since Speer wrote at about the same time the physics of the overtone series was discovered and more than 20 years before this discovery first appeared in an important work of music theory, he could have just as easily considered *f#'* as being in a very flat first position. In fact, in his explanation of how to play *c'*, he comments that *f#'* can be played in the same place. (Of course, for the note to be in tune, the slide position must be midway between those for *a* and *c'*.) A more likely correction would be to *g'* natural. All the other notes given for the principal positions are diatonic, and *g'* as a first position note would also conform with earlier treatises.[7] In either cases, *g#'* cannot be regarded as a first-position note by any stretch of the imagination, yet the same error was handed down from author to author for more than a hundred years.

Speer's measuring system requires some explanation. He describes the trombone as having four principal positions and three auxiliary ones, which are two *Querfinger* higher or lower than the principal ones. This word has caused much confusion, compounded by the fact that not every author uses it, and usage and available definitions are not consistent. "*Quer*" means transverse, across, oblique, and so the most literal translation would be "two transverse fingers."

If the index finger and the middle finger are extended and spread apart to form a "V", they are transverse to each other, and the distance between the finger tips is approximately the correct distance to move the slide for the interval of a semitone. Henry Howey showed me another method that has the advantage of being more comfortable and less variable in distance. He extended his index finger and his little finger from his fist, measuring across the inner fingers. The outer fingers are thus transverse to the inner ones. In either case, the distance is comparable, about three to three and a half inches.

While these ways of measuring both yield correct distances to

---

[7] David Guion, "The Pitch of Baroque Trombones," *Journal of the International Trombone Association* 8 (1980), 24–26.

interpret what Speer meant, they are not adequate for understanding later authors. Eisel, for example, refers to one *Querfinger* and three *Querfinger* (See page 40.) If the term is to be understood as two fingers in some kind of transverse relationship, Eisel's use of it presents more of a mystery than the sound of one hand clapping. Anthony Baines interprets one *Querfinger* as the width of two fingers.[8] Although this distance is comparable to the other interpretations, it is difficult to see what is transverse about the relationship between the two fingers. At least Baines's interpretation has the advantage of making sense of Eisel's use of the term.

Zedler's *Grosses vollständiges universal-Lexicon* includes an entry for *Querfinger* that, if anything, adds to the confusion. It claims that the term is the smallest unit of the Hebrew measuring system, cites Jeremiah 52:21 as an example, and defines it as "four barley-corns of average size placed side by side."[9] By this definition, two *Querfinger* are only half the distance needed to interpret Speer's use of the term correctly. The scripture it cites seems irrelevant. Luther's translation of that verse includes the phrase "und war vier Finger dicke," ("and was four fingers thick," which is just as the King James Version translates the verse); it does not use *Querfinger*.

Grimm's *Deutsches Wörterbuch* defines *Querfinger* as the width of one finger, the idea evidently being that the measurement goes across the finger.[10] This, too, fails to convey Speer's meaning. It is only half long enough. No modern dictionary I have seen has an entry for *Querfinger*. Good riddance!

Because Speer describes all the instruments in one book, it is necessary to study all of his articles on wind instruments in order to have the fullest possible picture of his ideas on the trombone, especially regarding pedagogical techniques and performance practice. His instructions for forming the embouchure, for example, are included in his description of the trumpet.

One important comment peculiar to the trombone deserves comment: when Speer says that it is better to tongue notes than slur them (see p. 20), he means a glissando rather than what modern trombonists would consider a slur. Anyone who has ever taught

---

[8] Baines, 114
[9] Zedler, vol. 30, 211.
[10] Jacob and Wilhelm Grimm, *Deutsches Wörterbuch* vol. 7 (Leipzig: S. Hirzel, 1889), col. 2359.

young trombonists knows that some hardly use their tongues at all. In Speer's day, when the chance to start learning to play musical instruments was so restricted, and everyone was required to play them all, some professionals, perhaps more comfortable on other instruments, played with the sloppy, lazy articulation that Speer and all competent teachers deplore. The translation below is Henry Howey's.[11] I have not copied his footnotes, but the comments in square brackets (except the last one) are his.

Von Posaunen:	Of Trombones
Wie pflege man eine Posaune zu *tracti*ren?	How is a trombone generally played?
Eine Posaun wird mit Blasen und Zügen *tracti*rt.	A trombone is played by blowing and moving the slide.
Wieviel hat eine Posaune Züg?	How many positions has a trombone?
Der Posaunen fürnehmste Züg seynd in drey Orten, ausser etlichen wenigen so auch sollen beygesetzet werden.	The trombone has three main positions, though a few more should be added.
Weil nun auf einer *Tenor-* Posaun *Alt*, *Tenor* und *Bass* kan geblasen werden, soll solche am ersten beschrieben werden.	Because the alto, tenor, and bass parts can be played on the tenor trombone, it should be described first.
Erstlich ist zu wissen, daß eine Posaun in zwey Theilen bestehet, nemlich im Hauptstuck und in Stangen, welche in einer Scheide stecken, es wird aber das Hauptstuck auf die Stangen eingezäpfft, und mit der linken Hand die gantze Posaun gehalten, welche bräuchliche Haltung der *Informator* seinem Lehrling schon zeigen wird, mit der rechten Hand	One must first know that a trombone has two parts, namely a bell section and a slide which is placed in an outer slide; however, the bell section is joined to the inner slide. The entire trombone is held with the left hand, a useful technique which a teacher will surely show his student. However, the slide is gripped between the fingers of the right hand. It has

---

[11] Howey, 174–78.

aber ergreifft man die Scheide zwischen die Finger; diese hat nun drey vornemliche Züge, der erste Zug ist beym Mundstuck, und bestehet in folgenden Buchstaben, so das beygesetzte Exempel weiset:

three main positions. The first position is next to the mouthpiece and consists of the following notes, which the accompanying example shows:

Ex. 1. Speer: Erster Zug (First Position).

Dieser Buchstaben Thon werden alle im ersten Zug gefunden, ausser, daß das *c.* um zwey quehr Finger etwas vorwarts muß gezogen werden, bey welchem Zuge auf das *f.#.* sich befindet.

These notes are all found in the first position, except that the *c'* must be played two transverse fingers [three inches] further out, in which position the *f#'* is found.

Der ander Zug ist beym Hauptstuck, und befinden sich folgende Buchstaben darinnen, wie zu ersehen:

The second position is next to the bell section and the following notes are found therein:

Example 2. Speer: Anderer Zug (Second Position)

NB. Bey diesem Zug ist zu mercken, daß das *b. mol,* nm [um] zwey quehr Finger hinaußwarts muß gezogen werden.

Note well: the *b*^b must be played about two transverse fingers beyond this position.

Der dritten Zug ist vier quehr Finger außwarts deß Hauptstucks, und hat folgende Buchstaben, wie zu ersehen:

The third position is four transverse fingers [six inches] beyond the bell section and has the following notes:

Example 3. Speer: Dritte Zug (Third Position)

Der vierdte Zug auf einer *Tenor*-Posaun, so man einen *Bass* darauf *tracti*ret, ist so weit draussen, als mans mit dem Arm fast erstrecken kan, und seyn folgender Thon-Buchstaben, wie zu ersehen:

On a tenor trombone the fourth position, in which one plays the bass part, is almost out as far as one's arm can be extended and has the following notes:

Example 4. Speer: [Vierdte Zug] (Fourth Position)

NB. B. mol muß noch um etwas weiters als die fördern zwey Buchstaben *E*. und *H*. gezogen werden.

Note well: The B^b must be played with the slide extended somewhat further beyond the *E* and *B* natural.

Wie werden die *Semitonia* gezogen?

How are the semitones played?

Die harten als mit #. bezeichneten hohen *Semitonia* werden von ihrem natürlichen Thon hineinwarts, die mit *b*. aber bezeichneten nidrigen *Semitonia*,

The hard, sharp-notated semitones are played two transverse fingers [three inches] higher than their natural pitch; but the lower semitones, notated with a flat, must

werden um zwey quehr Finger hinaußwarts gezogen. *NB.* Die Triller werden mit dem Kien, wie fornen bey der Trompeten gedacht worden, gemacht; theils schleiffen auch den Posaunen-Schall mit dem Athem, kommt aber besser herauß und lebhaffter, wann er mit der Zungen fein frisch gestossen wird; die *moderation* im *forte* und *piano* wird durch den starcken und schwachen außlassenden Athem gemacht, wie auf allen blasenden Instrumenten und braucht dieses Instrument keine sonderliche Leibs-Kräfften, sondern es kan ein Knab von acht, neun oder zehen Jahren, schon kecklich, Leibs-Kräffte halber, lernen, sonderheitlich einen *Bass* auf einer *Tenor* Posaune, welcher gar schlechten Wind gebrauchet.

be played two transverse fingers lower. As mentioned with the trumpets, trills are made with the chin. Some slur the trombone's sound with the breath, but it comes out better and livelier when it is cleanly articulated with the tongue. Control in loud and soft [playing] is made with the breath, as in all wind instruments. This instrument requires no special physical vigor. It can be learned quite soundly by a boy eight, nine, or ten years old, because he has enough physical strength to play a tenor trombone-- especially on a bass part, as this requires only a normal amount of air.

Von einer *Alt-* und *Quint*-Posaun.

Alto and Bass Trombones.

Eine *Alt-* und *Quint*-Posaun haben auch drey, und zwar einerley Züge, wieauß beygesetztem Exempel erscheinet:

Alto and bass trombones have the same three positions as the accompanying example brings out:

Example 5. Speer: *Alt-* und *Quint*-Posaunen erster Zug (Alto and Quint Trombone First Position).

Dieser erste in ersehender Buchstaben Zug, ist beym Mundstuck.

The first position consisting of the illustrated notes is next to the mouthpiece.

Example 6. Speer: Anderer Zug (Second Position).

Dieser andere in ersehender Buchstaben Zug, ist beym Hauptstuck.

The second position consisting of the illustrated notes is next to the bell section.

Example 7. Speer: Dritter Zug (Third Position).

Dieser dritte in ersehenden Buchstaben Zug, ist etliche Finger breit vor dem Hauptstuck hinaußwarts.

The third position consisting of the illustrated notes is a few fingers [about five inches] beyond the bell section.

NB. Und also hat auch eine *Quint*-Posaun ihre Züge, die Art der *Tromb*. wird durch folgende zwey *Sonaten* zu verhehmen und zu ersehen seyn.

Note well: The positions of a bass trombone are like these [one octave lower]. The trombone's style is perceived and illustrated through the following two sonatas.

[As Speer never makes explicit, the bass trombone he describes, the Quint trombone, is exactly one octave lower than the alto trombone.]

SÉBASTIEN DE BROSSARD

Dictionnaire de Musique[12]

(1703)

Brossard's *Dictionaire de musique*, the prototype of the modern dictionary of musical terms, appeared in preliminary editions in 1695 and 1701, and in its final form in 1703. It was immensely influential, not only in France, but all over Europe.

His definition of the trombone includes an accounting of the different sizes of trombone, the names of the trombone in other languages, and a curiously stilted and untechnical explanation of the slide mechanism. Absent from Brossard's article are any mention of what kinds of music trombones participated in (although implicitly they double voices) and the range of notes they could play.

It appears that Brossard derived his knowledge of the trombone from earlier writings and not from having even seen or heard one. Some sentences are copied from Marin Mersenne's *Harmonie universelle* (1636). A thorough study of seventeenth-century writings on the trombone would reveal his other sources. Certainly he cannot have known it well. His aim was to foster Italian influence on music in France. There is, however, little evidence, aside from the name of a trombonist in Venice[13] and an illustration of a trombonist at the court of Louis XIV that the trombone was well known in either France or Italy in his time. (See Plate 15.) Such was Brossard's influence that the same basic elements of his definition, and the same signs of lack of familiarity with the instrument, turn up in many of the definitions of later authors.

TROMBONE. C'est un espece d'Instrument à vent, que l'on embouche, & qui est fait à peu prés comme la *Trompette militaire*. Mais	TROMBONE. It is a kind of wind instrument that is blown with the lips, and is made almost like the military trumpet. But there is this

---

[12] Sebastien de Brossard, *Dictionnaire de musique* (Paris: Christoph Ballard, 1703), (no pagination).

[13] Eleanor Selfridge-Field, *Venetian Instrumental Music from Gabrieli to Vivaldi* (New York: Praeger, 1975), 303.

il y a cette différence que les branches du *Trombone* étant doubles & *emboitées* les unes dans les autres, de maniere qu'elles se peuvent aisément *déboiter*, on allonge & l'on racourcit l'étenduë de cette Trompette autant que l'on veut, selon les différens Sons qu'on luy veut faire marquer. C'est ce qui luy a fait donner en Latin le nom de *Tuba ductilis.* Les Allemands la nomment *Posaune*, & quelques François *Sacqueboute.*

difference, that the branches of the trombone are doubled and placed the one inside the other in such a way that they can easily be moved. The player lengthens and shortens the extension of this instrument as much as he wants, according to the different sounds that he wants to bring out. This is why it was given the Latin name *tuba ductilis.* The Germans call it Posaune, and some French *sacqueboute.*

Il y en a de plusieurs grandeurs qui peuvent servir à exécuter diverses Parties de la Musique. il y en a un *petit* que les Italiens nomment *Trombone piccolo*, & les Allemans *Cleine Alt-Posaune*, qui peut servir pour la *Haute-Contre*, & la Partie notée qui luy est destinée s'institue ordinairement *Trombone primo* ou I°.

There are several sizes that can serve to execute different parts of the music. There is a small one that the Italians call *trombone piccolo* and the Germans *clein Alt-Posaune*, which can be used for the counter-tenor. Its part is usually called first trombone.

Il y en a un autre un peu plus grand, qu'on apelle *Trombone maggiore* ou *majore*, qui peut servir pour la *Taille*. On intitule sa Partie *Trombone secondo*, ou II°, ou 2°.

There is another, a little larger, called *trombone maggiore*, which can serve as a tenor. Its part is called second trombone.

Il y en a un 3ᵉ encore plus grand, que les Italiens apellent *Trombone grosso*, & les Allemans *Grosse Quart-Posaune*, qu'on pourroit supléer par nos *Quintes* de *Violon* ou de *Haut-bois*. On intitule sa Partie *Trombone terzo*, ou III°, ou 3°.

There is a third still larger, which the Italians call *trombone grosso* and the Germans *grosse Quart-Posaune* that could be supplied by our violas or tenor oboes. Its part is called third trombone.

Enfin il y en a un qui est le plus grand de tous, que les Italiens apellent *Trombone grande*, qui se fait beaucoup entendre sur tout dans le bas. On intitule sa Partie

Finally, there is one that is largest of all, which the Italians call *trombone grande*, which is most often heard in the bass. Its part is called fourth trombone, or simply trombone

24   David M. Guion

Trombone quarto, ou IV°, ou 4°,   without modification. It ordinarily
ou simplement *Trombone* sans autre   uses the F-clef on the fourth line,
addition On luy donne   though frequently also on the fifth,
ordinairement la Clef de *F*, *ut*, *fa*, or top line, by reason of the depth
sur la 4ᶜ ligne, mais aussi fort   or gravity of its sound.
souvent sur la 5ᶜ ligne d'en haut, à
cause de la *gravité* ou *profondeur*
des ses Sons.

Plate 2. Mersenne: Illustrations from *Harmonie Universelle*.

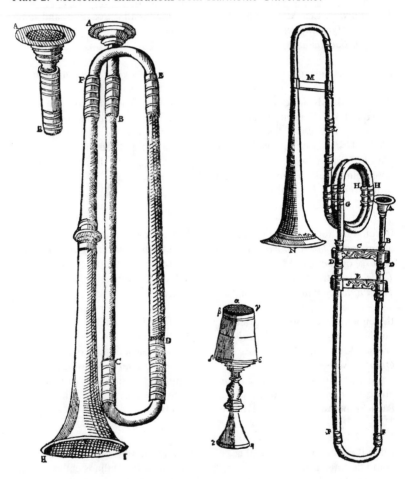

Reprinted from *The Trumpet & Trombone in Graphic Arts: 1500–1800* by
Tom L. Naylor © 1979 The Brass Press. Used by permission.

JOHANN MATTHESON

Das neu-eroffnete Orchestre[14]

(1713)

Mattheson was one of the more original writers represented in this chapter, never content merely to repeat earlier writings. *Das neu-eröffnete Orchestre* sought to show "the galant man how he can achieve a complete idea of the majesty and merit of the noble art of music."[15] In the comment on the trombone, therefore, we find no extended description of the construction or technique of the trombone. Essentially, Mattheson wrote not for composers, performers, or scholars, but for listeners. Perhaps for this reason, he comments on the sound of the trombone and mentions the narrow restrictions on its use. He appears to have had first-hand knowledge of the trombone, but not tremendous enthusiasm for it. His nomenclature is unorthodox; he calls the tenor a large alto trombone and the smaller of two basses the tenor.

Mattheson's later writings do not include a description of the trombone, although there are some passing references.[16]

Die prächtigst-thönende Posaune, *Ital. Trombone. Gall. Saqueboute*, ist eine Art Trompeten, auff welchen nebst dem Winde, vermittelst Aus-und Einziehung der Tohn *formi*ret wird. Es sind der Posaunen groß und kleine, nemlich: Kleine Alt, grosse Alt- *Tenor*- oder grosse *Quart*- und *Bass*- Posaunen, welch vor sich selbst ein vollständiges Chor ausmachen können, aber ausser in	The most magnificent-sounding trombone (Ital. Trombone, Fr. Saqueboute) is a type of trumpet, on which the notes are produced by pulling out and in, in conjunction with blowing. There are large and small trombones, namely: small alto, large alto, tenor or large quart, and bass trombone, which can form a full choir by themselves, but which are used very rarely, except in church pieces and solemn music.

---

[14] Johann Mattheson, *Das neu-eröffnete Orchestre* (Hamburg: The Author, 1713), 266–67.

[15] George J. Buelow, "Mattheson, Johann," *The New Grove*, vol. 11, 834.

[16] See, for example, Johann Mattheson, *Das beschützte Orchestre* (Hamburg: Schillerische Buchhandlung, 1717), 93, 301.

Kirchen-Sachen und *Solenni*täten
sehr wenig gebraucht werden.

FRIEDRICH ERHARD NIEDT

Musicalischer Handleitung[17]

(1721)

Niedt, an obscure and very likely failed musician, wrote a treatise
that became well known and widely quoted after his death, largely
because of Mattheson's revision of it.[18] His description of the trombone occurs in the second volume, which he published in 1706 and
which Mattheson revised and published in 1721. I have not located
the first edition, but from Mattheson's footnotes, it is clear that the
second edition includes some important amplifications and changes.

In a sense, this description summarizes all previous writings presented in this chapter. The basic definition comes from Brossard and
the technical description from Speer. Mattheson repeats his own
comments on the trombone's rarity and magnificent sound. This
treatise was intended for musicians rather than "galant men," and so
it is longer and more detailed than Mattheson's own brief comments.

Mattheson's second footnote hints that some composers would
have gladly used the trombone, but did not understand how to
compose for it. Possibly the notorious jealousy of the *Stadtpfeifer*
accounts for this condition as well as for the fact that the trombone
remained a rare instrument, limited to roles that required the participation of *Stadtpfeifer* until the end of the century, by which time
the guilds had largely lost their political clout and musical monopoly.

It appears that Mattheson added the details on the slide postions.
They may not have been as helpful to composers as he intended.
Where Speer neglected to state explicitly that the alto and bass
trombones were an octave apart, Mattheson seems to imply that

---

[17] Friedrich Erhard Niedt, *Musicalischer Handleitung*, 3 vols., 2nd ed. ed.
Johann Mattheson (Hamburg: Benjamin Schillers Wittwe, 1721; facs., s.l.:
Frits Knuf, 1976), vol. 2, 112–13.

[18] George J. Buelow, "Niedt, Friedrich Erhard," *The New Grove*, vol.
13, 222.

they are the same instrument. Also, where Speer said to move the slide out *Querfinger* from first position in order to play *c'*, Mattheson gives the distance as "the width of two fingers," less than half the proper distance.

Posaune, *Ital. Trombone, Lat. Tuba ductilis, Gall. Sacqueboute*: ein Blas-Instrument, das in zween Theilen bestehet, nemlich im Haupt-Stück und Stangen,* welche in eine Scheide stecken; es wird aber das Haupt-Stück auf die Stangen eingezäpfft, und mit der lincken Hand die gantze Posaune gehalten: da man indessen mit der rechten Hand die Scheide zwischen die Finger fasst und mit deren Auff- und Niederziehen den Ton *formi*rt.

Posaune (Italian, trombone; Latin, tuba ductilis; French, saqueboute): a wind instrument that consists of two parts, namely the bell section and the rods,* which are placed in a sheath. The bell section, however, is joined to the rods and the whole trombone is held with the left hand; for at the same time the slide is being held between the fingers of the right hand, which produces the notes by being moved in and out.

Eine Posaune hat vornemlich drey a 4 Züge; einen bey dem Mund-Stück, welcher sieben *sonos* angibt, nemlich: das *contra A*, groß *A*, *e*, *a*, *c'*, *e'*, gl (*gis*) und *a'*. Bey dem *c'* muß ein paar-Finger-breit vorwärts gezogen werden. Der andere Zug ist beym Haupt-Stück, und gibt folgende Tone, *G, d, g, h, d*. Der drit-Zug ist vier-Finger-breit ausser dem Haupt-Stuck, und hat nur drey *sonos*, nemlich *F, c*, und *f*. Der vierte Zug auf einer *Tenor*-Posaune, wenn ein Baß darauf *tracti*rt wird, ist so weit hinaus, als man mit dem Arm fast abrecken kann, und hat diese drey Klänge: *E, H*, und *B*.

A trombone has three or four principal slide positions. One, by the mouthpiece produces seven notes, namely: A_1, *A*, *e*, *a*, *c'*, *e'*, *g#'*, and *a'*. For *c'* one must pull the slide forward the width of two fingers. The second position is by the bell and provides the following notes: *G, d, g*, and *b, d'*. The third position is the width of four fingers beyond the bell and has only three notes, namely: *F, c*, and *f*. The fourth position on a tenor trombone, when playing bass, is about as far out as one can extend the arm, and has three notes: *E, B*, and B^b.

Die zweyte Art der Posaunen ist eine Alt- oder Quint-Posaune, die drey Züge auf eben die Art hat, wie die *Tenor*-Posaune; allein sie gibt andere *Tonos* an, nemlich bey dem ersten Zug *d, a, d', f', a', c''*; bey

The second type of trombone is the alto or quint trombone, which has three positions in much the same way as the tenor trombone, except it provides different notes, namely in the first position, *d, a, d', f', a',*

dem andern c, g, c', e', g', h'; bey dem dritten nur f, und h.†

and c''; in the second, c, g, c', e', g', b'; in the third, only f and b^b.†

---

*In der ersten *Edition* stand, mit zweyen Auffgestecken oder Zügen. Es wähle sich einer das verständlichste und richtigste.

*The first edition reads: "with two things placed on it or slide positions." One must choose for himself the more understandable and correct version.

Man kann es mit diesen beyden Arten der Trombonen schon bestellen, ob gleich noch zwo andere, nemlich die grosse Quart-Posaune, und noch eine grossere, welche schlecht weg *Trombone* heisset, worhanden sind. *vid. Brossard, & Dan. Speer* Unterrich der Music-Kunst, *pag.* 108.

We can stop here already with these two types of trombones, even though two more are available, namely the large quarto trombone and an even larger one which is simply called Trombone. See Brossard and Speer *Unterricht der Music-Kunst*, p. 108.

---

†Weil die Posaune ein Instrument ist, das zwar Kunst-Pfeiffern, sonst aber wenigen bekandt, so habe den *ambitum* desselben um so viel ausführlicher vor Augen legen wollen, da in ersten *Edition* schrecklich darüber hingehüpffet worden ist, und mancher, der gerne etwas mit *Trombon*en setzte, weil es prächtig klinget, nicht weiß, was sich drauff schicket.

†Because the trombone is an instrument that is little known except perhaps to *Kunstpfeifer*, I have tried to present the range of it in much more detail, since, in the first edition, this is skipped over so terribly much, and many, who wish to try something with trombones because they sound so magnificent, do not know what is proper on it.

FILIPPO BONANNI

Gabinetto armonico[19]

(1722)

A librarian by profession, Bonanni turned to a musical subject only for his last book. His others had been about such topics as

---

[19] Filippo Bonnani, *Gabinetto armonico* (Rome: Giorgio Placho, 1722), 49−50.

natural history, architecture, and costume.[20] Although other articles in this chapter were written for amateurs, Bonanni's is one of the few written by an amateur. (Others are those of Ephraim Chambers, Johann Samuel Halle, and Joos Verschuere-Reynvaan.) The illustrations in *Gabinetto armonico* are of great interest and importance to modern scholars. The engraving labeled *tromba spezzata* (see Plate 3) shows a man holding a trombone that resembles the one in Mersenne's *Harmonie universelle* (1636). (See Plate 2.) The artist, Arnolt van Westerhout, cannot possibly have used a trombonist for a model. The "player's" right hand is holding both braces of the slide and therefore cannot possibly move it. The text itself is of so little interest that when Frank Ll. Harrison and Joan Rimmer brought out their edition, they substituted their own commentary for Bonanni's.

Bonanni's description of the trombone depends largely on the authority of three treatises: Marin Mersenne's *Harmonicorum libri* (1635–36), or, less likely, *Harmonie universelle*, (1636–37), Fortunato Scacchi's *Sacrorum elaeochrismaton Myrothecium* (1625–37), and Caspar Bartholin's *De tibiis veterum, et earum antiquo usu libri tres* (1677). No other writer in this chapter except La Borde cites Scacchi, an Italian theologian who seems to have been seriously misled, and no one else at all cites Bartholin, a professor of medicine at Copenhagen. Bartholin believed Scacchi mistaken. Bonanni, having no background to know who was correct, simply quoted both. Bonanni's citations include page numbers, but often make it difficult to identify the specific work he cites. He makes at least one mistake: the quotation from the *Metamorphosis* of Apuleius is from the eleventh book, not the second. It should be noted that Mersenne's foot (32.8 cm.) was longer than the modern foot (30.48 cm.)[21] Therefore, the lengths quoted by Bonanni and anyone else who relied on Mersenne need to be adjusted according to modern measurements.

The ceremonies at Castel Sant'Angelo in Rome remain a mystery

---

[20] Filippo Bonnani, *The Showcase of Musical Instruments*, introduction and captions by Frank Ll. Harrison and Joan Rimmer (New York: Dover, 1964), v.

[21] Marin Mersenne. *Harmonie universelle: The Books on Instruments* trans. Roger E. Chapman (The Hague: Martinus Nijhoff, 1957), 573.

Plate 3. Bonnani: Tromba spezzata.

Reprinted from *The Trumpet & Trombone in Graphic Arts: 1500–1800* by Tom L. Naylor © 1979 The Brass Press. Used by permission.

to me, because I cannot be sure whether Bonanni described a contemporary practice or merely repeated what he found in a book somewhere. Certainly wind music was performed there. I cannot take Bonanni's word that the band included trombones in his lifetime, but as mentioned in the section on Italian music in Chapter 3, the trombone had not completely disappeared from Italy at the time; there was still a trombonist on the payroll at San Marco in Venice.

Tromba spezzata: A' Questa composta di Canale doppiamente piegato un'altra ne fù aggiunta communemente detta Tromba spezzata: è questa composta di doppio Canale, inserito l'uno nell'altro, e sostenuto dalla mano sinistra in modo, che la bocca possa animarlo col fiato, la mano destra ora allunga, ora scorta la parte mobile e con ciò si ottiene il suono, che si desidera dalla Musica, e non si può ottenere con la Tromba di sopra accennata. Parlò di questa il P. Mersenne nel libro degl'Istromenti armonici, e disse, che li Francesi la chiamano *saquebute*, e agginuse, che se fossero le volute di esso poste in linea retta, sarebbe la lunghezza di quindici pièdi. Descrisse quest'Istrumento anche lo Scacchi mirot. 3. cap. 54., e affermò che tal sorte di Tromba fù usata dagl'antichi Egiziani, fondato sù le parole di Apulejo, il quale nel libro secondo delle Metamorfosi, dice parlando delli Sagrifizii celebrati in onore dalla Dea Iside; *Ibant, & Tibicines dicati mango Serapi Tibicines qui per obliquum calamum ad aurem porrectum, dextera familarem Templi, Deique modulum frequentabant;* e della parola, *per obliquum calamum;*

Tromba spezzata: To this doubly folded compound tube [i.e. *Tromba doppia*, the previous article] another kind was commonly added, called *tromba spezzata* or broken trumpet. This is a compound double tube, inserted one inside the other, and held by the left hand in such a way that the mouth can give it life with the breath. The right hand now lengthens, now shortens the moving part, and with it, obtains the sounds desired by the music, which cannot be obtained with the above-mentioned trumpet. Mersenne spoke of it in his book on instruments and said that the French call it *Saquebute*. He added that if it were unbent into a straight line, it would be fifteen feet long. Scacchi also described this instrument in *Mirot*, book 3, chapter 54. He affirmed that such a trumpet was used by the ancient Egyptians, based on the words of Apuleius, who, in the second [sic, actually the eleventh] book of the Metamorphosis, says, speaking of the sacrifices celebrated in honor of the goddess Isis, "The temple pipers of the great god Serapis were there, too, playing their religious anthem on pipes with slanting mouth-pieces and tubes curving around their right

David M. Guion

arguisce tal sorte de Tromba ripiegata, e dall'altre: *Dextera familiarem Templi Deique modulum frequentabant*, stima significarsi il moto della mano, che ora allungava, ora accorciava la Tromba. *Dextera extendente* (dice egli) *vel retrahente Tubae canales musicales soni ab ea edebantur, in eaque extensione, & retractione Tibicines modulabantur*; e ne pone la figura a cart. 674, nella quale però non apparisce alcuna spezzatura, ed è in tutto simile a quella oggi di usata communemente, e da noi esposta al numero IV. stimò perciò il Bartolini essersi ingannato lo Scacchi, poichè (dice) di tal sorte di Tromba spezzata non se ne vede alcuna espressione antica, onde la stimò moderna: *Quod Istrumentum* (sono parole di lui) pag. 229. *nec dum mihi ex veteribus haurire licuit, licet nostris temporibus illud Tubae genus extare, atque in usu esse non ignorem.*

ears."[22] From the words "slanting mouthpieces" he deduces some sort of folded trumpet, and by others, "curving around their right ears," he considers is meant the way the right hand lengthens and shortens the trumpet. "Extending to the right," he says, "or drawing the musical pipes of the trumpet, sounds were drawn forth from it in its extension and retraction, played by the trumpeter." He puts a picture at figure 674, in which, however, no breaking appears, and it is in all respects similar to the one commonly used today and the one shown at number IV. Therefore, Bartolini considered that Scacchi was deceived, because, he says, such kind of broken trumpet is not seen in any ancient expression, so he considered it modern: "Although I have not found this instrument in antiquity" (these are his words on page 229) "I am not unaware that that type of trumpet exists in our times and is in use."

Al che noi potiamo aggiugere la Sinfonìa, che si fà nella mole Adriana in Roma, ora detta Castello S. Angelo in alcune feste principali dell'anno in una loggia eminente esposta verso il Ponte detto Elio da Elio Adriano, che lo fabbricò, da quattro Suonatori di queste Trombe spezzate, accompagnati col suono di due altri

To which we can add the symphony, which is done at the mausoleum of Adrian in Rome, now called the Castel Sant'Angelo, in some of the principal feasts of the year from a balcony facing the bridge called Elio, from Elio Adriano, who built it. This symphony is played by four players of this broken trumpet, accompanied by the sound of two

---

[22] Apuleius, *The Transformation of Lucius, Otherwise Known as The Golden Ass*, trans. Robert Graves (New York: Farrar, Straus & Young, 1951), 269.

detti communemente corni, delli quali a suo luogo si parlerà. Usano una simile sinfonia gl'istessi suonatori, qualunque volta il Senatore, e Conservatori di Roma offeriscono Calici d'argento nelle Chiese, ove si celebra la festa di qualche Santo, per anticha consuetudine a questo fine dal medesimo Senato stipendiati.

others commonly called horns, which will be spoken of in their own place. The same players use a similar symphony any time the senators and conservators of Rome offer chalices of silver in the churches, where the feast of some saints is celebrated, paid for by the same senate by ancient custom to this end.

EPHRAIM CHAMBERS

Cyclopaedia: or,
An Universal Dictionary of Arts and Sciences [23]

(1728)

Chambers's *Cyclopaedia*, the first work in this chapter not exclusively concerned with music, marks a major milestone in the history of reference books. It went through several editions in England and greatly influenced the great *Encyclopédie* of Diderot and d'Alembert.

The article on trombone amounts to a loose translation of Brossard's, although it does not acknowledge the earlier source. He mistranslated one sentence, saying that the largest trombone sometimes used an F-clef on the fifth line from the top, that is, the bottom line. An F-clef on that line would be an unorthodox alto clef.

Chambers's article contains some information not found in Brossard. It mentions the use of crooks and the length of the instrument, both with the slide closed and fully extended. Since this information is given in Mersenne's writings, Chambers either found it there or in some later work that was based on them. Once again,

---

[23] Ephraim Chambers, *Cyclopaedia, or An Universal Dictionary of Arts and Sciences*, 2 vols., 5th ed. (London: printed for D. Midwinter et al., 1743), vol. 2 (no pagination).

the lengths given are based on a foot that is longer than the modern standard. Also, the proportions are wrong. With the slide fully extended, the trombone produces a series of notes a tritone lower than the basic pitch. If the instrument is eight feet long in first position, it must be eight times the square root of two, or just over eleven feet long, not fifteen, in modern seventh position.

The following text comes from the fifth edition of 1743. The chief differences between the first and fifth editions in the article on the trombone are typographical, with the many fewer capitalized and italicized words in the later edition. Only two words are different, and neither affects the sense of the article.

SACBUT, a musical instrument of the wind kind; being a kind of trumpet, though different from the common trumpet both in form and size.

The Sacbut is very fit for playing bass; and is contrived so as to be drawn out or shortened, according to the gravity or acuteness of the tones. -- The Italians call it *Trombone*, the Latins, *Tuba Ductilis*.

It takes asunder into four pieces, or branches; and hath frequently a wreath in the middle; which is the same tube, only twisted twice, or making two circles in the middle of the instrument; by which means, it is brought down one fourth lower than its natural tone. It has also two pieces or branches on the inside, which do not appear, except when drawn out by means of an iron bar, and which lengthen it to the degree requisite to hit the tone required.

The Sackbut is usually eight foot long, without being drawn out, or without reckoning the circles. When extended to its full length, it is usually fifteen foot. The wreath is two foot nine inches in circumference. It serves as bass in all concerts of wind musick.

There are *Sackbuts* of different sizes, serving to execute different parts; particularly a small one, called by the Italians, *Trombone picciolo*, and by the Germans, *Cleine alt-posaune*, proper for a counter-tenor. The part assigned it, is usually called *Trombone primo* or I°. There is another large[er one], called *Trombone maggiore*, which may serve as a tenor: its part is usually called *Trombone secondo*, or II°. or 2°. There is a third still bigger, called *Trombone grosso*; its part is called *Trombone terzo*, or III°. or 3°. Lastly, there is another which exceeds all the rest, and which is much heard in the music, especially in the bass; its part is called *Trombone quarto*, or IV°. or 4to. or simply *Trombone*. It has usually the key of *F, ut, fa* on the fourth line; though frequently also on the fifth line from the top, by reason of the gravity or depth of the sounds.

JOHANN WALTHER

Musikalisches Lexikon[24]
and

JOSEPH F. B. C. MAJER

Museum musicum theoretico practicum[25]

(both 1732)

After Brossard, the next major musical reference work was Walther's *Musikalisches Lexikon*, the prototype for modern dictionaries that combine terms and biography. The article on trombone is copied verbatim from Mattheson's revision of Niedt's *Musicalischer Handleitung*, but without the footnotes. It is titled "Trombone," not "Posaune," which demonstrates the influence of Italian music in Germany. Shorter entries, which describe such Italian terms as "trombone grande" are the same as those in Zedler. See p. 59.

Majer's *Museum Musicum*, which appeared the same year, was intended as a self-instruction book in basic theory and the techniques of various instruments. Although considered an important work of late Baroque musical writing, it is largely derivative.[26] His article on the trombone, copies both Mattheson's original article and his revision of Niedt, with some minor word changes, but without attribution. The illustrations are very similar to Speer's, demonstrating the continued influence of his treatise 35 years after its publication, although neither Walther nor Majer acknowledge him. Of all the authors whose writings can be traced back to Speer, only Majer corrects his typographical error, showing *g'* and not *g#'* as a first position note. (See Plate 4). Although these two articles are not

---

[24] Johann Gottfried Walther, *Musikalisches Lexikon* (Leipzig: W. Deer, 1732; facs., Kassel: Bärenreiter, 1953), 619.

[25] Johann Friedrich Bernhard Caspar Majer, *Museum musicum theoretico practicum* (s.l.: Georg Michael Majer, 1732; facs., Kassel: Bärenreiter, 1954), 41–43.

[26] George J. Buelow, "Majer, Johann Friedrich Bernhard Caspar," *The New Grove*, vol. 11, 542–43.

Plate 4. Majer: Page from *Museum Musicum...*

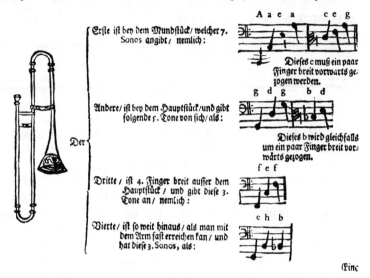

identical to Niedt's, the differences are minor enough that there is no need to reproduce them here.

Majer's treatise was revised and published under the title *Neueröffneter theoretischer und practischer Music-Saal* in 1741; the article on the trombone was unchanged.

JOHANN CHRISTOPH AND JOHANN DAVID STÖßEL

Kurtzgefaßtes musicalisches
Lexicon[27]

(1737)

Appearing within five years of Walther's *Musikalisches Lexikon*, the *Kurtzgefaßtes musicalisches Lexicon*, published by and usually attributed to Johann Christoph and Johann David Stößel, depends

---

[27] Johann Christoph and Johann David Stößel, *Kurtzgefaßtes musicalisches Lexicon* (Chemnitz: Stößel, 1737), 292–95, 406.

heavily on it. The Stößels' book can be regarded both as an attempt to capitalize on Walther's success and as a popularization of its model.[28] It includes two articles about the trombone. The first and longest, entitled "Posaune," copies some passages from Walther and some from Speer. Occasionally, the wording, although not the content, is original. The second, entitled "Trombone," shows no evidence of mere copying, although it likewise shows little evidence of original thought.

The final sentence presents a puzzle. No other eighteenth-century article makes a comparison between the trombone and the horn. The writer seems to prefer trombones played with more of a horn-like sound than a trumpet-like sound, but does not develop his thought sufficiently for modern readers to be quite sure what he had in mind.

Posaune, ist ein blasendes Kling-Spiel von meßingenen Blech, mit einem Mundstück, gleich einer Trompete, nur daß es aus einander geschoben, länger und kürtzer gemacht werden kan, nachdem es der Thon erfodert. Sie sind von unterschiedener Grösse nach der Stimme, zu welche sie dienen sollen, haben einen nicht so scharffen, aber lieblichern Schall, als die Trompeten. Sie bestehen in zwey Theilen, nehmlich im Hauptstück und in Stangen, welche in einer Scheide stecken; Es wird aber das Hauptstück auf die Stangen eingezapfft, und mit der lincken Hand die gantze Posaune gehalten, mit der rechten Hand aber ergreifft man die Scheide zwischen die Finger.

Trombone is a wind instrument made of brass with a mouthpiece like a trumpet, except that it is pushed apart and can be made longer and shorter according to what the note requires. They are of various sizes, according to the voice that they serve, and have a sound that is less sharp and more lovely than the trumpet's. They consist of two parts, namely the bell section and the rods, which are placed in a sheath. The bell section, however, is joined to the rods and the whole trombone is held with the left hand, but with the right hand, one grips the sheath between the fingers.

Es kan aber auf einer *Tenor*-Posaune *Alt, Tenor,* und *Bass* geblasen werden. Diese hat nun

Alto, tenor, and bass parts can be played on a tenor trombone. Now this one has four principal slide

---

[28] James B. Coover, "Dictionaries and Encyclopedias of Music," *The New Grove*, vol. 5, 436.

drey vernehmliche Züge. Der erste
Zug ist beym Mundstück, und
befinden sich folgende Buchstaben
darinnen, als *A*, *A*, *e*, *a*, *c'*, *e'*, *g.#'*
und *a*. Dieser Buchstaben Thone
werden alle im ersten Zuge
gefunden, ausser, daß das *c* um
zwey qver Finger etwas vorwärts
muß gezogen werden, bey welchem
Zuge auch das *f*, *#* sich befindet. Der
andere Zug ist beym Hauptstück,
und hat folgende Buchstaben, *G*, *d*,
g, *h*, *d'*. Bey diesem Zug ist zu
mercken, daß das *b moll* um zwey
qver Finger hinauswärts muß
gezogen werden. Der dritte zug ist
vier qver Finger auswärts des
Hauptstücks, und hat folgende
Buchstaben, *F*, *c*, *f*. Der vierdte
Zug auf einer *Tenor*-Posaune, so
man einen *Bass* darauf *tractir*et, ist
so weit draussen, als mans mit dem
Arm fast erstrecken kan, und seynd
folgender Thone Buchstaben, als *E*,
H, *B*. *b moll* muß noch um etwas
weiters als die fördern zwey
Buchstaben *E* und *H* gezogen
werden.

Die *Semitonia* werden gezogen: als
die harten mit # bezeichneten
hohen *Semitonia* werden von ihrem
natürlichen Thon hineinwärts, die
mit *b* aber bezeichneten niedrigen
Semitonia werden um zwey qver
Finger hinauswärts gezogen. Die
Triller werden mit dem Kien
gemacht, wie bey der Trompeten
gedacht wird; theils schleissen auch
den Posaunen-Schall mit dem
Athem, kommt aber besser und
lebhafter heraus, menn er mit der
Zunge fein frisch gestossen wird.
Die *moderation* im *forte* und *piano*,
wird durch den starcken und

positions. The first is by the
mouthpiece, and the following notes
are found there: A_1, *A*, *e*, *a*, *c'*, *e'*,
g#', and *a'*. These notes are all
found in first position, except that
the *c'* must be drawn about two
Querfinger forward, in which
position *f#'* is also found. Second
position is by the bell and has the
following notes: *G*, *d*, *g*, *b*, *d'*. The
b^b must be drawn out about two
Querfinger. Third position is four
Querfinger beyond the bell and has
the following notes: *F*, *c*, *f*. Fourth
position on a tenor trombone, so
one can play a bass on it, is about as
far out as one can extend the arm
and has the following notes: *E*, *B*,
B^b: the B^b must be drawn out a
little farther past the two notes *E*
and *B*.

Semitones are played as follows: the
hard, sharp-noted semitones are
played two *Querfinger* higher than
their natural pitch, but the lower
semitones, notated with a flat, must
be played two *Querfinger* lower.
Trills are made with the chin, as
mentioned with the trumpet. Some
slur the trombone's sound with the
breath, but it comes out better and
livelier when it is cleanly articulated
with the tongue. Control in loud
and soft playing is made with the
breath, as in all wind instruments.
This instrument requires no special
physical vigor. It can be learned

schwachen auslassenden Athem gemacht, wie auf allen blasenden Instrumenten. Dieses Instrument braucht keine sonderliche Kräffte, sondern es kan ein Knabe von neun oder zehn Jahren solches ohne Schaden lernen und blasen, sonderlich einen *Bass* auf einer *Tenor*-Posaune, welche gar schlechten Wind brauchet.

Eine *Alt*- und *Qvint*-Posaune haben auch drey, auch zwar einerley Züge, als: *d, a, d', f', a', d''*. Der andere Zug: *c, g, c', e', g', c''*. Der dritte *f, h*. Und also hat auch eine *Qvint*-Posaune ihre Züge. Theils *Musici* heissen den gantzen *Accord* dieser vier Posaunen *Tromboni*. In den Orgelln ist auch ein Pedal-Register so das Posaunen-Register heißt, wegen des Lauts.

Trombone, eine gemeine Posaune. *Trombone grosso*, eine grosse *Qvart*- oder *Qvint*-Posaune. *Trombone piccolo*, eine kleine Alt-Posaune. Die Posaune, Trommete, sind mehr *martial*ische als musicalische Instrumenta, denn sie schneiden gar zu scharf ins Gehör, darum solche einige gleich denen Jäger-Hörnern *æstimir*en.

quite soundly by a boy nine or ten years old, because he has enough physical strength to play a tenor trombone--especially on a bass part, as this requires only a normal amount of air.

Alto and bass trombone have the same three positions, with *d, a, d', f', a'*, and *d''*, in first position; *c, g, c', e', g', c''* in second; and *f* and *b* in third. A quint trombone also has its positions. Musicians call the whole gamut of these four [!] *Posaunen* trombones. In the organ, there is also a pedal register, the so-called trombone register, because of its sound.

Trombone: an ordinary trombone. Trombone grosso: a large quart or quint trombone. Trombone piccolo: a small alto trombone. The trombone and trumpet are more martial than musical instruments because they cut too sharply in the ear, therefore, such few like the hunting horn should be preferred.

JOHANN PHILIPP EISEL

Musicus autodidactos,
oder der sich selbst informirende Musicus[29]

(1738)

From the title, it is evident that Eisel's intention was the same as Majer's: to enable students of music to learn theory and technique on their own. The second word of his title is printed in Greek letters on the title page. Not surprisingly, the article is stuffier and more pretentious than any reproduced in this chapter so far. He was not considered important enough for inclusion in *The New Grove*, but unlike Majer, he wrote his own prose rather than copy someone else's.

This is not to say that Eisel broke new ground or showed much originality. He is the earliest author (of those whose works I have located) to ascribe the trombone to Biblical times. Otherwise his article seems to be based on Speer and/or Stößel, although he does not mention his sources.

At first glance, Eisel's description seems to point to a change in practice since Speer's time, for he does not follow Speer in mentioning the seventh partial in first position (*g'*, misprinted in Speer as *g#'*). His description of first position as being "next to the mouthpiece" is traditional enough, but in the section on the bass and alto trombone, he asserts that the slide is not extended at all for first position. It is a slight extension of the slide for first position, mentioned as early as Praetorius,[30] that makes the seventh partial possible in first position. Otherwise, it is far too flat to be useful. Therefore, if there was no change in practice between Speer's time and Eisel's, Eisel must be wrong. In all likelihood, Eisel was merely careless in his description; the list of first position notes for the bass and alto trombones includes the seventh partial.

Another bit of carelessness left over from Speer is Eisel's failure

---

[29] Johann Philipp Eisel, *Musicus autodidactos, oder der sich selbst informirende Musicus* (Erfurt: Johann Michael Funcken, 1738), 70–74.

[30] Michael Praetorius, *Syntagma musicum. Tomus secundus: De organographia* (Wolfenbüttel: Holwein, 1619), 232.

to make it explicit that the bass trombone plays an octave lower than the alto trombone. Eisel's system of measuring distances looks like Speer's at first glance, but it appears that he did not study his model very carefully. Speer gave the distance the slide must travel to raise or lower a given pitch one semitone as "two *Querfinger*" (see page 15 for a discussion of this difficult term.)

In the last section of his article, Eisel gives one *Querfinger* as the distance for one sharp of flat, two *Querfinger* for a double sharp or flat, and three *Querfinger* as the distance between the bell and second position. Assuming that Eisel and Speer meant the same thing by *Querfinger*, these distances are incorrect. Eisel likewise failed to differentiate octaves, printing all note names in capital letters. If his entire treatise is as flawed as his section on the trombone, it is easy to see why he was omitted from *The New Grove*.

VON DER POSAUNEN.	**ON THE TROMBONE**
1. Wer is der Erfinder der Posaunen?	1. Who is the inventor of the trombone?
AUch dem Zeugnisse *Philonis* soll die Posaune von dem grossin Gottbeliebten Propheten Mose um das Jahr der Welt 2400. seyn erfunden worden, gleichwie den Psalter und Cyther eben dieser Jüdische *Scribent* dem ersten *Musico* dem *Jubal*, zuschreibet. So viel ist ausser Streit. daß die Posaune eines der allerältesten *musicalis*chen *Instrument*en ist. *Conf. Josephus L. 1. Antiquit.*	According to Philo's testimony, the trombone is supposed to have been invented by God's beloved prophet Moses around the year 2400 of the world, just as this same Jewish writer ascribes the psaltery and zither to the first musician, Jubal. This much is indisputable: that the trombone is one of the very oldest musical instruments. See Josephus, L. 1 *Antiquities*.
2. Wie vielerley hat man Posaunen?	2. How many kinds of trombone are there?
Die Posaune, welche ein *Instrument* von Meßinge, das durch Blasen und Ziehen *tractir*et wird, ist dreyerley: Denn man hat *Tenor- Alt-* und *Quint-* Posaunen. Auf der	The trombone, which is an instrument made of sheet metal and played through blowing and pulling, comes in three types: for there are tenor, alto, and bass trombones. On

Tenor-Posaunen kan man so wohl
den *Tenor* als *Bass*, zur Noth auch
gar den *Alt* blasen.

3. Wie viel hat eine Posaune Züge?

So wohl die *Quint-* als *Alt-* und
Tenor-Posaunen hat 3. Züge,
welche vornehmlich zu *observir*en
sind: Denn die übrigen bedeuten
nicht viel. Und weil jede Posaune
ordinair aus 2. Theilen bestehet,
nemlich dem Haupt-Stück und den
Stangen, welche gleichsam in einer
Scheide stecken, daran das
Haupt-Stück eingezäpffet ist, so
muß man dahero, wenn dieses
Instrument soll recht *tractir*et
werden, mit der lincken Hand
allezeit die gantze Posaune halten,
und mit der rechten die Scheide
zwischen die Finger fassen, daß man
damit die Züge verrichten kan.

4. Kan ich nicht von jedem Zuge
der *Tenor*-Posaune deutlicher
*informi*ret werden?

Gar wohl: Und zwar, was den
Ersten Zug belanget, so ist derselbe
gleich oben bey dem Mund-Stück,
und hat im *Bass* das tiefe *A*.
ingleichen den *Accord A. Cis E. A.*
aber *C*. muß um 2. Qver-Finger
etwas vorwärts gezogen werden.

Der Andere Zug ist bey dem
Haupt-Stück, und hat im *Bass G. H.
D. G.* im *Tenor* aber *H*. und *D*. bey
welchem zugleich das *B*. wenn es
vorkommt, allezeit um 2.
Qver-Finger auswärts muß gezogen
werden.

the tenor trombone, one can play
bass as well as tenor, and even alto
if necessary.

3. How many slide positions does a
trombone have?

The bass, as well as the alto and
tenor trombone, has three slide
positions, that can be seen as
primary; for the others do not mean
very much. And since every
trombone normally consists of two
pieces, namely the bell section and
the rods, which are stuck in a sheath
at the same time, on which the bell
section is attached, so it is that one
must always hold the whole
trombone with the left hand, if it is
to be used properly. With the right
hand, the sheath is held between the
fingers, so that one can set up the
slide positions.

4. Could I not be more clearly
informed about each slide position
of the tenor trombone?

Of course: and so, concerning the
first slide position, thus it is up next
to the mouthpiece and has in the
bass low *A*, and at the same time the
range *A*, *C#*, *E*, and *A*, but *C* must
be pulled about two *Querfinger*
forwards.

The second position is next to the
bell section, and has *G*, *B*, *D*, and
G in the bass, but *B* and *D* in the
tenor, with which the *B^b*, if it
appears, must at all times be pulled
forwards about two *Querfinger*.

Der Dritte Zug ist 4. Qver-Finger breit auswärts dem Haupt-Stück, und hat im *Bass F. C. F.* Und dieses sind die gewöhnlichen Züge; worzu aber noch kommt:

The third position is four *Querfinger* forward from the bell section and has *F, C,* and *F* in the bass. Now these are the common slide positions, to which also comes:

Der Vierdte Zug, wenn man nemlich einen *Bass* auf einer solchen Posaunen *tracti*ret. Dieser gehet so weit hinaus, daß mans mit dem Arm kaum erreichen kan, und hat im *Bass E. H.* und *B.* welches letztere aber noch um etwas weiters als jene beyden muß gezogen werden.

The fourth position, if anyone plays a bass part on just such a trombone. This goes out so far that one can barely reach it with the arm and has *E, B,* and *B^b* in the bass, the last of which, however, must be pulled somewhat further still than the other two.

5. Was hat eine *Alt-* und *Quint*-Posaune vor Züge?

5. What kind of slide positions do an alto and bass trombone have?

Wie vorgedacht eben auch 3. welche mit den erstbeschriebenen auf einerley art gemachet werden, wie denn

As anticipated, they also have three positions, which are done in one and the same way as the first ones described.

Der Erste Zug, oder deutlicher davon zu reden, wenn die Posaune gar nicht ausgezogen wird, der *Accord* hat *D. A. D. Fis A. D.* und im *Alt* die *Claves* oder Tone nach einander *D. A. D. Fis, A. C. D.*

The first position, or to speak more clearly of it, if the trombone is not extended at all, the range has *D, A, D, F#, A, D,* and in the alto clefs or notes after each other are *D, A, D, F#, A, C, D.*

Der Andere Zug, welcher aber besser der erste genennet wird, befindet sich in der Mitte, hat den *Accord C. E. G.* und in dieser Stimme die Tone *C. G. C. E. G. H.*

The second slide position, which would better be named the first, however, is located in the middle, and has the range *C, E, G,* and in the latter [alto], *C, G, C, E, G, B.* [N.B. The German word here translated "position" (*Zug*) can also be translated "draw". Eisel is saying that since the slide is not drawn out at all for the first position, this second position is really the first "draw." As mentioned in the introduction to this article, his

description of first position is in
error.]

Der Dritte Zug, oder eigentlich zu
reden der andere, ist etliche Finger
breit von dem Haupt-Stück
hinauswärts, hat die *Claves H. F. H.*
aber *Dis* muß um 2. Finger breit
einwärts gezogen werden.

The third position, or to put it
closer to the truth, the second, is
many finger-widths forward from
the bell and has the notes *B*, *F*, and
B, but *D#* [surely he means *F#*]
must be pulled inward about two
finger-widths.

6. Wie werden die *Semitonia* auf der
Posaune gezogen?

6. How are semitones pulled on the
trombone?

Die mit # bezeichneten hohen
Semitonia werden von ihrem
natürlichen Ton hineinwärts, die mit
einem *B*. bezeichneten niedrigen
Semitonia hergegen um 2.
Qver-Finger hinauswärts gezogen.

The high semitones marked with a
sharp are pulled in from their
natural tone about two *Querfinger*;
the lower semitones marked with a
flat are pulled out about two
Querfinger.

7. Was ist wegen der *Clavium* oder
Zeichen zu mercken?

7. What is to be noted concerning
the clefs?

Nichts weiter als dieses, daß die *Alt-*
Posaune den *Alt-Clavem* oder
Zeichen, die *Quint-* und *Quart-*
Posaune aber gemeiniglich den
Clavem des *Basses* in Stücken
vorgezeichnet hat. Wer also das
vorhergesagte verstehet, wird sich
auch leichtlich hierein finden
können.

Nothing more than this, that the
alto trombone has the alto clef as
prescribed in the parts, where as the
quint and quart trombones generally
have the bass clef as prescribed in
the parts. Whoever understands
then that which was stated before
will also be able to find their way
easily in this.

8. Ist nichts weiters auf diesem
Instrument zu *marqvi*ren?

8. Is there nothing more to note
about this instrument?

Ja, nemlich die Triller und
Moderation. Die Triller werden mit
dem Kinne gemachet, wie unten
von der Trompete mit mehrern wird
gesaget werden. Einige schleissen
auch den Posaunen-Schall mit dem
Odem; es kommt aber allezeit
besser heraus, und ist viel lebhaffter

Yes, namely trills and dynamics.
The trills are made with the chin,
just as it will be said below in more
detail concerning the trumpet. Some
also slur the trombone sound with
the breath, yet it always comes out
better and is much livelier and more
pleasant if it is forced out carefully

und angenehmer, wenn er mit der
Zungen fein frisch gestossen wird.

Die *Moderation*, welche im *Forte*
und *Piano* statt findet, wird durch
den starck oder schwach
ausgelassenen Odem, wie auf allen
andern blasenden *Instrument*en,
gemachet, und braucht dieses
Instrument ins besondere vor den
übrigen gar keine starke
Leibes-Kräffte; sondern es kan ein
Knabe von 8. 9. und 10. Jahren
schon kühnlich wegen seiner Leibes-
Kräffte sich auf dessen *Tracti*rung
ohne Gefahr *applici*ren, zumal wenn
er von der *Tenor*-Posaune den
Anfang machet, welche ohne diß

and brightly with the tongue.

Dynamics, which occur in forte and
piano, are produced through
strongly or weakly released breath,
as on all other wind instruments.
This instrument does not
particularly need any more physical
strength than others. On the
contrary, a boy of 8, 9, or 10 can
apply his strength boldly to playing
it without danger, especially if he
starts with the tenor trombone,
which requires in any case only
modest and little air.

Example 8. Eisel: *Schema* der *Quint*-Posaune nach deren 3. Haupt-Zugen.
Toni naturales. (Diagram of the Quint Trombone with Its Three Principal
Positions. Natural Tones.)

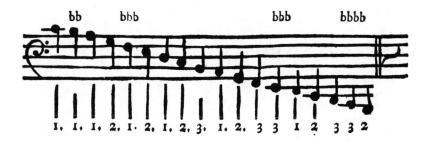

Example 9. Eisel: *Semitonia* (Semitones).

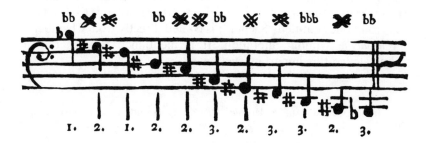

gar schlechten und wenigen Wind
erfordert.

9. Ist auch ein *Schema* nöthig?

9. Is a diagram necessary?

Ja: Solches ist aus folgenden zu
sehen.

Yes, and it follows:

Hierbey ist zu *marqvir*en, daß jede
Ziffer einen Zug bedeute; als z. E.
1. ist der erste Zug, 2. der andere
Zug, 3. der dritte Zug.

It should be noted here that each
number means a slide position: 1 is
the first position, 2 the second one,
and 3 the third.

Der erste Zug ist drinne, der andere
ist drey Qver-Finger breit von
Haupt-Stücke hineinwärts, der dritte
ist zwey Qver-Finger hinter den
Haupt-Stück hinauswärts. Ein jedes
zeiget 1. Qver-Finger breit
hineinwärts, zwey ## zeigen an
zwey Qver-Finger breit hineinwärts

The first position is pulled in, the
second is three *Querfinger* pulled in
from the bell, the third is pulled out
from the bell two *Querfinger*. Each
sharp shows one *Querfinger* pulled
in, two sharps show two *Querfinger*
pulled in.

So viel, *b.*, hier befindlich, so viele
Qver-Finger hinauswärts werden
dadurch vorgestellet.

However many flats are found here,
this represents how many
Querfinger to pull out.

JAMES GRASSINEAU

A Musical Dictionary[31]

(1740)

Grassineau's dictionary, the first important musical dictionary in the
English language, amounts to an adaptation of Brossard's dictionary,
with important information added from other sources. His article on
the trombone (entitled "Sacbut") is copied directly from Chambers's
Cyclopaedia without alteration. It is mentioned here merely to
acknowledge this important dictionary.

---

[31] James Grassineau, *A Musical Dictionary* (London: J. Wilcox, 1740),
206.

JOHANN HEINRICH ZEDLER

Grosses vollständiges Universal-Lexicon[32]

(1741)

Zedler, a Leipzig book seller, brought out this milestone in the history of encyclopedias between 1732 and 1750. It was issued in 64 volumes under the direction of nine editors, and was the first encyclopedia to include biographical information about living people.[33]

It was printed in columns with no paragraph breaks, and so I have supplied them. There are four substantial articles about the trombone: "Posaune," "Posaune Gottes," "Posaunen," and "Posaunen-Fest." In addition, there are five cross references beginning with the word "Posaune" and seven short entries, apparently copied from Walther's dictionary, beginning with the word "Trombone." Judging from the cross-reference at the end of the first article, these last are less substantial than the author's original intention. (There is also an article entitled "Contra-Posaune," which describes a 32-foot organ stop.)

Only the first two paragraphs of the first article contain any relevant information about the trombone in the eighteenth century. The author, whose identity is unknown to me, did not use any of the articles already given in this chapter as source material except for Walther's brief translations of certain Italian terms and two sentences from Stößel, or perhaps a common source. Most of the information given in earlier works does not occur here. There is some new information, much of which is not repeated in later articles.

Of all the articles examined, only Zedler's places trombones in Thuringia or mentions their use in dinner music. The use of the trombone to double voices was too commonplace for most eighteenth-century authors to mention. The writer in Zedler does not directly mention it either, but he alludes to the practice more clearly than do most authors in his enumeration of the different sizes of trombone.

---

[32] Johann Heinrich Zedler, *Grosses vollständiges Universal-Lexicon* 64 vols. (Leipzig: Zedler, 1732–50), vol. 6, col. 1145; vol. 28, col. 1695–1700; vol. 45, col. 1089–90.

[33] *The New Encyclopaedia Britannica: Micropaedia*, 1975 ed., "Grosses vollständiges Universal-Lexicon."

The rest of the article, and those that follow, contain no practical information at all. The author indulges in all kinds of fanciful speculations on the use of the trombone in ancient and Biblical times, centuries before it even existed.

The reason for these speculations is not hard to find. Luther's translation of the Bible rendered the Hebrew *shophar* as *Posaune*. Luther did not have the modern trombone in mind, but rather the medieval *busine*, which disappeared not long afterwards. Generations after Luther knew only one instrument called *Posaune*, the modern trombone. Zedler's writer on musical subjects, being a good scholar, recognized that the various ancient trumpets and horns he described in his articles on the trombone were not the same as the modern trombone. Nonetheless, he counted them as trombones of some sort rather than as trumpets or horns.

Other writers of various nationalities (see Bonanni, Eisel, Tans'ur, La Borde, and Schubart) also placed the trombone in ancient times, but with no glimmer of recognition that the ancient "trombone" was in any way different from the modern ones. Except for Bonanni, all base their views on Scripture. But where the English (and French?) Bible includes "sackbut" in only one chapter (Daniel 3:5, 7, 10, 15). Luther's Bible makes frequent reference to *Posaune*. Zedler's author was both a good scholar and a good Lutheran, as reflected in the heavily theological orientation of his articles.

Of the many sources cited, only one appears to be primarily about music. They are of slight enough interest to the majority of readers of this book that I will not mention them here. Such sources as I have been able to identify can be found in Appendix 1.

Beyond the first two paragraphs, then, the articles have no value in describing the trombone, but great value in demonstrating what the best of eighteenth-century German scholarship believed important. Although they do not explain the role of the trombone in the eighteenth century, they illuminate the background against which trombones were played.

POSAUNE, *Buccino, Trompe*, wird von den Stadtpfeifern auf den Thürnen; Rathhaußgänglein, in Kirchenmusiqven und bey andern Gelegenheiten gebraucht. Die tiefste und größte hießt eine Octavposaune, die andere, so etwas höher geht, eine Quartposaune, der dritte ist die gemeine Posaune, die

POSAUNE, *Buccino, Trompe* is used by the *Stadtpfeifer* of Thuringia in the towers, city hall corridors, in church music, and for other occasions. The deepest and largest is called an octave trombone; the second one, which goes somewhat higher, is the bass [i.e. quart-] trombone; the third is the common

vierte aber die Altposaune. Theils Musici heissen den gantzen Accord dieser vier Posaunen Tromboni. In den Orgeln ist auch ein Pedalregister von sechzehen biß zwey und dreyßig Fußtonen, so das Posaunenregister heißt, wegen dergleichen Lautes.

Die Posaunen werden von meßingenem Bleche, mit einem Mundstücke gleich einer Trompete bereitet, nur daß sie auseinander geschoben, langer und kurtzer gemacht werden können, nachdem es der Ton erfordert. Sie sind von unterschiedener Grösse, nach der Stimme, zu welcher sie dienen sollen, haben einen nicht so scharfen, aber lieblichern Schall als die Trompeten, und werden bey Kirchen- und Tafelmusicen gebrauchet.

Es sind die Posaunen schon ehemahls so wohl bey dem Volcke Gottes, als dey denen Heyden im Gebrauch gewesen. Von diesen, schreibt Sal. van Till, in der Dicht-Sing- und Spiel-Kunst der Alten, p. 141 u. f. wurden sie bey ihrem Götzendienst gebrauchet, dem Volcke nicht allein von dem vorhabenden Opffer Anzeigung zu geben, sondern auch die Opfferthiere bey ihrer ansehnlichen Umherführung anzufrischen, dem Hauffen zu folgen, auch die Proceßion desto ansehnlicher zu machen.

Wenn also Eustachius in *Homerum, ad Iliadem* Σ, die gekrümmete Posaune des Osiris beschreibet, so füget er hinzu, daß man solche gebrauchet, das Volck zum Opffer

trombone; the fourth is the alto trombone. Musicians call the whole gamut of these four *Posaunen* trombones. On the organ, a pedal register of sixteen to thirty-two feet is called the trombone register because it has the same sound.

The trombones are made from sheet-metal, with a mouthpiece like a trumpet's. But they can be made longer and shorter by pushing them apart, according to what the note requires. They are of differing sizes, according to the voice which they are supposed to serve. They have a sound more lovely than, if not as sharp, as the trumpet's, and are used for church and table music.

The trombones were used previously by the people of God and the heathen. Of these Salomon van Til writes in his *Dicht- Sing- und Spiel-Kunst der Alten*, p. 141 ff., that they were used in their idol worship, not only to inform the people of the impending sacrifice, but also to enliven the sacrificial animals at their stately parading, to make them follow the crowd and thus to make the procession even more stately.

Thus when Eustathius (in *Homeri Illiadis et Odysseae libros* Σ) describes the curved trombone of Osiris, he also adds that one uses such things for calling the people to

zu beruffen; wie es etwan heut zu Tage bey uns durch Glockenklang von der Zeit des Gottesdienstes benachrichtiget wird. Und Apulejus, da er im XI Buche von solcher Proceßion redet, spricht, daß die Trompeter, welche dem grossen Serapis geweihet gewesen, mitgegangen mit einer krummen Posaune, welche, da sie an den Mund angesetzet über den Kopff bißwieder an das Ohr herum gedrehet gewesen auf welchen sie die diesem Götzen gewidmete Stückgen oder Lieder gespielt. Aus welchen zu ersehen, daß sie gantz anders, als unsere heitigen Posaunen, und wie Krumm-oder Waldhörner gestaltet gewesen.

the sacrifice. This is roughly similar to the present-day announcement of religious services through the ringing of bells. And Apuleius, when he speaks of such a procession in Book XI [of *The Golden Ass*], says that the trumpeters, who had been dedicated to the great Serapis, went along with a large curved trombone, which they had set on the mouth and which was wound over and around the head down to the ear, and on which they played pieces or songs dedicated to this idol. From this, we can see that these were shaped quite differently from our present-day trombones and were more like crumhorns or hunting horns.

Wie denn gedachtet Eustachius die alten Posaunen in sechs Arten, nach dem Unterschied der Völcker, die solche gebrauchet, abtheilet.

And then the previously mentioned Eustathius divides the ancient trombones into six types, according to the different peoples who used them.

1) Zeiget er, daß unter den Argivern eine gerade Posaune gebräuchlich war, welche die Griechen vor der Minerva Erfindung hielten.

1) He shows that a straight trombone was in use among the Argives, which the Greeks claimed was invented by Minerva.

2) Unter den Libyern und Egyptern war die gekrümmte Posaune (die kurtz vorher Apulejus beschrieben worden) gemein, welche von ihnen zu den Griechen und Römern übergekommen war. Man glaubt, daß Osiris diß Kunststück erfunden hätte.

2) Among the Libyans and Egyptians, the curved trombone (as just described by Apuleius) was common. This came over from these groups to the Greeks and Romans. It was believed that Osiris had invented this work of art.

3) Unter den Celten war eine Trompete im Gebrauch, deren ausserstes Stücke einem Ochsen-Maul gleichete, oder dem

3) Among the Celts, a trumpet was in use, whose outermost piece resembled an ox-mouth or the mouth of some other monster or

Munde eines andern Monstri oder
Unthiers. Diese war in die
Morgenländer kommen durch die
alten Gallier, da sie in Asien
übersetzten, und sich in Galatien
niederliessen.

4) Die Paphlogonier gebrauchten
auch Trompeten von grossem und
grobem Laut, viel heßlicher als die
vorhergehende, deren ausserstes
Stücke einen gantzen Kopff eines
Ochsens vorstellete, und in die
Höhe nach der Lufft gehalten ward,
wenn es geblasen wurde.

[5)] Unter den Medern war ein
besonder Instrument, dessen Röhre
aus einem grossen und steiffen
Riedstock gemacht war, und ein
erschrecklich Gethön machte,
nachdem ein grob klingend
Mundstück daran gestecktet wurde.

6) Die Tyrrhener hatten eine
Trompete erfunden, welche der
Phrygischen Pfeiffe in Gestalt gleich
war, hatte ein auf Lippen Art
krumm gebogenes äussertes Stück
von sehr hellem Klang.

Was den Gebrauch der Posaunen
bey dem Volcke Gottes anlaget, so
pflegte man dieselben zu blasen

1) um das Volck damit zusammen
zu ruffen, wenn etwas
hochwichtiges, das den gemeinen
Nutzen betraff, zu berathschlagen,
oder anzukündigen war, 4 B. Mos.
X, 2. 3. 7;

2) wenn die Fürsten und Obersten
über tausend in Israel solten
zusammen kommen, v. 4;

creature. This had come into the
orient through the ancient Gauls
when they moved to Asia and
settled in Galatia.

4) The Paphlagonians also used
trumpets with a great and rough
sound, much uglier than the
previous one. The outermost piece
of these represented the whole head
of an ox, and it was held straight
up in the air when being played.

5) Among the Medes, there was a
special instrument, whose pipes
were made out of a large, stiff reed
stalk. After a coarse sounding
mouthpiece was stuck on it, it made
a horrible noise.

6) The Tyrrhenians had invented a
trumpet, which was the same shape
as the Phrygian whistle and had an
outermost piece bent like lips and a
very light sound.

Which brings us to the use of
trombones among the people of
God. They played it for the same
reasons:

1) to call together the people in this
way whenever something highly
important that concerned the
common needs was to be discussed
or announced, Numbers 10: 2, 3, 7.

2) whenever the princes and heads
over thousands in Israel should
come together, v. 4.

3) wenn die Läger solten aufbrechen, v. 5. 6;

3) whenever they should break camp, v. 5, 6.

4) wenn sie wolten im Streit ziehen, v. 9;

4) whenever they marched into battle, v. 9.

5) in Erlangung des Sieges, und hatte alsdenn alle Feindseligkeit ein Ende, so bald die Posaunen geblasen wurden, 2 B. Sam XVIII, 16; Cap. XX, 21;

5) in the winning of victory, and all hostilities had an end as soon as the trombones were played, 2 Samuel 18:16; 20:21.

6) bey Krönung der König, 1 B. Kön. I, 34;

6) at the coronation of kings, 1 Kings 1:34.

7) wurde das Volck damit zusammen beruffen an den Festen und Neumonden, 4 B. Mos. X, 10. 11; sonderlich wurden sie gebraucht am Tage der Versöhnung, bey Abkündigung des Jubel-Jahrs, und am Posaunen-Feste, jedoch nicht unter dem Singen der Sänger, weil derselben starcker Laut die Singstimmen und Säytenspiele zu sehr betäubet hätte. Woraus sie aber gemacht gewesen, ist in dem Artickel Neu Jahr der Ebräer, im XXIV Bande, p. 203. sonderlich p. 207. zu sehen.

7) when the people were called together at the festivals and new moons, Numbers 10:10−11. They were used especially on the Day of Atonement, at the proclamation of jubilee years, and at trombone festivals, however not with the singing of the singers, because this same powerful sound would have drowned out the singing voices and the string players too much. What these consisted of can be seen in the "Hebrew New Year" in volume 24, page 203, and especially page 207.

Wie es übrigens auch gebräuchlich war, daß die auf hohe Thürme und Warten bestellte Wächter, mit der Posaune ein Zeichen geben und blasen musten, wenn sich was feindliches oder gefährliches spüren ließ, so nimmt GOtt der HErr daher ein Gleichniß, und sagt zu dem Propheten Hosea, Cap. VIII, 1: Rufte laut, wie eine Posaune; oder wie es eigentlich heist: *ad palatum tuum buccinam seu tubam, scil. da, adhibe, admove*, nimm die Posaune in deinen vollen Mund.

As it was otherwise common that the guards placed in high towers and watchtowers had to blow the trombone to give a sign whenever something dangerous or hostile was spotted, so it is that the Lord God makes the simile and says to the prophet Hosea (Hosea 8:1), "Set the trombone to your mouth." The Syriac translator, which Luther follows, gave the figurative meaning, "from the voice of a caller or preacher" (Isaiah 40:3).

Der Chaldäis. Dollmetscher hats
gegeben *Gutture tuo clamita, velot
tuba*; welchem Luther nachgefolget;
und ist eine figürlich Rede, *de voce
clamantis*, von der Stimme eines
Ruffers oder Predigers, Es. XL, 3.

Denn eine Posaune kan ja das nicht
sagen, was hier zu sagen war; daher
wird durch die Redens-Art,
buccinam ad palatum admovere, die
Posaune in den Mund nehmen,
nichts anders verstanden, als eine
Sache entweder schriftlich oder
mündlich sagen und kund thun,
oder etwas deutlich und öffentlich
vorbringen, daß es zu jedermans
Wissenschaft komme. Denn wie ein
Wächter, wenn er sichet das
Schwerd kommen, muß die
Drommeten blasen, und das Volck
warmen, Es. XXXIII, 3. so solte
auch heir der Prophet seine
erheben, öffentlich und nicht in
einem Winckel predigen, daß es
jedermann hören, und sich für dem
instehenden Unglück entsetzen
möchte. Den obwol einige wollen,
GOTT rede das gantze Volck an,
wie es vorher geheissen: Blaset
Posaunen zu Gibea, ja drommetet
zu Rama, Hos. V, 8. so giebt doch
der Context ein anders hier zu
erkennen. Den GOtt befahl es dem
Propheten.

Da Amos von GOtt Befehl bekam,
die Posaune zu blasen, so kam ein
unangenehmer Thon heraus: Man
wird dieß Land, hieß es, rings
umher belagern, und dich von
deiner Macht herunter reissen, und
diene Häuser plündern, Amos III,
11. Nicht besser klang es bey
Hosea. Gräfens *Conc. in Hos.* p.

For naturally a trombone cannot say
what was to be said here; therefore,
the idiom "take the trombone to
your mouth" is understood as
nothing else than to announce or
say something, either in writing or
orally, or to bring up something
clearly and publicly, so that it
becomes everyone's knowledge.
The just as the guard, when he sees
the sword coming, must sound the
trumpet and warn the people
(Ezekiel 33:3), similarly the prophet
here should also raise his voice
publicly, and not preach in a corner,
so that everyone can hear and be
shocked in the face of the
misfortune herein. For even if some
claim that God speaks to the whole
people, as was stated earlier,
"Blow ye the trombone at Gibeah
and the trumpet in Ramah" (Hosea
5:8), so it is however that the
context provides a distinction to be
recognized here. For God
commanded the prophet to do it.

When Amos received the command
from God to sound the trombone,
an unpleasant sound came out. It
proclaimed that the land around
them would be placed under siege
and that you would be torn out of
your power and your houses will be
plundered (Amos 3:2). It did not
sound better for Hosea. See Gräfe's

743. u. f. Sieh auch den Artickel: Trombone.

Conc. in Hos., p. 743 ff. See also the article "Trombone."

POSAUNE (alt-) siehe Posaune.

POSAUNE (alto) see Posaune.

POSAUNE (contra) siehe Contra-Posaune im VI B. p. 1145.

POSAUNE (contra) see Contra-Posaune in Vol. 6, p. 1145.

POSAUNE (gemein) siehe Posaune.

POSAUNE (ordinary) see Posaune.

POSAUNE (Octav-) siehe Posaune.

POSAUNE (octave) see Posaune.

POSAUNE (Quart-) siehe Posaune.

POSAUNE (quart) see Posaune.

POSAUNE GOttes. Wenn Paulus die majestätliche Ankunst CHristi zum jüngsten Gericht beschreiben will, so spricht er I Thessal. IV, 16: der HERR wird mit einem Feldgeschrey, und Stimme des Ertz-Engels, und mit der Posaune GOttes hernieder kommen von Himmel. Anderweit, da er davon redet, nennet ers ein Geheimniß, I Corinth. XV, 51. 52. darum auch die Gelehrten untershiedene Meynungen davon geheget. Amelius sagt, es ziele Paulus auf die Gerichte der Juden so wohl als Heyden, in welchen die Posaunen gebraucht wurden, das Volck bey der Hinrichtung der öffentlichen Ubelthäter zu versammelen. Siehe dessen Erklärung dunckler Schriftstellen N. Test. I Th. p. 20.

POSAUNE GOTTES. When Paul wants to describe the majestic arrival of Christ at the Last Judgement, he says in 1 Thessalonians 4:16, "For the Lord himself shall descend from heaven with a shout, with the voice of the archangel and with the trombone of God." Elsewhere, when he speaks of this he calls it a mystery (1 Corinthians 15:51, 52), and for this reason, the scholars also foster differing opinions of it. Amelius says that Paul is aiming at the courts of Jews as well as heathens, in which trombone were used to gather the people together for the execution of exposed evil-doers. See his *Erklärung dunckler Schriftstellen Neues Testament*, Part I, p. 20.

Andere haben es von einer rechten naturlichen Posaune erkläret, und das darum, weil Paulus ausdrücklich von einer Posaune rede, und man in Geheimnissen nicht so leicht von dem Buchstaben weichen dürffe;

Others have explained it as a quite natural trombone for the reason that Paul explicitly speaks of a trombone and because one must not wander from the letters so easily with mysteries, for John also, when

wie den Johannes, da er im Geschichte das letzte Gerichte gesehen, den Schall der Posaunen gehöret, Offenb. Joh. VIII, 2. 6. u. ff. Cap. IX, 1. 13.

Wieder andere verstehen es im Gegentheil verblümter Weise von schrecklichem Donner, der alsdenn solle gehöret werden, weil die Schrift allewege, so sie von GOttes Stimme redet, melde, daß Donner unt Blitz darbey fürgegangen, 2 B. Mos. XIX, 16. Noch andere sehen auf die vernehmlich Stimme Christi, mit welcher er die Todten aus den Gräbern auferwecken werde: Der HERR HERR wird die Poaune blasen, Zach. IX, 14. und die in den Gräbern werden seine Stimme hören, Joh. V, 28.

Was es nun eigentlich für eine Posaune seyn werde, können wir in diesem Leben nicht erforschen, wir werdens aber dereinst schon erfahren. Darum ists eine unnützte Frage, wenn die alten Schul-Lehrer Suarez und Thyräus disputiren wollen, ob diese Posaune aus Gold, Silber, Kuppfer oder Ertz, aus einer Wolcken oder anderm *meteoro* seyn werde? Die beste Meynung ist, daß Christus und die Engel drommeten werden, das ist, einen Schall oder Klang erschallen lassen, daß mans allenthalben in der Luft hören wird, und die Todten alsbald auf Christi Befehl aus den Gräbern herfür kommen werden. Adami *Delic. Dict. P. V.* p. 908. u. f.

Ein anderer Gottesgelehrter macht hierüber folgende Auslegung: Vorzeiten, schreibet er, ist der

he saw the Last Judgment in the face, heard the sound of trombones (Revelation 8:2, 6ff.; 9:1, 13).

Others still understand it in a figurative manner, by contrast, as a terrible thunder because the Scriptures, everywhere that they speak of God's voice, report that thunder and lightning precede it (Exodus 19:16). Still others look to the audible name of Christ, with which he will resurrect the dead out of the graves. The Lord of Lords will sound the trombone (Zechariah 9:14) and those in the graves will hear his voice (John 5:28).

Now what kind of trombone it will actually be, we cannot research in this life, but we will some day find out. For this reason, it is a useless question when the old scholastics Suarez and Thyraeus want to dispute whether the trombone will be made of gold, silver, copper, or brass, or whether it will come from a cloud or some other heavenly phenomenon. The best opinion is that Christ and the angels will trumpet, that is, they will have a resonance and sound produced which people will hear everywhere in the air, and the dead will come forth from the graves at Christ's command. (Adami, *Delic. Dict. P. V.* p. 908ff.)

Another scholar of God makes the following interpretation concerning this. He writes: previously the use

Gebrauch der Posaunen sehr üblich gewesen: da GOtt sein Gesetz auf dem Berge Sinai geben wolte, da hörete das Volck einen Ton einer starcken Posaune, welcher immer stärcker ward, 2 B. Mos. XIX, 16. 19. besiehe Offenb. Joh. VIII, 2. Jos. VI, 16. Es. XXXIII, 3. Jerem. IV, 19. 4 B. Mos. X, 8. 10. 1 B. Kön. I, 34. B. Richt. VI, 34. Cap. VII, 20; und dadurch wird auch die Ankunft des majestätischen Richters verkündiget werden; und heistet eine Posaune GOttes, weil sie mächtig tönen wird, so daß von solchen Stimmen zusammen Himmel und Erden in einander brechen, die Gräber sich eröffnen, und die Todten lebendig hervor gehen werden; und halten die alten Lehrer meistentheils dafür, daß solches alles nicht werde seyn ein unverständlicher Klang, sondern eine Sprache und Rede, die man vernehmen werde.

of the trombone was very common. When God wanted to give his law on Mount Sinai, the people heard the sound of a powerful trombone, which became ever more powerful (Exodus 19:16, 19; see also Revelation 8:2; John 6:16; Ezekiel 33:3, Jeremiah 4:19; Numbers 10:8, 10; 1 Kings 1:34; Judges 6:34; 7:20). And in this way, the advent of the majestic judge will also be announced; and it is called a trombone of God, because it will sound mightily, so that Heaven and Earth will collapse into each other from such voices. The graves will open, and the dead will procede alive. The old teachers mostly believe that this will not all be incomprehensible noise, but rather a language and speech which one will hear.

Und schreibet Luther hierüber: "Ich "lasse mirs gefallen, daß es eine "solche Stimme seyn werde: Stehet "auf ihr Todten, wie Christus den "verstorbenen Lazarum aus dem "Grabe ruffet, Joh. XI. 43. und zu "dem Mägdlein und Jüngling Matth. "IX, 25. u. Luc. VII, 14. sprach: Ich "sage dir, stehe auf; also werde er "auch durch das Feldgeschrey, die "Stimme des Ertz-Engels und der "Posaune GOttes die Todten "auferwecken; daß, wie jetzt auf "Erden des Predigers Stimme, der "GOttes Wort predigt, nicht des "Menschen, sondern GOttes Wort "heisset; so ist auch die Stimme des "Ertz-Engels GOttes Stimme, welche "aus seinem Befehl und Kraft gehen

And Luther writes about this. "I can accept that there should be such a voice: arise, you dead, and Christ called the dead Lazarus from the grave (John 11:43), and said to the maiden and boy (Matthew 9:25 and Luke 7:14), I say to you, arise. Thus he will awaken the dead through the password, the voice of the archangel, and the trombone of God, so that, as now the voice of the preacher on earth who preaches the word of God, that word is called God's and not man's, so it is that the voice of the archangel is the voice of God, which will procede and sound from his command and power." Also, the ideas of Chysostom and Theophylactus tend

"und tönen wird." Dahin auch Chrysostomi und Theophylacti Gedancken gehen. Weihenmeiers Fest-Pos. II Th. p. 57. u. f.

in that direction. See Weihenmeier's *Fest-Posaune* Part II, p. 57ff.

POSAUNEN, Matth. VI, 2. Ob die Pharisäer im Gebrauch gehabt, daß, wenn sie haben Allmosen gegeben, sie zuvor durch öffentlichen Posaunen-Schall solches haben ausblasen lassen, zwar mit dem Vorgeben, daß es den armen Leuten wissend gemacht werde, damit nicht leichtlich ein Armes übergangen werden möchte, da es doch in der Wahrheit von ihnen zu dem Ende geschehen, daß ihre Freygebigkeit jedermann kund gethan würde, und also sich viele Leute als Zuschauer und Verwunderer bey der Spende versammeln sollen? da sind etliche, die es bejahen: Lightfot aber bekennet, daß, ob er wohl allenthalben fleißig nachgeforschet, so habe er doch nirgends nichts davon finden können.

POSAUNEN (Matthew 6:2). Did the Pharisees maintain the habit that, whenever they gave alms, they first had this sounded through public trombone playing? And was it with the pretense that it should be made known to the poor people, so that a poor person would not be easily passed over, although it was truly done so by them, so that their generosity would become known to everyone, and thus should assemble many people as spectators and admirers at the donation? There are many who assert this. Lightfoot claims, however, that he has never found any evidence of that anywhere, even though he diligently searched just about everywhere.

Dahero andere wollen, Christus ziele hiermit auf die *Histriones*, Comödianten und dergleichen Leute, welche mit Posaunen- und Trompeten-Schall pflegten die Leute zusammen zu ruffen, damit die Zuschauer möchten bekommen; als wolte Christus sagen: machts nicht wie die Gauckler und Spieler, wenn ihr wolt Allmosen geben, die durch den Posaunen-Schall die Leute zusammen ruffen.

Thus, others maintain Christ is pointing with this analogy at the actors and such people who call the others together with trombone and trumpet playing, so that they have spectators, as if Christ meant to say, "When you want to give alms, do not do it like the jugglers and actors who call the people together through trombone playing."

Chrysostomus und Theophylactus wollen, Christus sehe auf die Weise der Juden, welche zum Gottesdienste die Leute durch der

Chrystostom and Theophylactus maintain that Christ is looking at the ways of the Jews, who like to encourage the people to gather for

Posaunen-Schall, wie heut zu Tage durch die Glocken, pflegten zusammen zu fordern; also sollen sie es nicht machen, will der HErr sagen, wenn sie Allmosen geben; sie sollen nicht vor sich posaunen lassen, daß es jedermann höre und zulauffte, und sehe, wie sie so reich Allmosen austheilen, denn sonst haben sie ihren Lohn dahin. Weihenmeiers Evang. Buß, und Trost-Pred. I Th. p. 121. u. f.

the worship services through trombone playing as is done in the present day by means of bells. They should not do it this way when they give alms. That is, the Lord intends that they should not have the trombone played before them so that everyone hears and comes running to see how they distribute alms, for otherwise, they have lost their reward. See Weihenmeier's *Evangelische Buß- und Trost-Predigten* Part I, page 121ff.

POSAUNEN-FEST, welches sonst auch genennet wird das Fest des Blasens, das Fest der Drommeten, wie auch das Fest des neuen Jahres war ein Fest bey denen Jüden, welches einfiel auf den ersten Tag des siebenden Monden, und also im Neumonden; daher dieser Neumond von denen ordentlichen Neumonden unterschieden war, sowol wegen des Blasens, Posaunens oder Drommetens, welches an andern Neumonden nicht so lange auch nicht so oft geschahe; als auch wegen der Opffer, weil auf diesen Tag mehr Opffer geopffert wurden, als auf andere Neumonden.

POSAUNEN-FEST, which is also called the festival of wind playing, the festival of trumpets, and the festival of the New Year, was a festival among the Jews, which fell on the first day of the seventh month and thus during the new moon. For this reason, this new moon was different from the ordinary ones: for the wind-playing, tromboning, or trumpeting, which did not last as long or happen as often on other new moons, as well as for the sake of sacrifices, because on this day, more sacrifices were offered than on other new moons.

Denn, neben den ordentl. u. gewöhnl. monatl. u. täglichen Opffern, geschahe ein Brandopffer von einem jungen Farren, einem Widder, sieben jahrigen Lämmern, einem Ziegenbock zim Sündopffer, mit ihren Speiß- und Trankopffern, 4 B. Mos. XXIX, 1–6. Mehrere Nachricht von diesem Feste, als worinnen se bestanden, wenn es gefeyert, warum und wie es gehalten worden, u. s. w. ist in dem Artickel Neu-Jahr der Ebräer, im XXIV B. p. 203 u. ff. zu finden.

For, next to the ordinary and customary monthly and daily sacrifices, a burnt offering of a bullock, a ram, seven young lambs, and a goat was made as an atonement, along with their grain and drink offerings (Numbers 29: 1–6). More information about this festival, such as what it consisted of, when it was celebrated, why and how it was held, etc., can be found in the article "Hebrew New Year" in volume 24, pages 203ff.

TROMBONE, ist ein Italienisches Wort, und heist eine Posaune, davon im XXVIII Bande, p. 1695 u. f.	TROMBONE is an Italian word and means *Posaune*, concerning which, see volume 28, columns 1695ff.
TROMBONE GRANDE, ist Italienisch, und heist schlechtweg und ohne Zusatz: *Trombone*, die Baß oder Octav-Posaune.	TROMBONE GRANDE is Italian and means simply and without addition, trombone, the [contra-] bass or octave trombone.
TROMBONE GROSSO, ist Italienisch, und heist die grosse Quart-Posaune.	TROMBONE GROSSO is Italian and means the quart trombone.
TROMBONE MAGGIORE, heist die grosse Alt-Posaune.	TROMBONE MAGGIORE means the large alto trombone.
TROMBONE PICCOLO, ist Italienisch und heist die kleine Alt-Posaune.	TROMBONE PICCOLO is Italian and means the small alto trombone.
TROMBONI, seihe Posaune, im XXVIII Bande, p. 1695.	TROMBONI, see *Posaune* in volume 28, columns 1695ff.
TROMBONISTA, Trombonisti, ist Italienisch, und heist: der oder die die Posaune blasen.	TROMBONISTA, Trombonisti, is Italian and means he or they who play the trombone.

GIOVANNI BATTISTA MARTINI

Storia della musica[34]

(1761)

Martini's primary influence on music was as a teacher. He was also a prolific composer and respected writer. His history of music seems to be more important for the library he collected while doing the research for it than for its contents. Howard Brofsky dismisses it as being less practical than his other works.[35] Vincent Duckles, although

---

[34] Giovanni Battista Martini, *Storia della musica*, 3 vols (Bologna: Lelio dalla Volpe, 1757 [i.e. 1761]), vol. 1, 429–31.

[35] Howard Brofsky, "Martini, Padre Giovanni Battista," *The New Grove*, vol. 11, 724.

acknowledging the history's influence and its value as a source for later authors, criticizes Martini's archaic methodology.[36] Part of the impracticality of this work results from the fact that Martini did not live to complete it, and only the volumes on ancient music ever appeared.

The first volume, although dated 1757, appeared in 1761. It includes descriptions of the various instruments. The brief passage on the trombone serves to demonstrate the weakness of Martini's methodology. His entire description is based on an appeal to the authority of earlier writers, and he supplements his own rather wandering prose with lengthy footnotes which, for the most part, quote the authorities.

Martini relies most strongly on Gioseffo Zarlino's *Sopplimenti musicali* (1588) and Marin Mersenne's *Harmonicorum libri* (1635–36). This latter is an odd choice, being essentially a first draft of his definitive *Harmonie universelle* (1636). That the former was written in Latin and the latter in French may have influenced Martini's decision. The footnotes quote from three sources not mentioned in the text: Giovanni Maria Artusi's *Delle imperfettione della moderna musica* ... (1600), Ercole Bottrigari's *Il desiderio, overo de' concerti di varij strumenti musicali* (1594), and Aurelio Virgiliano's *Il dolcimielo* (c. 1600). None of Martini's sources are well known to trombonists today.

Since the focus of this chapter is on what eighteenth-century writers, and not sixteenth- or seventeenth-century writers, wrote about the trombone, I have omitted Martini's footnotes. Even in the text, Martini has little if anything original to say. His only interest in the trombone is that it fills in notes that, before the invention of valves, were impossible on the other brass instruments. He makes no attempt to describe the workings of the slide mechanism and includes no information about what kind of music trombones were used in. Therefore, he provides possibly the least useful eighteenth-century description for the purposes of modern readers.

One odd feature of Martini's description, copied from Mersenne, is the implication that the trombone was at some time in C. Beginning the scale and overtone series on C_1 was convenient for Mersenne, allowing him to pursue the analogy with notes available on the trumpet. He could not have meant to say that trombones were actually built in that key. Martini found it more convenient to copy

---

[36] Vincent Duckles, *Musical Reference and Research Materials*, 3rd ed. (New York: Free Press, 1974), 431.

Plate 5. Martini: Illustration from *Storia della musica*.

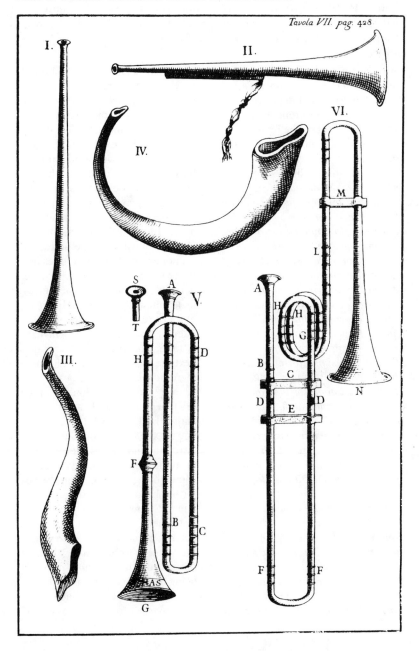

Reprinted from *The Trumpet & Trombone in Graphic Arts: 1500—1800* by
Tom L. Naylor © 1979 The Brass Press. Used by permission.

Mersenne than use any more accurate information he may have had. He seems to have understood the hypothetical nature of Mersenne's description, closing his first paragraph with the words "supposing a lowest note of C_1.

A discorrer per tanto in primo luogo del *Trombone amovibile*, come più esteso in lunghezza e larghezza, dimostreremo colla scorta del Zarlino, che lo descrive esattamente, la qualità e quantità de' *Suoni*, di cui è capace. *Il Trombone*, dice egli, *il che è veramente cosa degna di considerazione, nel quale, come mi fu fatto vedere et udire più fiate da quelli, che lo sanno adoperar bene, incominciandosi a sonare dalla voce o suono gravissimo, che può fare cotale istrumento; eßendo (come dicono) tutto serrato, senza punto alterarlo; non si può salire all'acuto per ordine et per altri gradi, che per quelli che poco fa ho dimostrato. Perciocchè prima salendo verso l'acuto, non si può formare altro Intervallo, che sia miore della Diapason, dopoi, formato questo salendo pure a tal modo; quello della Diapente; ne da questo si può passare ad altro più vicino, che a quello della Diatessaron: similmente dopo la Diatessaron non si può formare se non il Ditono: dopo il quale, senz'alcun mezzo si forma il Semiditono; et ultimamente gli è conceßo di formare il Grado o Intervallo del Tuono. Volendo poi paßare più oltra, et formare altri Intervalli: fa bisogno di alterare, muovere et aprire (come dicono) l'Istrumento; altramente il tutto tornarebbe vano. Il P. Mersennio,*

Before we speak at length about the movable trombone, we would testify with the guidance of Zarlino, who describes exactly the quality and quantity of sounds of which it is capable. "The trombone," he says, "is truly worthy of consideration. I have lately seen and heard the blowing of those who play it well, starting to play with the deepest sound or voice the instrument can make. Being, as is said, a closed instrument wihtout tone holes, it cannot climb to the high notes by the scale and other degrees I have demonstrated already. Therefore, at first climbing towards the high notes, it cannot form any other interval smaller than the octave. After having formed that, it climbs next the interval of a fifth. From there, it can pass to the next nearest, the fourth. Similarly, after the fourth, it can only form the major third, after which, without any middle step, it forms the minor third, and finally it is allowed to form the degree or interval of the whole tone. Wanting, then, to pass farther beyond and form other intervals, one needs to alter the instrument, to move, or as they say, open it; otherwise it is all in vain." Mersenne, carrying on research on this instrument, describes it to us as being movable by means of the shortening and lengthening of its lower part. It forms a series of

prosegundo le richerche sopra questo *Strumento* ci descrive, come essendo *amovibile* col mezzo dell'abbreviare o allungare la parte inferiore dello stesso, si forma una *Serie* di quindici *Voci*, la quale nell'Esempio seguente esponiamo, supponendo il di lui *Suono* più *grave* in *C sol faut gravissimo*.

fifteen notes, which we present in the following example, supposing a lowest note of C_1.

Example 10 Martini: [Scale of the Trombone]

Descritte le qualit e quantità de' *Suoni* o *Voci* del *Trombone*, facilmente rilevansi quelle della *Tromba ripiegata*, le quali *Voci* secondo l'esatta ricerca fattane dal lodato P. Mersennio, riduconsi ad esser simili a quelle del *Trombone amovibile*, con questo divario, che alla *Tromba ripiegata*, non essendo ella per se stessa *amovibile*, mancano i frapposti all' *Ottava*, alla *Quinta*, alla *Quarta Quarta acuta*, dopo la quale forma la serie de' *Tuoni* e *Semituoni Diatonici* per il corso di otto *Voci*, talchè si estende in tutto fino al numero di tredici *Voci*, secondo l'uso comune dei Suonatori; la qual *Serie* espressa viene nell'esempio seguente, in cui si stabilisce il *Suono* più *grave* in *C sol faut*.

He describes the quantity and quality of sounds or notes of the trombone, obviously those of the folded trumpet. These notes, according to the research of the acclaimed Mersenne, are reduced to be similar to those of the trombone. There is this difference: the trumpet, not being similarly movable, lacks the sounds that fill in the intervals. It makes the octave, fifth, fourth, the two thirds (major and minor), and the augmented fourth, after which it forms the series of diatonic whole steps and half steps for the course of eight notes, so that it is extended all the way to the number of 13 notes according to the common usage of players. This series is shown in the following example, in which the sound is fixed on a lowest note of C_1.

Example 11: Martini: [Overtone Series]

Sotto Baſſo .   Baſſo .Vurgano. Striano   toccata quinta do re mi fa fol   re   mi   fa

JOHANN SAMUEL HALLE

Werkstätte der heutigen Kunst[37]

(ca. 1764)

Halle was not a musician, but he was a prolific author on scientific, technological, and magical subjects. *Werkstätte der heutigen Kunst* is a survey of various arts and crafts as they existed in the middle of the eighteenth century. The third volume (of four) includes a lengthy section on instrument making, with a paragraph on the trombone. In spite of its brevity, there are two points of interest. Halle is the first author to mention the discant (soprano) trombone. He also mentions the handle needed to reach the outer positions on the bass trombone, a detail more often encountered in pictures than in prose.

Posaunen gibt es vier; Diskant- Alt- Tenor- und Qvart- oder Qvintposaunen, die Qvartposaunen von 4 Fus Orgelthon. Ihr Mundstükk ist, wie an den Trompeten, blos ein Kessel, dessen Boden ein enges Loch hat, das aber weiter ist. Sie bestehen aus einem weiten Schallstükk, zwo Spillen, zween Krummbögen, zwo Stosspillen, zween Krummbögen, die gezogen, d. i. weiter vorgerükkt	There are four kinds of trombone: discant, alto, tenor and quart or quint bass trombones. The quart trombones have a four-foot organ tone. As on the trumpet, their mouthpiece is simply a cup with a hole in the bottom, except it is wider. They consist of a broad sounding piece [i.e. bell section], two cylinders, two bent arcs, two movable cylinders, and two bent arcs that are pulled, that is, moved

---

[37] Johann Samuel Halle, *Werkstätte der heutigen Kunst*, 4 vols. (Brandenburg: J. W. Halle, 1761–65), vol. 3, 371.

werden. Je länger der Auszug, desto tiefer der Thon. An den grossen 16 füssigen ist ein Drat mit einem Gelenke und Griffe feste, um die Spillen, weil der Arm nicht so weit hinreicht, damit herauszuziehen. Sie steigen durch drei Oktaven, und werden blos durch die Gewalt des Athems und der Lippen geblasen, welcher Athem zu jedem Thon sein gewisses Maß von Luft haben mus.

forward. The further out it is pulled, the deeper the tone. On the large sixteen-foot one, a wire is fastened with a joint and handle for pulling out the slide, because the arm does not reach far enough. They ascend through three octaves and are played simply with the force of breath and lips, by which each breath must have a definite amount of air.

[JEAN-JACQUES ROUSSEAU]

Encyclopédie, ou Dictionnaire raisonné...[38]

(1765)

Inspired by the success of Chambers's *Cyclopaedia*, a group of French writers under the leadership of Denis de Diderot and Jean d'Alembert collaborated on a similar but more ambitious project, the first volume of which appeared in 1751. Jean-Jacques Rousseau wrote most of the musical articles.

Rousseau provided not one, but two articles on the trombone, entitled "Sacquebute" (in volume 14) and "Trombone" (in volume 16). (Both volumes appeared in the same year.) The latter consists only of Brossard's article, minus the first paragraph, and so is of no further interest. The former merely describes the appearance and length of the trombone, although its last sentence mentions its role as a bass instrument. This brief description foreshadows the way the trombone would be used in French music after the Revolution, but does not describe any music known to me from the time Rousseau wrote the article.

If Rousseau ever heard a trombone, it must have been in the private orchestra of La Riche de Pouplinière, which performed

---

[38] [Jean-Jacques Rousseau], "Sacquebute," "Trombone," *Encyclopédie, ou Dictionnaire raisonné des sciences, des arts, et des métiers*, 35 vols., (Paris: Briason [et al.], 1751–80), vol. 14, 474; 16, 692.

selections of Rousseau's opera-ballet *Les muses galantes* in 1745.[39] As will be seen in Chapter 4, it is a matter of controversy whether Pouplinière actually had trombones in his orchestra, so it is impossible to determine when he had them or what they played. Two possible sources for Rousseau's comment on the trombone as a bass instrument are Mersenne's *Harmonie universelle* or Chambers's *Cyclopaedia*.

As late as 1780, when the index appeared, the trombone had very little importance in the eyes of the encyclopedists. The index has no entry for "Trombone"; it refers readers to this article with the comment "Trompette des italiens appellée trombone. XVI. 692.a." [Trumpet of the Italians called trombone, volume 16, p. 692.]. Under "Sacquebute," the index merely says, "sorte d'instrument de musique à vent. Sa déscription. XIV. 474.a." [Type of musical wind instrument. Its description, volume 14, p. 474.] In contrast, there are several entries under "Trompette" promising to tell the etymology of the name, to describe both ancient and modern trumpets, to explain the eight principal ways of playing the military trumpet, and to explain the use of the trumpet in church music and chamber music. There is no recognition, either in the index or text, that the articles on "Sacquebute" and "Trombone" in fact describe the same instrument.

SACQUEBUTE, s.f. (*Musique instrum.*) instrument de Musique qui est à vent, & une espece de trompette harmonique, qui differe de la militaire en figure & en grandeur. Elle a son embouchure ou son bocal & son pavillon semblables; mais elle a quatre branches qui se démontent, se brisent à l'endroit des nœuds, & souvent au tortil, qui est le même tuyau qui se tortille deux fois, ou qui fait deux cercles au milieu de l'instrument; ce qui le fait descendre d'une quarte plus bas que son ton naturel. Elle contient aussi deux branches intérieurs, qui ne

SACKBUT: musical wind instrument and type of harmonic trumpet, which differs from the military trumpet in shape and size. It has a similar mouthpiece and bell, but it has four branches that come apart and break at the place of the knots, and often at the crook, which is the same pipe twisted twice, or which makes two circles in the middle of the instrument, which makes it descend a fourth below its natural pitch. The trombone also contains two interior branches, which can be seen only when they are drawn by means of a bar that one pushes as far as it can go, and

---

[39] Daniel Heartz, "Rousseau, Jean-Jacques," *The New Grove*, vol. 16, 270.

paroissent que quand on les tire par le moyen d'une barre qu'on pousse jusque vers a potence, & qui l'allonge comme on veut, pour faire toutes sortes de tons; les branches visibles serve d'etui aux invisibles. La *sacquebute* ordinairement a huit piés, lorsque'elle n'est point alongée, & qu'on n'y comprend point son tortil. Quand elle est tirée de toute sa longeur, elle va jusques à quinze piés. Son tortil est de deux piés neuf pouces; elle sert de base dans toutes sortes de concerts d'instrumens à vent, comme font le serpent & la fagot ou basson, & elle sert de basse-taille aus hautbois. (D. J.).

that lengthens it as desired in order to make all kinds of notes. The visible branches serve as a sheath for the invisible ones. The sackbut is ordinarily eight feet long when it is not lengthened at all and when no crook is used. When it is pulled out to its full length, it is nearly fifteen feet long. Its crook is two feet nine inches. It serves as the bass in all kinds of consorts of wind instruments, as do the serpent and the bassoon, and it serves as baritone to the oboe.

Encyclopaedia Britannica[40]

(1771)

It is almost a shock to look at the beginnings of what is now one of the most comprehensive and authoritative encyclopedias in the world and see how short and uninformative so many of the articles are. In its first edition, it was greatly inferior to Chambers's *Cyclopaedia*, which had already gone through several editions. The greatly expanded third edition, which appeared between 1790 and 1797, is generally of much greater interest to musicians than the first two editions. The article on the sackbut, however, was carried over from the first edition without change.

> SACKBUT, a musical instrument of the wind kind, being a sort of trumpet both in form and size: it is fit to play a bass, and is contrived to be drawn out or shortened, according to the tone required, whether grave or acute. The Italians call it *trombone*, and the Latins *tuba ductilis*.

---

[40] "Sackbut," *Encyclopaedia Britannica* 3 vols., 1st ed. (Edinburgh: Bell and Macfarquhar, 1771), vol. 3, 560.

WILLIAM TANS'UR

The Elements of Musick Display'd[41]

(1772)

Tans'ur was essentially a country church musician writing for other country church musicians.[42] As the trombone could not have been known in the English countryside or used in churches even in London (see the section on English music in Chapter 3), it is pretension, not utility, that led him to include half a chapter about the trombone. (The first half of the chapter describes the marine trumpet.)

This volume consists of five books, each with a separate title page, but with continuous pagination. The preface to the whole book is dated 1766. The title page for Book III, which contains Tans'ur's comments on the trombone, is dated 1767. The title page for the entire volume, however, carries the date 1772.

Tans'ur owes much to either Chambers or Grassineau, but does not copy verbatim. He could not have read very carefully, however. His list of the various sizes of trombone omits the alto trombone entirely. The reference to the second-trombone and the third-trombone likewise betrays that Tans'ur either was careless or did not understand his source. He must have had access to some source that I have not yet located; the reference to the sackbut makers' scale and the comparison with pitch pipes is without precedent otherwise, and Tans'ur seems to have lacked either the scholarship or the imagination to make any original contributions. The scale he refers to may have been some kind of drawing or chart. It is hard to imagine any kind of marking on the slide that would fulfill the same purpose.

The scriptural citation that opens Tans'urs description of the trombone shows his roots in church music; no other English author mentions it. In the King James Version, the translators mistranslated the Hebrew *sabbeka*, a stringed instrument, as "sackbut" in the third chapter of Daniel.

---

[41] William Tans'ur, *The Elements of Musick Display'd* (London: Stanley Crowder, 1772), 100–01.

[42] Nicholas Temperley, "Tans'ur, William," *The New Grove*, vol. 18, 567.

A glossary at the end of the book includes three entries of interest to this chapter. They are included as a sample of numerous glossaries and short-entry dictionaries published in eighteenth-century England.

> The *Sackbut*, or *Trumpet harmonious*, is mentioned in the Book of *Daniel*; it being a large *Trumpet* in Kind, tho' different in Form, and contrived to sound the *Basses* on; it being made longer or shorter, by drawing it out more or less, as the Tones require to be in *Acuteness* or *Gravity*, as we do our modern *Pitch-pipes*. It takes asunder in four Pieces or Branches, and has commonly a *Wreath* in the Middle, which is the same *Tube* only twice twisted; or making two *Circles* in the Middle of the Instrument; by which it may be brought down a *Fourth* lower than its *natural Tone*: Hence it is lengthened to hit any *Tone* you like, *Grave* or *Acute*, &c. It is generally 8 Feet long before drawn out; and will extend to 15 Feet long: And the *Wreath* is 2 Feet 9 Inches in Circumference; and serves for a *Bass* in *Concerts* of *Wind Musick* &c. There are several *Sizes*, viz. *Trombone-maggiore*, for the Tenor.--*Trombone-secundo*, a 2d.--*Trombone-secundo*, a 2d.--*Trombone-terza*, a 3d.--*Trombone-quarto*, a 4th; and the Key of each is generally *F-faut*; and to as many *Octaves* as its Length will admit; for which the *Sackbut* or *Serpent Makers* have a Scale, which they fix thereon, to shew how far they must be lengthened or shortened to sound the *Tones*, as we do our *Pitch-pipes*, &c.
> Sackbut. A Tubical Instrument play'd by drawing a Register.
> Sackbutist. A Player on the Sackbut.
> Trombone. A Sackbut.

JEAN BENJAMIN DE LA BORDE

Essai sur la musique ancienne et moderne[43]

(1780)

Jean-Benjamin de la Borde, born to an aristocratic family, pursued many varied interests, including politics, finance, literature, geography, and music. As a musician, he played a violin, composed music of minor interest, and wrote treatises of great value. The

---

[43] Jean Benjamin de la Borde. *Essai sur la musique ancienne et moderne.* 4 vols. (Paris: Ph.-D. Pierres, 1780), vol. 1, 203, 232, 272, 275–76, 278, 407.

four-volume *Essai sur la musique ancienne et moderne*, perhaps his most important work, covers a wide range of musical topics.[44]

La Borde mentions the trombone several times in the first of the four volumes of his treatise, both in the discussion of ancient and modern instruments. Where he relies on written sources, he merely passes on their errors. What makes his writings of value to modern trombonists, however, is that he is the first French author to demonstrate any first-hand knowledge of the trombone.

The "Saquebute" is listed among the instruments mentioned in the Bible (p. 203). La Borde gives no scriptural citations for any of the instruments, but as the translators of the King James Version erroneously translated *sabekka*, a stringed instrument, as "sackbut" in the third chapter of Daniel, it is possible that French scholars committed the same error.

Later (p. 232), La Borde comments that the trumpet of the Greeks and Romans was not different from that of the Hebrews. Facing this page is a plate of engravings based on, but not identical to those in Bonanni's *Gabinetto armonico* and labeled "*Trompettes antiques.*" One of these is a trombone, here captioned "*Trompette à plusieurs morceaux.*" The promised description of this "ancient trumpet" was somehow omitted. It is not on the page mentioned in the caption or anywhere else in the chapter on ancient trumpets. (See Plate 6.)

Among the modern instruments, La Borde includes articles entitled "*Saquebute.*" "*Tromboni, en Allemand, Posaunen,*" and "*Trompette rompue,*" with no cross references to acknowledge that all three describe the same instrument. The first includes measurements that can be traced back to Mersenne and a quotation from Rabelais, not mentioned by any other author in this chapter. The second seems to be based largely on an interview with one of the Parisian trombonists. The third is a summary of Bonanni's article, probably based on the French translation published in 1776. It contains the same basic description, the same comment based on Mersenne, and the same reference to Apuleius (with the same mistake in citing the second book instead of the eleventh.) Regarding Apuleius, La Borde cites one Scaschi Mirot. This is actually Fortunato Scacchi, who was also cited by Bonanni. In Bonanni's article, "Mirot." is an abbreviation of the title, not part of the author's name.

---

[44] Frederick Merritt, "La Borde [Laborde], Jean Benjamin (-François) de," *The New Grove*, vol. 10, 342–43.

Plate 6. La Borde: Trompettes Antiques

Reprinted from *The Trumpet & Trombone in Graphic Arts: 1500–1800* by
Tom L. Naylor © 1979 The Brass Press. Used by permission.

Near the end of the volume (p. 407), La Borde compares the
orchestra of the Opéra in 1713 and 1778, listing the instruments
available. Neither list mentions trombones, but under the 1778 list,
La Borde writes:

Tous les instrumens comme Tymbales, Trombone, Tambourins, Hautbois de forêt, &c, se remplissent par quelqu'uns des 64 Musiciens que composent l'Orchestre.	All of the instruments like timpani, trombones, tambourines, and English horns are supplied by certain ones of the 64 musicians who make up the orchestra.

As there is a no record of trombonists employed at the Opéra
before the 1774 production of Gluck's *Iphigénie en Aulide*, La
Borde here includes information more up to date than any other
writer in this chapter. He was an operatic composer himself, and his
brother-in-law was director of the Opéra.[45] Therefore, it is very
likely that he knew a number of the personnel of the Opéra person-
ally. As Chapter 4 will show, all of the trombonists were German.
The second of La Borde's articles, "*Tromboni*, en Allemand,
Posaunen," is the most reliable of his three articles on the trombone.
It is the only non-German writing that mentions the trombone's role
in German church music and the first French writing to attempt to
describe the character of the trombone and the music most suitable
for it. Furthermore, it mentions the soprano trombone, an instrument never used in France. La Borde must have heard trombones at
the Opéra and spoken with at least one of the Opéra's trombonists before he wrote this article.

The ranges he gives, however, are most unusual. The lower end
of the range for the alto and tenor is too high. The upper end of all
but the bass trombone are likewise much higher than any given by
any previous author.

Saquebute	*Saquebute*
Espece de Trompete dont le tuyau s'allonge & se racourcit à la volonté de celui qui en joue, ce qui fait les différens tons. C'est le même instrument que les Allemands & les	Kind of trumpet of which the tube can be lengthened and shortened at the will of whoever plays it in order to make different notes. It is the same instrument that the Germans

---

[45] Ibid., 342.

Italiens appelent *Trombona*. Les Latins l'appelaient *Tuba ductilis*.

and Italians call *Trombona*. The Latins called it *Tuba ductilis*.

La Saquebute a ordinairement huit pieds de long sans être tirée, & peut aller à seize quand elle est déployée. Cependant il y en a de différentes grandeurs. C'est par un anneau de fer qu'on la tire, & qu'on la fait rentrer.

The trombone is ordinarily eight feet long without being pulled, and it can go to sixteen when it is extended. Meanwhile, there are different sizes. It is by a loop of iron that one pulls it and makes it come back again.

Cet instrument était connu des Hébreux.

The instrument was known by the Hebrews.

Il en est parlé dans Rabelais, liv. I, chap. 23.

It is spoken of in Rabelais, [*Gargantua and Pantagruel*] Book I, Chapter 23.

Voici ce qu'il dit: "Ils "s'ébaudissaient à chanter "musicalement à quatre & cinq "parties, ou sur un thême à plaisir "de gorge (*probablement le chant "sur le livre*). Au regard des "instruments de Musique il aprint à "jouer du *Luct*, de l'*Epinette*, de la "*Harpe*, de la *Flûte d'Allemant*, & à "neuf trous, de la *Viole* & de la "*Sacquebute*."

Here is what he says: "They amused themselves by singing musically in four and five parts, or on a theme to their throat's content" (probably the song on the book). "In regard to the musical instruments, he learned to play the lute, the spinet, the harp, the German flute, the nine-holed flute [recorder], the viol, and the sackbut."

Tromboni, en Allemand, *Posaunen*

Trombones, in German, Posaunen

Instrument de cuivre jaune. Il y en a cinq.

Instrument of brass. There are five:

Canto.
Alto.
Tenor.
Basse.
Contre-Basse.

Soprano.
Alto.
Tenor.
Bass.
Contrabass.

On s'en sert beaucoup en Allemagne dans la Musique d'Eglise. On peut exécuter tous les tons & demi-tons par gradation presqu'insensible.

It is much used in German church music. It is possible to play all tones and semitones by almost inaudible gradations.

Example 12. La Borde: [Range of Trombones]

La maniere de les écrire est la même que pour les voix, & les *Tromboni* ont la même portée.	The manner of writing for them is the same as for voices, and the trombones have the same range.
La contre-basse est d'une quinte plus bas que la basse ordinaire. On ne s'est servi à l'Opéra que de l'*Alto, Tenor & Basse.*	The contrabass is a fifth lower than the ordinary bass. Only the alto, tenor, and bass are used at the Opéra in Paris.
Cet instrument fait le plus grand effet dans les marches funebres, & en général dans la Musique triste.	This instrument makes its greatest effect in funeral marches and, in general, sad music.

Trompette rompue

Trompete rompue

Instrument moderne, composè d'un double canal entrelacé l'un dans l'autre. On la tient avec la main gauche, & la droite soutient la partie supérieure qui est mobile, & qu'on peut allonger ou racourcir à volontè.

Modern instrument made of a double canal, one intertwined in the other. It is held in the left hand, and the right supports the upper part, which is mobile, and which can be lengthened or shortened at will.

Le P. Mersenne dit que les Français l'appelent Saquebute, & que si les voûtes étaient placées en ligne droite, elle aurait quinze pieds de long.

Mersenne said that the French call it *saquebute*, and that if the curves are straightened out, it will be fifteen feet long.

Scaschi Mirot en attribue l'invention aux Egyptiens, sur ce qu'Apulée

Scaschi Mirot attributes its invention to the Egyptians, which

semble la décrire dans son secod livre des Métamorphoses lorsqu'il parle des sacrifices qu'on célébrait en l'honneur d'Isis. Cependant il ne nous reste aucun monument ancien qui nous représente cette Trompete.

Apuleius seems to describe in his second [i.e. eleventh] book of Metamorphoses, when he speaks of sacrifices celebrated in honor of Isis. Meanwhile, there remains to us no ancient monument that portrays this trumpet for us.

JOHANN GEORG ALBRECHTSBERGER

Anweisung zur Composition[46]

(1790)

Johann Georg Albrechtsberger, well known to trombonists as the composer of a trombone concerto, is best known to music history in general as one of Beethoven's composition teachers. The textbook in composition that he wrote includes descriptions of various instruments. Albrechtsberger wrote a substantial paragraph about most of them. Of the trombone, he says only, "Posaunen gibt es dreyerlei, als Baß-, Tenor- und Altposaune; ihre mögliche Töne siehe bey No. 7." [Of trombones there are three: bass, tenor, and alto. For the notes they can play, see No. 7.]

Albrechtsberger gives the range of each trombone as a chromatic scale. He gives c to d'' for the alto trombone, commenting that $c\#''$ and d'' are difficult, A to a' for the tenor, and G to c' for the bass. These ranges are conservative but reasonable, although the low end of the tenor and bass ranges is high. Speer gave c to c'', E to a', and C to c', respectively.

Comparison between Albrechtsberger's recommendations and Othon Vandenbroek's (the next article) is instructive. His upper limits for alto and tenor trombones are a step higher, with none of Vandenbroek's warnings that the top notes are nearly impossible. Albrechtsberger's upper limit for the bass trombone, however, is a fifth lower than Vandenbroek's, reflecting the fact that the true bass trombone, a fourth lower than the tenor, was still used in Vienna, but hardly ever in Paris.

I have seen only the third edition of this book (1821); I assume that the first edition has the same description of the trombone.

---

[46] Johann Georg Albrechtsberger, *Anweisung zur Composition*, 3rd ed. (Leipzig: Breitkopf und Härtel, 1821), 378, 387–78.

OTHON VANDENBROEK

*Traité général de tous les
instrumens à vent à l'usage des compositeurs*[47]

(ca. 1794)

Othon Vandenbroek, a Flemish-born hornist, held several important positions in Paris beginning in 1783, including from 1795 to
1800, professor of horn at the Conservatoire. He also composed in a
variety of forms, including opera and symphony.[48] His *Traité* was
intended to help composers write effectively for wind instruments.

Vandenbroek's title is somewhat misleading. Most of his treatise
(44 of 65 pages) concerns the horn. There is little more than a page
about the trombone. Comparison has already been made between
Albrechtsberger's recommendations about the trombone's range and
Vandenbroek's. If Albrechtsberger was conservative Vandenbroek was absolutely timid, declaring the upper two notes of the
alto and tenor trombone impossible unless approached by step. Yet
Vandenbroek's recommendations were almost universally followed
in French military music and generally observed in French opera.
Three statements can therefore be made with assurance.

First, Vandenbroek's bass trombone, like the tenor, was in B♭.
He does not actually describe it as such; the first author to do so was
Joseph Fröhlich. (See p. 92.) It is evident, however, that, because of
a low pitch standard in Paris, Vandenbroek's trombones must be
considered as B♭ instruments. (See p. 121 for a fuller explanation
of this point.) The bass trombone may have had a larger mouthpiece
and possibly a wider bore, but it was essentially the same instrument
as the tenor. Judging from the handful of parts that demand lower
notes than *E*, a true bass trombone must have been available, but
rare.

Second, the strongest and most proficient players in France must
have played the "bass" trombone. Otherwise, Vandenbroek would
hardly have given *g′* as the top note on the bass trombone without

[47] Othon Vandenbroek, *Traité général de tous les instrumens à vent à
l'usage des compositeurs* (Paris: Louis Marchand, 1794?), 54–55.
[48] Eric Blom, "Vandenbroek, Othon Joseph." *The New Grove*, vol. 19,
519.

comment after claiming that the same note on tenor trombone was impossible unless approached by step.

Third, the French tenor trombone player was so lacking in skill that notes now routinely written for high school students, or even younger students, had to be avoided or approached with great care.

The position of the alto trombone is less clear, but apparently it still had a higher fundamental pitch than the tenor. Vandenbroek's warning that b' and c'' were too hard to play unless approached from $b^{b'}$ indicates that French alto trombonists were note too proficient. (See Plate 7 for his musical examples.)

Plate 7. Vandenbroek: Page from *Traité général...*

Exemple

l'Alto   le Thénor   la Basse

Etendue ou Gamme de la partie d'Alto.

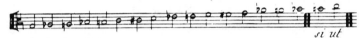

si ut

Il faut éviter les deux dernieres notes qui sont si et ut, c'est trop haut et trop difficile, on peut les faire après un si bemol;

Gamme de la partie du Thénor

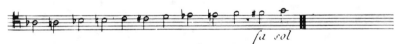

fa sol

Les deux dernieres notes fa et sol il faut les éviter, on ne peut les prendre qu'après avoir pris le fa naturelle; autrement c'est impossible c'est beaucoup trop haut

Gamme de la partie de Basse.

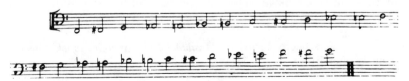

Les Trombonnes son divisés en trois parties s'avoir l'Alto, Thénor, et la Basse.	The trombones are divided into three parts: alto, tenor, and bass.

La partie d'Alto est la plus haute et censée premier dessus, le Thénor est le second dessus, la Basse est la Basse, aucune de ces trois parties ne fait du chant, c'est tous Accords preparés dans des morceaux déchirants, ou des morceaux lugubres. il n'y a que la Clef qui distingue les trois parties des Trombonnes.	The alto is the highest and called first treble. The tenor is second treble, and the bass is the bass. None of these three plays the melody, but rather chords prepared in heart-rending or gloomy pieces. Only the clefs distinguish the different trombone parts.

[See Plate 7]

Il faut éviter les deux dernieres notes qui sont si et ut, c'est trop haut et trop difficile, on peut les faire après un si bemol;	It is necessary to avoid the two last notes, b' c''. They are too high and difficult, but they can be played after $b^{b'}$.

[See Plate 7]

Les deux dernieres notes fa et sol il faut les éviter, on ne peut les prendre qu'après avoir pris le fa naturelle; autrement c'est impossible c'est beaucoup trop haut.	The two last notes, $f\#'$ g', must be avoided. They cannot be played except after f'. Otherwise, it is impossible. They are much too high.

[See Plate 7]
[Vandenbroek makes no comment about the bass trombone.]

JOOS VERSCHUERE-REYNVAAN

Muzijkaal Kunst-Woordenboek[49]

(1795)

Apparently, this dictionary is the earliest dictionary of musical terms in the Dutch language. The title page identifies the author as a

---

[49] J[oos] Verschuere-Reynvaan, *Musijkaal Kunst-Wooddenboek* Amsterdam: Wouter Brave, 1795), 75.

lawyer ("*practiseerand advocaat*"). An earlier edition appeared in 1789. The 1795 edition is greatly expanded (618 pages instead of 370 pages). Oddly enough, both editions contain articles only for the first half of the alphabet. The rest never appeared at all.[50] The article on the trombone is very brief, but it looks as if the author intended to supply a supplementary article entitled "Trombone" for some reason, in order to give the ranges.

BAZUIN; (*Een bekend Blaasspeeltuig van dien naam;*) zijnde eene soort van schuiftrompet, het welk bij vreugdebe drijven in kerken, enz., gebruikt wordt; en in Duitschland van de Stadsmuzijkanten op de torens: men heeft er verscheide soorten van: de grooste of laagste in toon, wordt genaamd een *Ocktaafbazuin*: de volgende, welke hooger in toon is, wordt genoemd, *Quart-bazuin*: de derde is de *gemeene Bazuin*: en de vierde, is de *Alt-bazuin*. Zie de schaale daarvan bij TROMBÓNE.

TROMBONE: (a wind instrument known by that name), being a kind of slide trumpet, which is being used at joyful occasions in churches, etc. and in Germany by the city musicians on towers. There are several kinds: the largest, or lowest pitch is called a contra-bass trombone; the next one, which sounds higher, is called a bass trombone; the third is the ordinary trombone; and the fourth is the alto trombone. Refer to the scale of it at "Trombone."

Men heeft behalven dit Speeltuig, ook een *Register* in het *Orgel*, welke zodanig genaamd is; zijnde een *Tongwerk*, een *Pedaalstem*, niet kleiner dan 16 voet in toon: hunne ligchaamen zijn van de grooste soort, die men onder de *Tongwerken* aantreft: van onder zijn ze spits; en loopen, allengskens, naar boven, wijd uit: het is eene overheerelijke stem; en, wanneer dezelve wèl is ingericht, moeten haare toonen of geluiden, posten en deuren doen dreunen.

Besides this instrument, there is also a stop on the organ, which is called similarly, being a reed stop, a pedal voice, not smaller than 16 feet in tone. Their bodies are of the largest kind of those one finds among the reed stops. At the bottom, they are pointed, and get bigger and bigger gradually, going upwards. It is a most delightful voice, and when it is well executed, its tones or sounds should cause doors and posts to tremble.

---

[50] Coover, "Dictionaries," 437, 445; *Music Lexicography* 3d ed., rev. and enlarged (Carlisle, Penn.: Carlisle Books, 1971), 149.

HEINRICH KOCH

Musikalisches Lexikon[51]

(1802)

Koch's musical dictionary is an excellent, highly regarded reference
tool. Although based, as all dictionaries must be, on earlier writings,
it is an original work, unsullied by mere copying of previous articles.
And yet the article on the trombone perpetuates an error that can
be traced all the way back to Speer, because Koch lists $g\#'$ as one
of the notes available in first position. He probably copied his list of
notes from Walther, who bodily lifted Mattheson's revision of Niedt's
book. Niedt (or Mattheson, as the case may be) copied it from
Speer, who, as a sometime *Stadtpfeifer*, undoubtedly knew better,
but did not catch the error in proof. Once again, the note should
be g'.

(This error is by no means the only one that I have found passed
from author to author in my research. Others have been reprinted
uncritically by men whose scholarly credentials are as impeccable as
Koch's, a sobering thought for anyone who publishes any kind of
nonfiction.) It should also be noted that Koch gives b' rather than
$b^{b'}$ as the seventh partial in second position on an alto trombone.
Apparently, he noticed a descrepancy and attempted to correct it,
altering the second position series of the alto trombone, which was
correct, instead of the misprinted first position series of the tenor
trombone. It would be necessary to move the slide in half a step
from the main position in order to play this note, and otherwise, this
position seems to have been considered a low first position rather
than a high second.

Like all dictionary articles on the trombone, Koch identifies the
different sizes, but mentions only the alto and tenor trombones. The
omission of the bass trombone is an oversight, because later in the
article, Koch gives the notes available in each position on a bass
trombone. The soprano trombone, on the other hand, has disappeared

[51] Heinrich Christoph Koch, *Musickalisches Lexikon* (Frankfurt am Main:
August Hermann dem Jüngere, 1802), col. 1163–65.

without a trace. Koch refers to a distant trombone, but he means not a soprano trombone, but a high alto (in e rather than in d). Koch ends his article with a description of how little the trombone was used in his day. By that time, Mozart's operas with trombones were well known. Koch apparently either did not know about Gluck's masterpieces or else did not recognize their influence.

Posaune, *Trombone.* Ein Blasinstrument von Blech ohne Tonlöcher, welches sich durch seine besondere Einrichtung von allen übrigen Instrumenten dieser Art sehr merklich auszeichnet, und dadurch ein ziemlich hohes Alterthum verräth. In Ansehung der Form und des Traktementes kömmt die Posaune der Trompete am nächten, sie unterscheidet sich aber auch sehr merklich von derselben dadurch, daß das Instrument aus zwey Theilen bestehet, die sich in zwey Scheiden enger zusammen und weiter aus einander ziehen lassen.

Trombone. A wind instrument made of sheet metal and without tone holes, which is markedly distinguished from other instruments of this type by its unique arrangement and thus betrays a rather great antiquity. In view of its shape and use, the trombone comes closest to the trumpet, yet it is also quite different in that it consists of two pieces that can be pulled closer together and further apart from each other in two sheaths.

Die Posaune bestehet nemlich 1) aus dem Hauptstüke, welches bey dem Traktemente derselben mit der linken Hand gehalten wird, und 2) aus den sogenannten Stangen, oder aus zwey verbundenen dünnen Röhren, die in die beyden Röhren des Hauptstückes passen, und vermittelst der rechten Hand bey dem Blasen weiter aus dem Hauptstücke heraus, oder weiter in dasselbe hinein gezogen werden. Durch dieses Ziehen bekömmt die Röhre des Instrumentes eine verschiedene Länge, wodurch mehr Töne auf demselben herausgebracht werden können, als außerdem möglich seyn würde.

The trombone consists namely of 1) the bell section, which is held with the left hand during use, and 2) the so-called rods, or two thin, connected tubes which fit into the two tubes of the bell section, and during the playing are pulled further out of or into the bell section with the right hand. Through this pulling, the tube of the instrument receives a different length, at which more tones can be produced on it than would be possible otherwise.

Man hat von diesem Instrumente verschiedene Dimensionen, die man mit dem Namen Alt- und Tenorposaune bezeichnet.* Jede Posaune hat drey Hauptzüge, nemlich einen bey dem Mundstücke, bey welchem das Instrument sieben Töne angiebt, nemlich das Contra *A* und die Töne *A, e, a, c', e, gis', a'*; der andere Zug ist bey dem Hauptstücke, und vermittelst desselben bringt der Spieler die Töne *G, d, g, h* und *d'* hervor; der dritte Zug ist ohngefähr 3 bis 4 Zoll lang außer dem Hauptstücke, und giebt die Töne. *F, c, f.* Auf der Tenorposaune ist noch ein vierter Zug gebräuchlich, bey welchem die Stangen so weit hinaus gezogen werden, als der rechte Arm reichen kann, und dann giebt das Instrument die Töne *E, H* und *B.* Auf der Alt- oder Quintposaune bekommen die Töne durch die drey vorhin beschriebenen Züge ein anderes Verhältniß unter einander, denn der erste Zug giebt *d, a, d', f', a', c''*; der zweyte *c, g, c', e', g', h'*, und der dritte *f* und *h.*

Das Mundstuck der Posaune gleicht dem Mundstücke der Trompete, hat aber eine weitere Bohrung und nach

There are different sizes for this instrument which are called alto and tenor trombones.* Every trombone has three main slide positions, namely one by the mouthpiece, at which the instrument provides seven notes, namely A_1, *A, e, a, c', e', g#'*, and *a'*; the second position is by the bell, by means of which the player produces the notes *G, d, g, b*, and *d'*; the third slide position is approximately three or four inches past the bell and provides the notes *F, c*, and *f.* On the tenor trombone, a fourth slide position is also common, at which the rods are pulled out as far as the right arm can reach, and the instrument provides the notes *E, B, B^b.* On the alto or quint trombone, the notes receive a different relationship to each other with the three just-described slide positions, for the first provides *d, a, d', f', a'* and *c''*; the second *c, g, c', e', g'*, and *b'*; and the third *f* and b.

The mouthpiece of the trombone resembles the mouthpiece of the trumpet, but it has a wider bore and

*Vor Zeiten hatte man, außer der damals ganz gewöhnlichen Posaune, noch eine Alt- order Discantposaune, eine Quartposaune und eine Oktavposaune, die um eine Oktave tiefer stand, als die gewöhnliche oder gemeine Posaune. S. *Praetor. Syntag. Music. T. II.* S. 31.

*Years ago, they also had, aside from the then quite common trombone, another alto, or discant, trombone, a quart trombone, and an octave trombone, which was one octave lower than the normal or common trombone. (See Praetorius, *Syntagma Musicum*, Vol. 2, p. 31.)

Verhältniß der Größe der Alt- oder Tenorposaune einen weitern Kessel.

a broader cup in proportion to the size of the alto or tenor trombone.

Vor Zeiten war dieses Instrument eines der vorzüglichsten bey allen Arten der Ausübung der Musik, und besonders der Kirchenmusik. Zeither bedienten sich desselben nur noch hier und da einige Stadtpfeifer zur Begleitung des Zinken bey dem sogenannten Abblasen, oder bey dem Neujahrblasen. Von aller übrigen Musik war es längst entfernt, bis Mozart in seiner Zauberflöte von neuem darauf aufmerksam machte. Diese neu erregte Aufmerksamkeit hat aber noch keine merklichen Folgen für die Wiedereinführung dieses Instrumentes haben können, weildas Traktement desselben zu sehr vernachläßigt worden war, und weil man wahrscheinlich geneigter ist, lieber Blasinstrumente zu erlernen, deren Gebrauch anjetzt allgemeiner ist.

Years ago, this instrument was one of the most excellent of all types for the performance of music, particularly church music. Since that time, only a few *Stadtpfeifer* have continued to play it here and there as accompaniment for the cornetts at the New Year's celebration. It was long kept out of all other kinds of music until Mozart made us aware of it anew in his *Zauberflöte*. This newly generated attention, however, has not yet been able to have any marked results for the reintroduction of this instrument, because it has been neglected too much, and because people are probably inclined to prefer to study wind instruments whose use is more common now.

CHRISTIAN FRIEDRICH DANIEL SCHUBART

Ideen zu einer Aesthetik der Tonkunst[52]

(1784–85, published 1806)

Schubart, a poet and journalist as well as a musician, wrote his *Ideen* while in prison for insulting the mistress of the Duke of Württemburg.[53] It was not published until 15 years after his death, and so it had no influence on his contemporaries.

---

[52] Christian Friedrich Daniel Schubart, *Ideen zu einer Aesthetik der Tonkunst*, ed. Ludwig Schubart (Vienna: J. V. Degen, 1806), 315–17.

[53] David Ossenkop, "Schubart, Christian Friedrich Daniel," *The New Grove*, vol. 16, 750.

Since Schubart was concerned with esthetics and not history, pedagogy, or physical description, his comments on the trombone are significantly different from the others in this chapter. He describes the trombone and mentions some of the standard ideas about its origin, including the common misidentification of the trombone with the Hebrew *shophar*. His primary purpose in writing about it, however, is to plead for its revival as a sacred instrument, and that it not be used for secular purposes. The footnote reference to Mozart's operas must have been added by Ludwig Schubart, who edited the manuscript for publication. The manuscript itself predates *Don Giovanni* and *Die Zauberflöte*, the only operas Mozart wrote with important enough trombone parts to attract the attention of other composers to the trombone. Christian Schubart must have known at least the operas of Gluck, and possibly other operas, most likely from Austria, that included trombone parts. He protested vigorously this "profaning" of a sacred instrument, while admitting that it was used effectively.

Of particular interest is Schubart's comment that there were still excellent trombonists in Saxony and Bohemia. He lived and worked all his life in the districts of Württemburg and Bavaria, yet he does not mention trombones there. Christoph Friedrich Nicolai of Berlin, whose comments are cited by Ottmar Schreiber,[54] wrote that trombones were still used in Bavaria. Either they were concentrated in parts of Bavaria that Schubart never visited (he did not live there long), or else he was not favorably impressed with the caliber of their playing.

Schubart declined to describe the workings of the trombone in detail on the grounds that an earlier author, Haider, had already done so. Regrettably, I have not been able to locate any other references to such an author, and cannot present Haider's description in this chapter.

Dieses Instrument ist ganz kirchlich, und verbreitet sich in drey Zweige, in die *Alt- Tenor-* und *Bass-posaune*. Es ist eigentlich eine Trompete, nur mit dem Unterschiede, dass durch hin- und herschieben alle fehlenden Töne

This instrument is entirely ecclesiastical, and is divided into three branches: alto, tenor, and bass trombones. It is actually a trumpet, only with the difference that all missing tones can be produced by sliding back and forth. The

---

[54] Schreiber, 139.

hervor gebracht werden können.
Das Instrument ist uralt, und wie es
scheint, eine Erfindung der Juden:
denn schon im alten Testamente
kommen Bemerkungen vor von
Tonveränderungen auf blasenden
Instrumenten; und diese lassen sich
ausser der Posaune nicht denken.
Jedes blasende Instrument hat nicht
mehr und nicht weniger Töne als
das Kuhhorn. Was über den vollen
Accord geht, ist ausser dem Bezirke
seines Wirkungskreises. Die
Gebrechen der Natur müssen also
durch Erfindungen der Kunst
ersetzt werden. Diess geschah bey
der Posaune, wo durch das Ein- und
Ausziehen alle möglichen Töne
hervorgebracht werden können.
Der rechte Arm befiehlt durch
Schieben dem Hauche, und lenkt so
den ganzen Harmoniesturm der
Posaune. Diess Instrument ist durch
Jahrtausende nie profanirt worden,
sondern immer gleichsam als ein
Erbtheil dem Tempel Gottes
geblieben. Man hing die heilige
Posaune am Pfosten des Tempels
auf, liess sie nur an Festtagen tönen,
oder geboth ihr, den Flug des
Kirchengesangs zu tragen. Aber in
unsern Tagen hat man sie zum
Operndienste entweiht; und die
Posaune ist nicht mehr ein
Eigenthum des Gottesdienstes.--
Man gebraucht sie nun auch mit
grossem Effect bey den Chören
grosser Opern.

instrument is ancient, and, as it
would seem, an invention of the
Jews: for there appear references
already in the Old Testament to
tone changes on wind instruments,
and this is unthinkable aside from
trombones. Each wind instrument
has neither more nor fewer tones
than a cow's horn. Whatever
exceeds the full range is outside the
realm of its jurisdiction. The defects
of nature therefore must be
corrected through the invention of
art. This is also the case with the
trombone, with which all possible
tones can be produced by drawing
in and out. The right arm
commands the breath through
sliding, and thus guides the
trombone's entire harmonic gamut.
This instrument has never been
profaned throughout the millenia,
but rather has always remained a
heritage of God's temple. The holy
trombones were hung on the
doorpost of the temple and allowed
to be sounded only on festival days
or bidden to bear the soaring of
church music. In our days, however,
they have been desecrated for the
service of opera, and the trombone
is no longer the property of God's
worship. It is also used now with
great effect in the choruses of large
operas.

Der Ton der Posaune ist
durchschneidend, und weit dicker
als Trompetenton; liegende Noten
können auf keinem Instrumente der
Welt so ausgedrückt werden, wie
auf diesem.

The trombone's tone is piercing and
much thicker than a trumpet's.
Sustained notes can be expressed on
this instrument as on no other in the
world.

Man hat jetzt nicht nur Kirchengesänge für die Posaune gesetzt, sondern auch Concerte, Sonaten, Solis; und diess immer mit bewundernswerther Wirkung. Die Katholiken in Deutschland allein begünstigen indess diess Instrument noch, und wenn nicht in Wien Rath geschafft wird;* so müssen wir fürchten, solches allmählig ganz zu verlieren. --

Not only church music has now been composed for trombones, but also concertos, sonatas, and solos, and these always have an admirable effect. Only the Catholics in Germany still favor this instrument, and unless help is forthcoming from Vienna*, we must fear the gradual and complete loss of this instrument.

Die Theorie der Posaune ist schon vor dreysig Jahren von Haider zu Dresden, in ein so helles Licht gesetzt worden, dass man kaum noch etliche Grundsätze hinzusetzen kann. Da sie heutiges Tages so gewaltig verabsäumt wird, und man nur armseligen Zinkenisten die Ausübung überlässt; so sollten unsere Musiklenker vorzüglichen Bedacht darauf nehmen, dieß göttlich autorisirte Instrument wieder zu wecken; Genies für sie zu beflügeln, und dadurch der Posaune den Donnerton wiederzugeben, den sie zu Salomos Zeiten hatte. Inzwischen gibt es doch noch jetzt sonderlich in Sachsen und Böhmen treffliche Posaunisten.

The theory of the trombone was placed in such a clear light thirty years ago by Haider of Dresden that one can hardly add any more basic principles. Since it is so greatly neglected today and the performance is left to wretched cornett players, so it is that our music directors should take into preferential consideration the reawakening of this divinely authorized instrument, and to urge geniuses in its favor, and thereby return the thunderous sound of the trombone, which it had in Solomon's time. Meanwhile, there are nevertheless still outstanding trombonists in Saxony and Bohemia.

Ausgemacht aber ist es, *dass der Posaunenton ganz für die Religion und nie fürs Profane gestimmt ist.*

But is is certain *that the sound of the trombone is truly intended for religion and not at all for secular use.*

---

*Auch hier hat *Mozart* Rath geschafft, und man findet seit ihm in den meisten neuern Opern Posaunen angebracht.

*Here, too, Mozart has had influence, and one finds trombones in most new operas after him.

JOHN MARSH

Hints to Young Composers of Instrumental Music[55]

(1807)

John Marsh led a highly active musical life as violinist, organist, conductor, composer, and writer on musical subjects. His comments on the trombone are highly practical and represent a middle-of-the-road approach to using the trombone, taking their place between the enthusiasm of certain musicians who overwhelmed performances by having the trombones play too much and too loudly and the undisguised antipathy of musicians like Charles Burney (next article). Both Marsh and Burney agree, however, that Handel made very effective use of the trombone.

Oddly enough, in trying to explain why Handel's practice was preferable to that of later composers, Marsh took *Messiah*, which has no trombone parts, as his example, not *Saul* or *Israel in Egypt*. Marsh has very little to say about the technique or description of the trombone. He is concerned mostly with good taste.

For the modern scholar, perhaps Marsh's most enlightening observation is that composers seldom included trombone parts in their scores even when they intended for them to take part in the performance. This practice may have also been widespread on the continent, in which case trombones may have been heard much more frequently than surviving music indicates.

The original publication includes two movements for orchestra as illustrations of Marsh's principles. I have not seen them, but they apparently both include trombone parts, judging from Marsh's defensive comments.

---

[55] John Marsh, *Hints to Young Composers of Instrumental Music* (London: Clementi, Banger, Hyde, Collard & Davis, ca. 1807); reprinted with an introduction by Charles Cudworth in *The Galpin Society Journal* 18 (1965), 57–71.

There yet remains one other instrument, which, since the commemoration of Handel in 1784, when it was first introduced in
England, has been admitted in very large orchestras, viz, the
TROMBONE; of which there are three different sizes, forming respectively, a counter-tenor, tenor, and bass to the trumpet, to the scale of
which they are however not confined, having sliding tubes attached to
them enabling the performer to play the common diatonic intervals, in
most of the common keys.

These instruments, being the most powerful of any in the orchestra,
are only used in the very full, or tutti parts, when the bass-trombone
plays as simple a part as can be formed from the general bass, the other
two playing at the same time in harmony and making a kind of
thorough bass with it; except in choral fugues, when each occasionally
takes and enforces the points of its own part.--The trombones being
therefore not in general use, composers seldom insert parts for them in
their scores, but leave them to be added afterwards, as may be
required, which can easily be done from the score by any composer or
judge of composition.--Except however in orchestras of the very first
magnitude, the bass-trombone is the only one used; which many then
play from the common ripieno bass, or contra-bass.

The trombones, trumpets, double drums and full organ may therefore together be reckoned to form the *corps de reserve* hinted at in
page eight, which by augmenting the chorus at particular parts much
increases the effect of the softer parts in contrast with it. In this
respect the great Handel has set a good example; for by a perusal of
the scores of his oratorios, it will at a glance be perceived, that the
trumpets and drums are but sparingly resorted to, in order that,
whenever they are brought in, the effect may be the more striking.
This observation is particularly exemplified in the sacred oratorio of
the Messiah, throughout which the trumpet is but four times, and the
kettle-drums but twice brought into action. And here I cannot but
notice an injudicious criticism I have actually heard upon this popular
oratorio, which the critic seemed to wonder had not commenced with
such an overture as that of the Occasional Oratorio.--So far however
was Handel himself (it appears) from being of this opinion, that he
introduced it by one of his gravest overtures, and in a minor key,
being a simple composition in four parts, without even the aid of a
single wind instrument. And in this he undoubtedly showed his
judgment by coinciding with the compiler of the words to the oratorio, who does not at once usher in the Messiah in all his glory, but,
going back to a distant prophecy, gradually proceeds onwards to the
nativity.--The composer therefore in like manner after a simple and
plaintive opening (which by-the-bye, is succeeded by a beautiful and

striking transition to the major key at the accompanied recitative--
'Comfort ye') advances with much simplicity of style, 'till he comes to
the chorus--'For unto us'--which is wrought up with much ingenuity;
and the emphatical words 'Wonderful, counsellor', etc., are repeated
four times by the whole force of the orchestra. None of the more
powerful instruments are introduced however, 'till the annunciation
of our Saviour to the shepherds; when in the chorus of angels the
trumpets are used, and yet not the drums and trumpets together, 'till
the grand Hallelujah at the end of the second part, when they unite to
produce a most striking and grand effect. In the third part the
trumpet is again introduced, when expressly alluded to in the words,
and the drums and trumpets together are once more brought forward
in the concluding chorus and amen, which with the Hallelujah are the
only two *grand* choruses, as they are pre-eminently termed in the
whole oratorio.

For want of attending to this example in making *selections*, as is
now done, instead of performing complete oratorios, too many of the
grand choruses are generally brought into one performance; and thus
so great a glare produced, that after hearing two or three of them, the
remaining ones lose their effect. And again, through the growing
practice of over-straining the choruses, by trombones and double
drums too forcibly beaten, what should occasionally produce an awful
and grand effect, degenerates into continued noise and clatter, with
which the audience frequently become fatigued before the performance is over.--This I cannot help thinking to be in some measure the
case, in particular with the Oratorio of Redemption, in other respects
judiciously complied by the late Dr Arnold from Handel's works; as,
after employing the whole strength of the instrumental band at the
opening, no less than eight or nine of the fullest and most forcible
choruses are introduced, which by the original author were dispersed
throughout different oratorios.

Composers therefore in general cannot do better than conform to
the example of Handel, in making but a sparing use of the more
powerful instrument. Should it be thought I have myself indeed, in
some measure, deviated from this rule in the pieces here published, I
have to reply, that being in themselves very short, and consisting each
of but a single movement, they are to be considered, not as forming a
whole of themselves, like a symphony or concerto of several movements, but as either a concluding or introductory *part* of an act, or
concert, contrasted to immediately preceded or succeeded by music
of an opposite quality, as songs, glees, &c. --They can only be liable
therefore to the objection above stated, when injudiciously attached
to other *full* pieces.

CHARLES BURNEY

Cyclopaedia (ed. Abraham Rees)[56]

(1819)

After learning about the process of making encyclopedias by revising
Chambers's *Cyclopaedia*, Abraham Rees decided to issue his own,
and asked Charles Burney to write the musical articles. The encyclopedia appeared volume by volume between 1802 and 1820.
Burney's article on the trombone was probably written in 1804 or
1805, but was not published until 1819. The encyclopedia also
contains the article entitled "Sacbut" from Chambers. As is the case
with Rousseau and La Borde, there is no cross reference and no
indication that there are two articles that describe the same instrument. In Burney's case, however, there is no possibility of ignorance
being at the root of the duplication. When writing about the Handel
Festival of 1784, Burney included a paragraph on the sacbut, which
is quoted below on page 144–45, and mentioned that the Italian
name is trombone. As Rees's *Cyclopaedia* is essentially a greatly
enlarged revision of Chambers's, the decision to include the old
article on the sacbut must have been Rees's and not Burney's.

Burney, of course, had traveled widely and read old treatises
voraciously in preparation for his *General History of Music*. His
articles for Rees were largely based on this research. He must have
had first-hand knowledge of such early authorities as Zarlino and
Mersenne, but his quotations of these two authors parallel Martini's
article so closely that it must have been Martini that Burney had
open in front of him as he wrote. There is one striking difference
between Zarlino's original text as quoted by Martini and Burney's
translation. Burney makes Zarlino say that after the minor third,
the next available interval is the fourth, thus omitting the seventh
partial. In Martini's treatise, this particular sequence of intervals
occurs in the paragraph about Mersenne.

As already mentioned in the commentary on Martini's article, it is
easy to misread Mersenne, and Burney does so, implying that he

---

[56] [Charles Burney], "Trombone," *Cyclopaedia*, ed. Abraham Rees, 39
vols. (London: Longman et al., 1802–20), vol. 36 (no pagination).

discovered certain pitches rather than assuming them for the sake of argument.

Burney's last two paragraphs seem to be based on his personal experience. He visited Germany while soprano trombones still found occasional use, and being a lover of Handel's music, he knew the Dead March from *Saul* well. Closer examination, however, reveals that, except for the reference to *Saul* and the closing opinion, everything is lifted from La Borde.

Burney closes his article with a deplorably opinioned statement that makes it clear that he did not like or respect the trombone. This opinion becomes understandable considering that most of the music that Burney could have heard with trombone parts was either French music or influenced by French music. Not only were these parts generally tasteless, but Burney passionately hated French music.

TROMBA, in the *Italian Music*, either denotes the common trumpet, the buccina of the ancients, or the modern sacbut, but more properly our trumpet.

TROMBONE, a wind-instrument blown by the mouth, and resembling in form the military trumpet, of which it is the base, the name implying the *great trumpet*. It differs, however, from the trumpet in being divided into two branches or parts fitted to sockets, giving the performer power to lengthen and shorten the general tube at his pleasure, according to the different tones which he wishes to produce. On which account it is called in Latin, *tuba ductilis*. The Germans call it *pausaune*, and the French *sacqueboute*.

Zarlini has described this instrument under the title of *trombone amovibile*, and the quantity and quality of the sounds it is capable of producing, very exactly.

"The trombone," says he, Supplimenti Musicali, lib. iii. cap. 5. "is an instrument truly worthy of consideration, which I have seen and often heard by good performers, beginning at the lowest sound which it is capable of producing; when, being closed in all the joints, it can produce no sound less than the octave; then from the octave to the 5th; nor from that can it produce a less interval than the 4th; and from the 4th to the 3rd major, then the 3d minor, after which another 4th, the keynote, from which it can form a complete series of eight notes. No other sounds than these can be produced without altering, moving, and lengthening the instrument."

Père Mersenne, in his experiments on this instrument, (Harmon. Instrum. lib. ii.) found it capable, by lengthening or shortening the lower part of the instrument, of forming a regular series of fifteen sounds, from double C in the base, to C on the sixth line.

The instrument is made of brass, of which there are five sorts: canto, alto, tenor, base, and double-base. It is much used in the large churches of Germany. They can produce all the tones and semitones in gradation. The manner of writing for them is the same as for different voices, and on the same staff of five lines. [See Example 13.]

The double-base of this instrument goes a 5th lower than any other base. It has the finest effect in funeral processions, and in general in melancholy strains. We never hear it with more pleasure in England than in Handel's dead march in Saul. Its use should be rare, and its effects would be more striking. But tromboni and double-drums are now so frequently used at the opera, oratories, and in symphonies, that they are become a nuisance to lovers of pure harmony and refined tones: for, in fact, the vibrations of these instruments produce noise, not musical sounds.

Example 13. Burney: [Range of Trombones]

JOSEPH FRÖHLICH

Vollständige theoretisch- pracktische Musikschule[57]

(1811)

Joseph Fröhlich marks a major turning point in the history of writings about the trombone. As mentioned in Chapter 1, he was

---

[57] Joseph Fröhlich, *Vollständige theoretisch- pracktische Musikschule*, 4 vols. (Bonn: Simrock, [1811]), vol. 3, 27−35.

the first to describe the modern system of seven chromatic slide positions instead of four diatonic ones, and the first to describe a tenor trombone in B^b instead of A. He is also the first author of those described in this chapter who was primarily an educator. Where previous works were addressed to composers, theorists, amateurs, or scholars, Fröhlich addressed his to performers and students.

It would be too much to claim that Fröhlich wrote the first trombone tutor. Speer clearly believed that his treatise would benefit performers and teachers. Fröhlich himself cites a *Posaunenschule* by Braun, which I have not been able to locate. Robert MacDonald cites a method for trombone by Andre Braun that, he says, was published in 1815.[58] If it is this Braun that Fröhlich cited, and if the date always given for the publication of Fröhlich's treatise is correct, the date MacDonald found is at least five years too late. Precise dating of musical publications of that generation is extremely difficult in that publishers did not include dates on the title page, so scholars must guess according to plate numbers, prices, addresses, advertisements, and other clues that, even taken together, are not always entirely reliable.

In describing the modern seven-position system, Fröhlich takes pains to compare it with the old system, showing how the new positions correspond to the old ones. His prose style is not as clear as one would like, however, and so the following chart may be helpful:

New System	Old System
1	–
2	1
3	–
4	2
5	–
6	3
7	4

Adam Carse reproduced a similar chart, but then committed a major blunder in projecting it back to the time of Speer.[59] But while

---

[58] MacDonald, vol. 1, 345, n.505.
[59] Adam Carse, *Musical Wind Instruments* (New York: Da Capo, 1965, reprint of 1939 ed.), 255.

Fröhlich places B^b in first position and builds his series of first position notes on it, Speer placed B^b out beyond fourth position, where it is definitely the third partial.

Clearly, Fröhlich advocated a new numbering for the slide positions, but did not even acknowledge the new pitch level that his system implied. Some time between Speer and Fröhlich the pitch of the tenor trombone changed from A to B^b. The opening section of Chapter 3 explains how this change came about with no deliberate change in either the manufacture or playing of trombones.

Among other important differences between Fröhlich and his predecessors are his recommendations about musicianship, how to hold the instrument, and what music to practice. Fröhlich is the first author in this chapter to describe alternate positions, give any details about the mouthpiece, or explicitly state that the bass trombone, like the tenor, was in B^b. This latter point is implicit in Vandenbroek's description and apparently explicit in Braun. Braun may have anticipated some of the other points that I have attributed to Fröhlich.

Fröhlich's trombone method was not a separate publication, but rather a long chapter in a four-volume set of books about singing and all the instruments. To save repeating himself, he includes frequent cross-references. The trombone method refers back to the sections on singing and the trumpet. While the trombone method is sufficient to establish Fröhlich as an important innovator, it does not include his every remark relevant to the trombone.

Some of the volumes of this treatise are set in type, Roman, not *fraktur*, but the one with the *Posaunenschule* is engraved in italics and includes an astounding number of errors. I hope that all of the typographical errors that follow constitute faithful copying, but a few may be mine. Most of the musical examples, tiny and hard to read even in the original, can be found recopied in Appendix 2.

Von Der Posaune.

On the Trombone

§1 Werth des Instrumentes

§1 Value of the Instrument

Das der Trompete sowohl in Hinsicht des Alterthums als der Behandlungsweise nächste Instrument ist die Posaune, von den Italiänern desswegen Trombone genannt.

The trombone is the instrument that is closest to the trumpet in the regard of the ancients as well as in treatment. Therefore, the Italians call it trombone [i.e. big trumpet].

Der Volle feyerliche Ton derselben, und die grössere Ausdehnung, welche dieses Instrument durch die beÿ demselben anzubringenden verschiedenen Züge erhält, wodurch man auch in den Stand gesetzt wird, aus allen Tonarten in ihrem ganzen Umfange spielen zu können, erheben es zu einem besonders brauchbaren musik-Werkzeuge. Der in ihm liegende volle klangreiche Ton befähigt den Spieler zum Ausdruck aller erhabenen eingreifenden Empfindungen, zur Darstellung und zur Unterhaltung der feÿerlichsten Gemüthsstimmungen. Daher es auch in den ältern Zeiten gewöhnlich zur Erhebung der Singstimmen in den Kirchenmusiken gesetzt wurde, und allerdings zur Erweckung der Andacht und Erbauung Vieles beÿtragen musste. Sein Gebrauch schien in den neuern Zeiten im Allgemeinen ziemlich abgekommen zu seyn, als Mozart, welcher so trefflich den Charakter aller Instrumente zu seiner Darstellung zu benutzen wusste, dieses würdige Instrument in mehreren seiner Werke anwand, damit die vortrefflichsten Wirkungen hervorbrachte, und so das Meiste zu seiner Wiedereinführung beÿtrug.

Its full, solemn tone (and the greater extension that it receives through its ability to play all kinds of notes over its entire range) exalt it to an especially useful musical tool. Its full, sonorous tone enables the player to express all noble and effective sentiments for the exhibition and maintenance of the most solemn states of mind. Therefore, it was usually played in the olden days for the exaltation of singing in church music, and to be sure, must have greatly contributed to the inspiration of prayer and devotion. In modern times, its use seemed in general to have fallen somewhat into disuse when Mozart, who knew how to take such excellent advantage of the character of all instruments in his compositions, used this worthy instrument in many of his works, with which he brought forth the most excellent effects, and so contributed the most to its reintroduction.

Da dieses Instrument, wie die 3 Singstimmen Alt, Tenor, und Bass gebraucht wird, so ist es geeignet, eine ganz vollstimmige Harmonie hervorzubringen, die um so bestim̃tere Effecte erzeugt, als die Töne auf den verschiedenen

Because this instrument is used in three voices, alto, tenor, and bass, it is suitable for bringing forth full harmony, which produces such a definite effect when the tones of the various trombones blend because of their similarity, especially when they

Posaunen wegen ihrer Gleichheit
sich in einander verschmelzen
besonders, wenn sie von eineem
guten Meister gesetzt, und gehörig
behandelt werden.

are suitably handled and composed
for by a good master.

Der Charakter des Instrumentes,
besonders geeignet zum Ausdruck
des Erhabnen, Feyerlichen, welchem
auf der andern Seite das Sanfte
Ruhige entspricht, so wie die
gewöhnliche Bestimmung desselben,
jene der Begleitung von
Singstimen erfodert es, dass der
Vortrag auf demselben gehalten,
gesangvoll, und ja nicht zu grell
seyn dörfe, um so die möglichste
Annäherung an diejenige Stimme
zu bewirken, welche jede dieser
Posaunen im Satze begleitet, oder
vorstellt, der Alt-Posaune an die
Alt, der Tenor an die Tenor, und
der Bass-Posaune an die
Bass-Stimme. Soviele Wirkung eine
schöne Harmonienfolge auf diesen
Instrumenten mit Seele und einem
verhältnissmässig modificirten
Ansatze vorgetragen immer hat,
und haben muss, so wiederlich, und
allen guten Eindruch verderbend ist
es, wenn Posaunen mit einem
wilden schmetternden Tone
geblasen werden wenn es nicht
ausdrücklich von dem Tonsetzer
angezeigt ist.

This instrument is especially suitable
for the expression of the noble and
solemn, which suits the gentle and
calm, as well as its usual role of
doubling voices. Its character
requires that its execution be kept
melodious and not too shrill, in
order to bring out the closest
resemblance to the voice that each
trombone doubles or represents:
alto, tenor, and bass trombones
with alto, tenor, and bass voices
respectively. Just as a beautiful
result of harmonies always has, and
must have, so much effect on this
instrument when it is played with
soul and a gentle articulation, so it
is revolting and spoils all good
impressions when the trombone is
played with a wild and blaring tone,
if the composer has not expressly
indicated it.

Denjenigen, welche sich auf dieses
Instrument verlegen, ist daher nicht
genug anzuemfehlen, sich blos nach
der Singschule zu bilden, um so
mehr, als, wie schon eben gesagt
wurde, ihre Hauptbestimmung,
vorzüglich bey der Gesangmusik,
jene ist, Singstimmen zu begleiten,
die Wirkung derselben durch ihren

To those who devote themselves to
this instrument, it cannot be
recommended strongly enough that
they train themselves according to
vocal teaching, especially
considering that, as already
mentioned, their highest vocation is
in vocal music, that is, to
accompany voices and to reinforce

vollenen Ton zu verstärken, nicht aber sie zu verderben.

their effect with their fuller tone, but not to spoil it.

§2 Vom Baue des Instrumentes, und der Haltung desselben.

§2 On the Construction of the Instrument and How to Hold It.

In Hinsicht des Baues kömmt die Posaune der Trompete ziemlich nahe, und unterscheidet sich hauptsächlich dadurch, dass sie nicht wie jene bloss aus einer unveränderlichen Röhre, sondern aus mehreren ineinander geschobenen Cylindern besteht, durch deren Verlängerung oder Verkürzung die verschiedenen Töne erzeugt werden. Sie hat überhaupt folgende Theile:

Regarding construction, the trombone comes rather close to the trumpet. The main difference is that it is not merely an unchanging tube, but is made of cylinders, one pushed into another. By lengthening and shortening, one gets the different notes. It has the following parts: [See Plate 8.]

1) Die Röhre des Bechers A)
2) Die grosse Röhre B)

1) The bell section (A)
2) The large tube (B) [i.e. the part of the inner slide attached to the bell]

3) Die Röhre in welche das Mundstück gestzt wird C)

3) The tube in which the mouth-piece is put (C) [i.e. the other part of the inner slide]

4) Die grosse Schiebröhre, D) in welche die grosse Röhre B) und jene des Ansatzes C) eingesetzt wird, welche beÿde eingesetzte Röhren B und C man auch den Kern nennt.

4) The large sliding tube (D) in which tubes B and C are set (which two tubes are also called the core)

5) Das Mundstück F)
6) Das kleine Queerstück welches die grosse Röhre, und jene des Ansatzes zusamenhält G)

5) The mouthpiece (F)
6) The little crossbar that hold the large tube and that of the mouthpiece together (G)

7) Das kleine Queerstück, welches die grosse Einschiebröhre allein zusamenhält H)

7) The little crossbar that holds the sliding tube together (H).

Die Haltung des Instrumentes hängt zwar grösten-Theils von der Art ab, wie ist dem Spieler am gemächlichsten ist, doch ist es im Allgemeinen am bequemsten, u. auch der Regel der Haltung der

Holding the instrument depends, to be sure, chiefly on the way that is most comfortable to the player. In general, the most convenient way is according to the rule for holding the trumpet: the bell is held high and the

Plate 8. Fröhlich: Examples A–M from *Posaunenschule*.

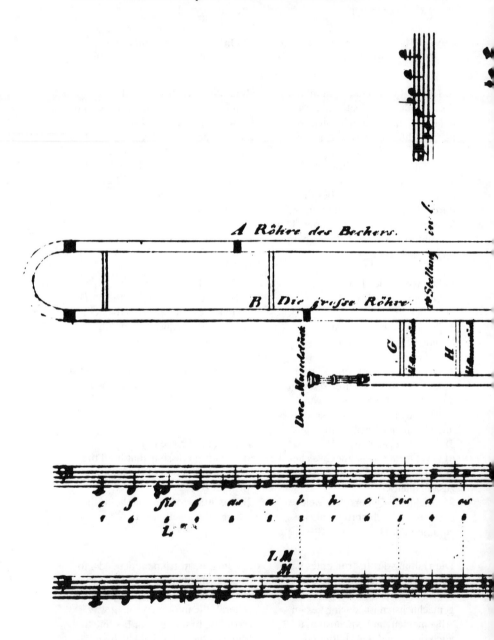

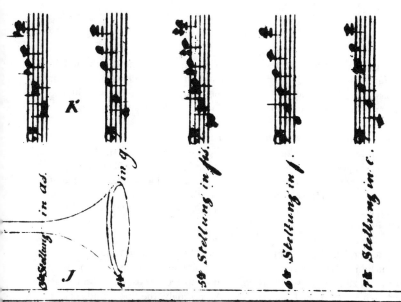

Trompete gemäss, dass die Röhre des Bechers in die Höhe gehalten werde, die 3 Röhren A, B, C, werden in der Form eines Triangels gerichtet.

three tubes A, B, and C are adjusted to form a triangle.

Man hält das Instrument mit der linken Hand an dem kl. Queerstück G, so, dass man das Mundstück sogleich an den Mund bringen kann.

The instrument is held with the left hand on the little crossbar G, so that the mouthpiece can be brought directly to the mouth.

Die grosse Einsetzröhre wird mit der rechten Hand an dem kl. Queerstück H gehalten. Diese Einsetzröhre ist beweglich, und durch das Hin- und Herschieben derselben erzeugt man die Verhältnisse der Töne.

The large insert tube [i.e. the outer slide] is held with the right hand on the little crossbar H. This tube is movable, and with its sliding in and out, the proportions of the tone are produced.

Wie bey jedem Blasinstrumente, so gehört auch hier der Bau des Mundstückes zu dem Wesentlichsten. Da nach den 3 Arten der Posaune das Mundstück verschieden seyn muss, so fügen wir hier 2 Zeichnungen desselben bey, und zwar a) für die Tenor, und b) die Bassposaune, indem jenes für die Alt Trombone das nämliche in der Regel wie jenes bey der Trompete mit der Verteifung des Kessels bey b ist. Siehe den §2 der Trompeten Schule.

As in the case of all wind instruments, the construction of the mouthpiece is most important. Accordingly, the three kinds of trombone must have different mouthpieces. We have attached here two drawings, one for the tenor (a) and the other for the bass (b), while the one for the alto trombone is the same, as a rule, as that of the trumpet, but with a deepening of the cup like (b). See §2 of the Trumpet School. [See Plate 9.]

§3 Art, Töne auf dem Instrument anzugeben.

§3 Description and Sound of the Trombone.

Die Töne werden auf der Posaune eben so wie auf der Trompete erzeugt, oder mit andern Worten der Ansatz ist hier der nämliche wie bey der Trompete.

The sound of the trombone is produced the same way as the trumpet's. In other words, the articulation is the same as on the trumpet.

Man lese hierüber das Nöthige in dem §3 der Trompeten Schule. Allein man sey sehr aufmerksam auf die dort gegebenen Vorschriften zur

Whatever is necessary can be read above in §3 of the Trumpet School. But be very attentive to the instructions given there for the

Plate 9. Fröhlich: Mouth pieces.

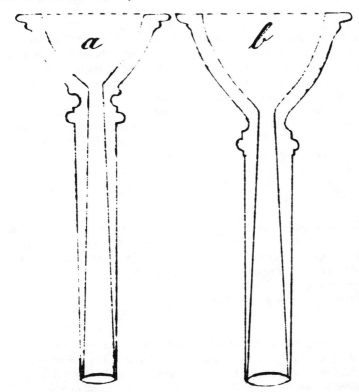

Erlangung eines gesangvollen Vortrags, welcher das Wesentlichste beÿ diesem Instrumente aus jenen in §1 gegebenen Gründen ist. Dieser Theil ist daher eigentlich der wichtigste beym Unterrichte, und derjenige, der diess Instrument gut behandeln will, muss mit aller Sorgfalt dahin trachten, Herr seines Ansatzes zu werden, um die nöthigen Modificationen allen Tönen und dem ganzen Vortrage verleihen zukönnen.

Besonders muss alles Grelle vermieden werden, und die stärker

achievement of a sonorous performance, for which the most essential principles are given for the trombone in §1. This section is therefore strictly speaking the most important in the instructions. Whoever wants to treat this instrument well must strive very conscientiously to become master of his articulation in order to lend the necessary inflection to all notes and the entire performance.

All harshness must be especially avoided. The loud passages must

gegebenen Stellen dörfen nicht schärfer genommen werden, als ein Sänger es zu thuen im Stande ist, welcher wohl stark singt, aber nicht schreiet, es seÿ dann, dass die Posaunen nicht sowohl zur Begleitung der Singstimmen, als vielmehr in Verbindung mit den übrigen Instrumenten scharfe Eindrücke, und starke Accente hervorbringen sollen. Der Posaunist muss sich daher ganz nach der Singschule bilden, und ein guter Sänger kann dessen einziges Muster seyn.

Was die Erzeugnung der verschiedenen Töne auf dem Instrumente selbst betrifft, so geschieht dieses, wie schon angegeben wurde, durch das Hin und Herschieben der grossen Röhre D.

Es ist bekannt, dass, je länger der Cylinder eines Instrumentes ist, ein desto tieferer Ton entstehe. Durch das Ziehen erhält die ganze Röhre der Posaune eine verschiedene Länge, durch dasselbe wird man also in den Stand gesetzt, alle die mannigfaltigen Töne aus derselben herausbringen zu können.

Das erste ist es also, zu untersuchen, welchem Grundton das Instrument in seiner Structur habe, denn besonders die ältern Posaunen waren verschieden gestimmt, und hatten verschiedene Dimensionen.

Die beÿ uns angezeigte Bass-Posaune stimmt B, sie gleicht also einer in B gestimmten

not be piercing, just as a singer is capable of singing very loudly but does not scream. Otherwise, when the trombone is not accompanying voices, but rather is in connection with the other instruments, it should bring forth a strong impression and a heavy accent. The trombonist must therefore model himself entirely according to vocal teaching, and a good singer can be his proper example.

As already stated, the production of different notes comes by means of the back and forth sliding of the large tube (D).

It is known that the longer the cylinder of an instrument is, the lower the fundamental. The entire tubing of the trombone gets different lengths by means of sliding, through which it is enabled to bring forth all the various notes.

First of all, it is necessary to examine which fundamental the instrument would have, because especially the older trombones were in different keys and had different sizes.

The bass trombone that we describe is pitched in B^b and thus resembles a B^b trumpet. We get, then, without

Trompete. Wir erhalten somit ohne Zug auf jener, wie auf dieser den Grundton B die Quinte F, die Octave b, die 10te d, die 12te F, u.s.w. wenn nicht das weite Mundstück des Bassposaunisten das Fortschreiten in die Höhe hindern würde, z.B.

the slide on the former as well as the latter, the fundamental B^b, the fifth F, the octave b^b, the tenth d and the twelfth F, etc. if the wide mouthpiece of the bass trombonist does not hinder the advance to the high register.

Example 14. Fröhlich: [B^b Trumpet and Trombone Compared]

(In dem Beyspiele bey LM ist diese Stellung der Posaune mit 1, und die andern sind mit den folgenden Nummern bezeichnet). Zieht man nun ohngefähr 3 Zoll heraus, (2te stellung) (welches eigentlich der erste Zug ist) so wird die ganze Röhre, soviel als es einen halben Ton beträgt, länger, sie wird gleich einer im A gestimmten Trompete, und wir erhalten wieder den Gundton A, die 5te E, 8te A, 10te Cis, und 12te E u.s.w.

In the example at LM, this position of the trombone is called 1; the others are designated with the following numbers. When the slide is drawn out about three inches (second position, which is actually the first draw), the entire pipe becomes longer by half a tone; it becomes like an A trumpet and we get again the fundamental A, fifth E, octave A, tenth $C\#$, and twelfth E, etc. [See Plate 8.]

Example 15. Fröhlich: [A Trumpet and Trombone Compared]

Der nächste Zug oder die 3te Stellung gibt as, der folgende, oder die 4te g, der weitere oder die 5te Fis, der folgende oder die 6te F, und der weiteste oder die 7te E, so dass jeder Zug, oder jede dieser

The next draw, or third position, gives A^b; the next, or fourth, G; the next, or fifth, $F\#$; the next, or sixth, F; and the farthest, or seventh, E; so that each draw or position of the trombone gives the same notes in

Stellungen der Posaune die nämlichen Töne im nämlichen Verhältnisse gibt, wie es oben bestimmt wurde, und wie es beÿ J und K deutlich angegeben ist, wo alle Stellungen dieses Instrumentes mit Nummern nebst dem dadurch bewirkten Absteigen durch halbe Töne bis ins e genau bezeichnet sind.

the same relationship as established above. It is clearly shown at J and K, where all the positions of this instrument are, the numbers together with the lowering of pitch by semitone until E is reached.

Beÿ N° 4 kömmt schon die Doppeltoctav dazu, welche der Bassposaunist beÿ gutem Ansatze schon eher erreichen kann. Es versteht sich, dass man, um die höhern Töne zu erlangen, die Lippen mehr schliessen müsse, wodurch die Luftmasse zusammen gedrängt, und so der Ton schärfer wird, da man im Gegentheile, um abwärts zu steigen, den Schluss der Lippen vermindert, und nach Verhältniss die Masse der Luft vermehrt, je nachdem man den Ton tiefer und voller haben will.

At number 4 comes already the double octave, which the bass trombonist with a good embouchure can surely reach earlier. It is understood that, in order to get the high notes, it is necessary to close the lips more, through which the mass of air crowds together, and the pitch becomes higher, because, on the other hand, the closing of the lips is reduced to go downward, and as a result, the amount of air increases as the tone gets deeper and fuller.

Sehr wichtig für den Schüler ist es, den Punkt der Abtheilung genau zu bemerken, weil er sonst nie rein spielen lernt, auch muss man die Schieb Röhre sehr leicht, und mit Sicherheit bewegen, damit der Ansatz fest bleibe.

It is very important for the student to observe the point of this section completely, because he will not otherwise learn to play purely. He must also move the slide very lightly and with certainty so that the articulation remains strong.

Mehrere theilen auch die Züge auf der Posaune in 3 Hauptzüge ein. Der erste davon (bey dem Mundstücke oben mit N° 2 bezeichnet) gibt das Contra A mit den oben angegebenen Tönen, der 2te beÿ den Hauptstücke (oben N° 4) das G, zwischen beyden liegt ein Nebenzug, (oben N° 3) welcher das as oder Gis gibt, der 3te ausser dem

Many divide the positions into three principal draws. The first, by the mouthpiece, called no. 2 above, gives contra A with the notes mentioned above. The second, by the bell (no. 4 above), gives G. Between the two lies an auxiliary position (no. 3 above), which gives A^b or $G\#$. The third is beyond the bell (no. 6), which produces F and

Hauptstücke, (N° 6) welcher das F mit seinen anhängenden Tonverhältnissen erzeugt, zwischen den 2ten und 3ten Hauptzug liegt der Nebenzug (N° 5) für das Fis oder Gis, und nach dem letzten Haupt-Zug (N° 6) der Nebenzug, (N° 7) welcher das E als Grundton mit seinen anneren Tönen erscheinen lässt.

its related notes. Between the second and third principal positions lies the auxiliary position (no. 5) for F# or G^b, and after the last (no. 6), the auxiliary position (no. 7), where the fundamental E and its other notes appear.

Setzen wir nun alle durch die verschiedenen Züge erhaltene Töne zusammen, so bekommen wir folgende vollständige Tonreihe bey L, wo zugleich durch Zahlen die Züge angezeigt sind, oder vielmehr durch die wievielste Stellung dieser oder jener Ton erzeugt werde. Doppelte Ziffern unter einer Note bedeuten, dass sich diese auf zweÿerley Art hervorbringen lasse, welches bloss von der Stelle, oder Passage abhängt.

Now if we set down all the notes together that are obtained by means of the various positions, we get the complete scale at L, where, at the same time, the positions are indicated by numbers, or rather, in which position this or that note is produced. Double numbers under a note mean that it can be played in either, depending on the technical demands of the passage.

Man nimmt aber immer in der Regel den nächsten Zug, um allen Aufenthalt in der Execution zu vermeiden.

The rule is that the closest position is chosen in order to avoid all delays in execution.

Beÿ M sind diejenigen Töne angegeben, welch, durch Erhöhung oder Erniedrigung den bey L angezeigten gleich, mit dem namlichen Zuge (oder derselben Stellung) gemacht werden.

At M, the same notes are given, which are made by raising or lowering the same as indicated in L, with the same draws or positions. [See Plate 8.]

Diese Scala mit allen Zügen lasse man den Schüler fleissig üben, und mache ihn dabey aufmerksam, dass er sowohl einen sanften klangwollen Ton zu erhalten suche, als auch so rein als möglich zu spielen trachte. Man sey hierauf um so sorgsamer bedacht, als es gewiss unerträglich,

This scale, with all the positions, allows the student to practice industriously and thereby makes him attentive, so that at the same time, he will seek to get a gentle, sonorous tone and strive to play as purely as possible. It should be considered all the more carefully, as

und alle Wirkung verderbend ist, mit solchen durchdringenden Instrumenten, wenn sie falsch intonirt werden, eine Harmonie oder gar Singstimmen durch ihre Begleitung unterstützen zu wollen.

it is certainly unbearable, and spoils all effect with such penetrating instruments, if the intonation is false in the accompaniment of a harmony or even a voice.

Um dem Schüler die hiezu gehörige Gewandheit beyzubringen, ist is gut, wenn man denselben die verschiedenenen Scalen bey V durchnehmen lässt, so dass man immer von den leichterern zu den schwerern übergehe.

In order to bring the student to the necessary skill, it is good to go through the various scales at V [see Plate 10], so that one always progresses from the easier to the more difficult.

Hierauf lasse man denselben die Terzen, Quarten, Quinten, Sexten, u.s.w. und zwar nach der nämlichen Methode durch alle Tonarten durchnehmen, genau nach der in der Singschule enthaltenen Anweisung, welcher man stets folgen muss, welches um so weniger darf versäumt werden, als der Posaunist aus allen Tonarten spielen muss.

Afterward, the student should go through the third, fourth, fifth, sixth, etc., in fact through all keys according to the same method where instruction has been received in the Singing School, which must always be followed. It must not be neglected, as the trombonist must play in all keys.

Ist der Ansatz des Schülers schon ziemlich fest, dann mache man ihn mit folgenden wichtigen Vortheilen bekannt, ohne welchen die Behandlung dieses Instrumentes nicht anders, als sehr beschwerlich werden kann.

If the student's embouchure is already rather strong, then one should acquaint him with the following important features, without which the handling of this instrument can only be very cumbersome.

Beÿ der nämlichen Stellung der Posaune erhält man, wie es schon oben angegeben worden ist, den Grundton, die 5te, 8te, 10te, und 12te. Dieses wird bloss durch den Ansatz, durch den schärfern oder mehr nachgelassenen Schluss der Lippen bewirkt. Ferner hörlen wir, dass das vermittelst der Züge

As has already been shown, the fundamental, fifth, octave, tenth, and twelfth are played in the same position. This is caused only by the embouchure, by the tensing or easing of the closing of the lips. Furthermore, by means of the position that lengthens the tube of the instrument about three inches,

geschehene Verlängern der Röhre des Instrumentes, ohngefähr um 3 Zoll, immer den ersten Ton ohne Zug, um einen halben vertiefe.

the first note without draw is lowered a semitone.

Beyde Vortheile, mit einander verbunden, setzen den Posaunisten in den Stand, bey einer und derselben Lage 4 bis 5 verschiedene Grundtöne, und somit ein 4 oder 5 faches Herabsteigen von demselben mit der nämlichen Art des Ziehens bewerkstelligen zu können, ohne erst nöthig zu haben, jeden Ton in einem andern Zuge suchen zu müssen, was die geschwinde Execution, hindern, somit den Zusammenhang des Vortrags selbst stören muss. Man sehe die Beyspiele bey P, Q, R, S, T.

Both features taken together enable the trombonist to bring about one and the same harmonic series with four or five different fundamentals, and therefore a four- or five-fold ascent from them without first needing to look for each note in a different position, which would hinder the rapid execution and thus disturb the unity of the performance. See examples P through T. [Plate 10]

Eben dieses findet bey jedem verschiedenen Grundtone seine Anwendung, und muss genau einstudiert werden, indem diess die wichtigsten Folgen für die Leichtigkeit der Ausführung von Seite des Schülers nach sich zieht.

Certainly this finds its use with each fundamental and must be practiced completely while it moves toward the most important results for the ease of execution on the part of the student.

Es würde zu weitläufig werden, wenn wir noch Beyspiele anführen sollten, wie man oft mit wenigen Zügen, besonders beÿ geswindem Zeitmaasse, ganze Stellen vortragen kann, es kann diess Fingerzeig für den denkenden Musiker genug seyn, um sich durch reifes Nachdenken, und darauf gebaute fleissige Uebung dieser Vortheile zu versichern.

It would be too lengthy if we should guide with additional examples how, especially at fast tempos, entire passages can be played, often with few positions. This cue will be enough for thinking musicians in order to assure this technique through mature consideration and the industrious practice that comes from it.

Hiebey kömmt freÿlich Vieles auf den Bau der Instrument selbst, besonders auf die Art an, wie selbe

At this point, of course, much depends on the structure of the instrument itself, especially the way

Plate 10. Fröhlich: Examples O–V from *Posauneschule*.

Beyspiel R.

...itern in dur und moll.

eingeblasen sind, wobey man vorzügliche Rücksicht darauf nehmen muss, auf welchem Zuge dieser oder jener Ton am festesten oder sichersten sey, um sich hierinn beym Aushalten der Töne, danach richten zu können. Es ergibt sich hieraus, wie nothwendig ein genaues Studium seines Instrumentes dem Bläser sey, und wie sehr Schüler und Lehrer darauf sehen müssen, nicht allein jeden Zug, sondern sogar jeden einzelnen Ton in jedem Zuge zu untersuchen, um ganz fest im Technichen zu werden, und sich in den Besitz zuverlässiger Mittel zu ihrer Darstellung zu setzen.

Hat der Schüler ganz genaue Kenntniss seines Instrumentes, hat derselbe schon einige Gewandheit in den verschiedenen Zügen, dann kann man schon leichtere Uebungsstücke mit ihm vornehmen.

Diese müssen aber alle sehr gesangwoll gesetzt seyn, so wie man auch im Anfange langsamere Stücke wählen muss, um dem Bläser Gelegenheit zu geben, alle Töne gehörig zu entwickeln, und eine feste Grundlage zu einem gesangvollen Vortrag zu erhalten. Man kann sich hiezu schon gesetzter Posaunen Stimmen bedienen, oder auch Singstimmen benutzen welche für jene Art der Posaune gesetzt sind, auf welche sich der Schüler verlegt.

Auch Arien und Gesänge aus Opern thun hier gute Dienste, wobey man den Text den Bläser in Erwägung ziehen lässt, um ihn so

it is played, for which reason one must consider carefully which position is firmest or most secure for this or that note in order to be able to determine in this way the sustaining of the tone. It follows that a thorough study of this instrument is essential to the player, and that the student and teacher must see not only every position, but even investigate each individual tone in each position, in order to become entirely strong in technique and to devote themselves to the possession of a dependable means to their performance.

If the student has complete familiarity with his instrument, and if he already has some skill in the various positions, then he can undertake the easier etudes.

But these must be very tunefully composed, so in the beginning, slow pieces must be chosen in order to give the player the opportunity to develop all suitable notes and to get a strong foundation for a sonorous performance. One can use already composed trombone parts or take advantage of vocal music, which is composed for whatever trombone the student devotes himself to.

Also, arias and songs from operas make good practice material, because the player takes the text into consideration in order to make

mit der Folge der Empfindungen bekannt zu machen, und deselben unvermerkt zur Entwicklung seines eignen Gefühles hin zu leiten.

the result of the sentiment known and to lead the player to the gradual development of his own sensitivity.

Hiezu ist ihm nöthig, die Kenntniss von den Vortheilen beym Athemhohlen, welche Lehre in der Singsch. S. 46 abgehandelt ist, die Lehre von den verschiedenen Articulationen, welche derselbe nach den §4 in der Trompeten Schule studieren kann, und hiernächst ist ihm dazu nothwendig die ganze Lehre vom Vortrage und den wesentlichen Manieren, welche er, in der Singschule von Seite 48 bis zur Seite 66 durchgeführt findet.

In addition, one needs to know how to breathe to good advantage, instruction in which is discussed on p. 46 of the Singing School. The teaching of the various articulations can be studied in §4 of the Trumpet School. After this, the entire instruction from the performances and the essential manners is important to him, and he will find guidance in the Singing School on pages 48—66.

Alle in diesen verschiedenen Lehren vorkommende Beyspiele müssen natürlich nach dem Schlüssel und den Umfang jener Art dieses Instrumentes übersetzt und eingerichtet werden, welcher der Schüler sich widmet.

All of the examples that happen in these various instructions must naturally be transposed into the right key according to the compass of each type of this instrument to which the student dedicates himself.

Wenn wir diese Bildnungsmethode nach der Singschule in allen diesen Anweisungen durchführen, so ist es bey dieser Art von Instrumenten für den Bläser vorzüglich in dem Falle zu verstehen, wenn derselbe, fest im Technischen, Lust und Anlage genug hat, das Höhere der Kunst zu ergreifen, welches freylich das Strben jedes Musikers seyn sollte.

If we follow through with this method according to the instructions in the Singing School with this kind of instrument, the player can very well understand that if he has strong enough technique, interest, and ability, he will be able to grasp the heights of the art, which should be the goal of every musician.

Wer sich besonders noch als Solo Bläser einspielen will, der kann auch die Lehre von den willkührlichen Auszierungen, welche in der Singschule von Seite 72 an behandelt ist, durchnehmen.

Whoever especially wants to become a soloist can study the instruction in optional embellishments, which are discussed on p. 72 of the Singing School.

Zwar sind alle bisher gegebene Regeln und Vorschriften für jede Art der Posaune gleich anwendbar, wobey nur hauptsächlich der Schlüssel und der Umfang mancher Uebungs-Stücke muss geändert, und der Natur jener Dimension dieses Instrumentes, welch man behandelt, angepasst werden, da aber oft sowohl die verschiedene Structur, als der verschiedene Ansatz, hauptsächlich aber das verschiedene Mundstück die Töne im andern Verhältnisse, z.B. mehr in der Höhe oder Tiefe erzeugen macht, als in welchem wir sie bisher auf der Bass-Posaune sahen, so ist es nothwendig, noch etwas über die Tenor und Alt-Posaunen zu sagen.

Indeed, all rules and instructions given so far for each kind of trombone are immediately usable, in connection with which, for the most part, only the clef and the range need to be changed and adapted to the nature of the dimensions of the instrument being used. But it is important to say something more about the tenor and alto trombones, because differences in structure, embouchure, and mouthpiece produce the notes under different conditions, such as higher or lower than what we have seen until now regarding the bass trombone.

In neuern Zeiten verfertiget man an manchen Orten die 3 Arten der Posaune in gleicher Grösse, und durchaus in einem gleichen Baue.

In modern times, the three kinds of trombone are made similar in size in many places, and always similar in construction.

Hier entscheidet nichts als das Mundstück, besonders für die Altposaune, wofür ein engeres nothwendig ist, damit der Posaunist die imer vorkommenden höhern Töne sicher haben kann.

Nothing is different but the mouthpiece, especially for the alto trombone, for which a narrower mouthpiece is necessary. With it, the trombonist can always have the high notes with confidence.

Besser ist es freÿlich, wo der Bau der Posaunen verschieden ist, so dass die Bass und Tenorposaune, wo nicht in Hinsicht des Grundtones, doch gewiss in Hinsicht der Grösse des Bechers, der Länge der Röhre, u.s.w. sich unterscheiden, denn jene hat es mehr mit den liefern, diese mit den Mitteltönen zu thuen.

It is better, to be sure, when the construction of the trombones is different, so that the bass and tenor trombones are distinguished not in regard to their fundamentals, but certainly in regard to the size of the bell, the length of the pipe, etc., because the former has more to do with low notes and the latter with middle notes.

Eine solche Verschiedenheit ist in der Posaunen Schule von Braun angegeben. Wir wollen sie hieher setzen, nebst den durch die verschiedenen Zuge bewirkten Accorden, welche aber sowohl bey der Tenor als bey der Altposaune nicht wie vorher mit Zahlen, sondern mit Buchstaben bezeichnet sind.

Such a difference is set forth in Braun's Method for Trombone. We wish to set it down here next to the chords caused by the various positions, which, however, in the case of both the tenor and alto trombones are designated not by numbers, as before, but by letters.

(Hieher gehört die Tenor Scala U)

(The tenor scale U belongs here.) [See Plate 11.]

Wegen des engeren Mundstücks spricht hier die Höhe mehr, weniger die Tiefe an, desswegen hat nur die erste Stellung a) den Grundton, indem derselbe bey allen folgenden weggelassen ist, weil er nur sehr schwer anspricht beÿ b) das a) bey c) as, bey d) G, u.s.w.

Because of the narrower mouthpiece, the high notes speak more and the low notes less. Therefore, only the first position (a) has the fundamental, which is lacking in all others because it is very difficult to get the A in (b), the A^b in (c), the G in (d), etc. to speak.

Die Töne, welche mit doppelten Buchstaben bezeichnet sind, können mit 2 Zügen oder Stellungen gemacht werden. Ganz unten sind in der Leiter alle jene Töne angegeben, welche als die nämlichen behandelt werden, was in den allg. Grundsätzen schon erklärt wurde.

The notes designated with double letters can be played in two draws or positions. Underneath, the chromatic scale is given, which is handled according to the general principles already given.

Beynahe alles das nämliche gibt auch von der Altposaune, nur steht sie nach dieser Angabe eine Quarte höher wodurch die höhern Töne noch leichter zu erhalten sind, und ihr Grundton ist Es.

Almost all of the foregoing is also true of the alto trombone, except that it is a fourth higher, making the high notes even easier to get, and its fundamental is e^b.

(Hieher gehört die Scala für die Altposaune V.)

(The scale for the alto trombone, V, belongs here.) [See Plate 12.]

Plate 11. Fröhlich: Tenor Scale, U from *Posaunenschule*.

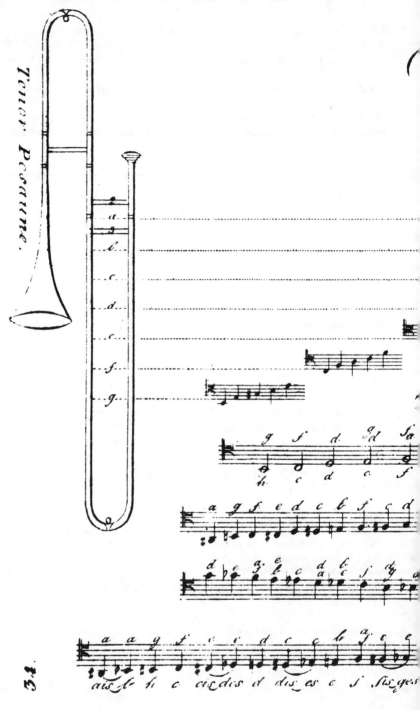

Plate 12. Fröhlich: Alto Scale, V from *Posaunenschule*.

CHAPTER 3

AN OVERVIEW OF THE TROMBONE IN THE EIGHTEENTH CENTURY (EXCLUDING FRANCE)

Early in the eighteenth century, trombones hardly differed from those described by Praetorius a hundred years earlier. The bell was shaped like a cone, with little or no terminal flare. The instrument as a whole was still held together by removable flat stays. Trombonists could use not only their basic trombone and mouthpiece, but could also add crooks. According to Anthony Baines, these lowered the fundamental pitch of the instrument a semitone; by combining crooks, it was possible to add enough tubing to lower the pitch as much as a fourth, which enabled the player to transpose as needed.[1]

It should be noted that Ephraim Chambers wrote that the crook, or wreath, was "twisted twice, or making two circles in the middle of the instrument." Rousseau's description is similar. (See Chapter 2 for the full texts.) Illustrations in Bonanni, and La Borde, based on Mersenne, also show two circles for the crook. In order for this configuration to lower the basic pitch a fourth, each semicircle must be long enough to lower it a whole tone. The picture may not be accurate in detail, and Chambers may have based his comments on

---

[1] Anthony Baines, *Brass Instruments: Their History and Development* (New York: Scribner, 1978), 116.

the picture rather than on other writings; it is unlikely that he had first-hand knowledge. In any case, the ability to add crooks was especially helpful, considering that there was no standard pitch at the time; each town had its own pitch level.

Soon, tubular stays, which are more comfortable to hold, began to replace flat stays.[2] In 1732, Johann Leopold Ehe III of Nürnberg made a bass trombone with a flaring bell; in this innovation, the trombone lagged behind the trumpet, probably because of its limited role in Germany.[3] By mid-century, however, the flaring bell became standard on trombones as well as trumpets. Little by little, crooks disappeared, so that by the end of the century, trombones differed from those of the middle of the nineteenth century only by lacking such minor features as stockings on the slide.[4]

The change in the tenor trombone's pitch from A to B^b, explained in Chapter 1, seems not to have been deliberate. Most likely, it was a combined function of the lack of an internationally accepted standard pitch and the disappearance of crooks.

According to Baroque practice, the slide in first position was not completely closed, but extended far enough that it was possible to play the seventh partial in tune.[5] With no crooks or tuning slide to lower the fundamental pitch, players in locations with low pitch had to extend the slide still farther in order to play the overtone series on A_1 in tune. If the local pitch was low enough, the slide was no longer long enough to produce the series on $E^b{}_1$ (modern seventh position or the extended fourth position of eighteenth-century writers), but a series of notes higher than those in "first" position, on $B^b{}_1$ became possible with the slide completely closed (all except the seventh partial, which is too flat to be used.) For example, Gossec wrote E^bs in his *Messe des morts*, possibly because his German trombonists told him that they could play it. Because of the low pitch used in France, it became necessary for the players to write "8va" in their parts over all of these notes.[6]

---

[2] Philip Bate, *The Trumpet and Trombone: An Outline of Their History, Development and Construction*, 2nd ed. (London: Benn; New York: Norton, 1978), 147.

[3] Willi Wörthmüller, "Die Nürnberger Trompeten- und Posaunenmacher des 17. und 18. Jahrhunderts," *Mitteilungen des Vereins für Geschichte der Stadt Nürnberg* 46 (1955), 392–93.

[4] Bate, 147.

[5] David Guion, "The Pitch of Baroque Trombones," *Journal of the International Trombone Association*, 8 (1980), 25.

[6] Baines, 242.

It is probably in this way that the old tenor trombone in A became the modern trombone in B^b in France and anywhere else that used similar pitch, with no modification in the practice of trombone makers. As Chapter 4 will show, French music, and especially military music, had an influence completely out of proportion to its musical worth, and nearly all of the military music was written in flat keys. This usage, as well as low pitch, became another reason to think of the tenor trombone as an instrument in B^b and not in A.

Although I have not been able to find specific information on the pitch standards of very many cities, Paris is probably not the only place where the transition just described took place. The trombone was a solo instrument in Austria. All of the concertos for trombone written in Vienna are in flat keys and all similar works written in Salzburg are in sharp keys. Presumably, composers would write virtuosic solos in convenient keys, and so it appears that the pitch standards in the two cities were different. In any case, when Fröhlich first described the B^b trombone in 1811, he clearly did not advocate a change in theory or practice, but merely described one that had already taken place.

The eighteenth century also saw the beginnings of the decentralization of trombone making. Nearly all extant trombones from the sixteenth and seventeenth centuries were made by various instrument makers who worked in Nürnberg.[7] Lyndesay Langwill's compilation of wind instrument makers[8] shows that the Nürnberg makers still dominated the industry, but that they no longer account for such an overwhelming majority of extant trombones. By the end of the century, there were also cities outside Germany where trombones were made.

Makers in Nürnberg included four members of the Ehe family, Johann Karl Kodisch, and Georg Friedrich Steinmetz. Other German cities with trombone makers included Berngrundt (Johann Christoph Fiebig), Breslau (Johann Florian Bittner), Dresden (Johann Gottfried Leuthold), Leipzig (Johann Heinrich Eichentopf), Neukirchen (Johann Georg Eschenbach), Neustadt bei Dresden (C. F. Riedel), and Pfaffendorf (Johann Joseph and Johann Simon Schmied). Breslau, now Wrocław, Poland, was then part of the Kingdom of

---

[7] Adam Carse, *Musical Wind Instruments* (New York: Da Capo, 1965, reprint of 1939 ed.), 253.
[8] Lyndesay G. Langwill, *An Index of Musical Wind-Instrument Makers*, 5th ed., (Edinburgh: Langwill, 1977), passim.

Prussia. All of the other cities were located either in Saxony or Bavaria.

At least three trombone makers (Anton Kerner, Michael Lei-chamschneider, and Franz Anton Purggraf) worked in Vienna. Jacob Plüs made at least one trombone in Aarburg, Switzerland. Two specimens survive made by Hos. J. G. Ahlgren of Stockholm, Sweden. A horn maker in Paris, Lefèvre (given without a first name), made at least one trombone in Paris at about the time of the Revolution.

The foregoing cannot be taken as a complete list of the trombone makers of the eighteenth century. It is intended merely to demon-strate the beginnings of the decentralization of trombone making.

For a period in the history of the trombone that is so commonly passed over without comment, the eighteenth century holds an unexpected wealth of trombone music. This chapter presents an overview of the use of the trombone everywhere in the world it was used except in France. A separate chapter on French music with trombone (Chapter 4) serves as an example of how much detail is available about this neglected century. A thorough study of the trombone in Germany would be at least as long. The Austrian empire could serve as the subject of an entire book as long as the present one.

Therefore, in no sense do any of the following sections constitute a complete survey. Moravian music in America, for example, has already been the subject of one doctoral dissertation[9] and several articles. Available information about other parts of the world ranges from the barest hints that the trombone was known at all in Italy to the plethora of as yet barely explored music and documentation in Austria and Bohemia.

AMERICA

The trombone played an important role in the civil and religious life of the Moravian settlements in Pennsylvania and North Carolina. It was unknown elsewhere. In 1822, when the Musical Fund Society of

---

[9] Harry H. Hall, *The Moravian Wind Ensemble: Distinctive Chapter in American Music* (Ph.D. dissertation: George Peabody College for Teachers, 1967).

Plate 13. Brass Instrument Maker's Workshop from *Encyclopédie*.

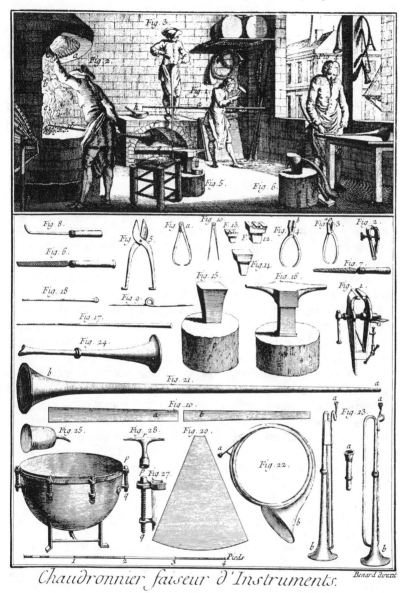

Reprinted from *The Trumpet & Trombone in Graphic Arts: 1500–1800* by
Tom L. Naylor © 1979 The Brass Press. Used by permission.

Philadelphia performed Haydn's *Creation*, not a single trombonist
lived in the city; the three trombone parts were played by members
of the trombone choir from Bethlehem.[10]

The Moravian church, descendant of a dissident Bohemian group
called Unitas Fratrum, was founded in 1722 in Saxony, a district
that Schubart would later identify as a center of excellent trombone playing. (See Chapter 2 for the full text.) The Moravians
founded the town of Herrnhut, which became the worldwide headquarters of their faith after they began to evangelize all over the
world.[11] In Germany at this time, as will be presented in more detail
later in this chapter, wind instruments played an important part in
the daily lives of the German people. Luther's translation of the
Bible uses "trombone" in many of the places where the English
Bible uses "trumpet." For this reason, the Germans regarded the
trombone almost as if it were the voice of God himself. (See the
section on German music for a more detailed explanation of this
point.) The Moravians seem to have embraced the trombone even
more than their Lutheran contemporaries.[12] They even made extensive use of the otherwise uncommon soprano, or discant, trombone
and continue to use it in their trombone choirs to this day.[13]

Moravian music in America differed greatly from all the rest of
the music discussed in this dissertation in one important way: music
was considered a necessary spiritual pursuit, but not a worthy profession. Therefore, all Moravian musicians, including the trombonists,
were amateurs.[14] Elsewhere, the trombone seems never to have
been played by amateurs.

A great missionary zeal characterized the Moravians, and they
established several settlements in the New World to spread the
gospel to the heathen. They founded their first colony in what is
now the United States in Savannah, Georgia in 1735, only two years
after it was founded by James Oglethorpe. Although the Moravians

---

[10] Joseph A. Maurer, "The Moravian Trombone Choir," *The Historical
Review of Berks County* 20 (Oct.-Dec. 1954), 3.

[11] Bernard J. Pfohl, *The Salem Band* (Winston-Salem, N. C.: Winston
Printing Co., 1953), 8.

[12] Harry H. Hall, "Early Sounds of Moravian Brass Music in America: A
Cultural Note from Colonial Georgia," *Brass Quarterly* 7 (Spring 1964),
117.

[13] Maurer, 3.

[14] Hall, "Moravian Wind," 46, n. 2.

got along well with Oglethorpe, the hostility of other Georgians forced them to abandon Savannah for the more tolerant colony of Pennsylvania in 1740.

While in Georgia, a Moravian brass choir functioned much as it had in Germany. Harry Hall singles out two especially important customs: the Easter dawn proclamation and the use of chorales as funeral music.[15] The Savannah choir apparently did not include trombones.[16]

Bethlehem

Bethlehem, the first Moravian settlement in Pennsylvania, was founded in 1741.[17] Others soon followed. As early as May 1744, Bethlehem had a choir of trumpets and horns. A quartet of slide trombones first performed for the Festival and Prayer Day of the Unmarried Brethren on August 31, 1754. Another set of trombones was purchased for the town of Nazareth in 1767. By the end of the century, Bethlehem had two trombone quartets, and there was another at Hope, New Jersey.

Two unusual features of these quartets remain unique to this day. One, the soprano trombone, an instrument tonally inferior to the trumpet, is now obsolete except in Moravian churches and as a novelty instrument in a few jazz bands. The other, the bass trombone in F, used to be the standard bass trombone, but, except in Moravian churches, has been replaced by a large-bore B^b trombone with, preferably, two triggers.

Trombones played for funerals, the Easter liturgy, and other occasions in the church year when brass music would add dignity and interest. They announced deaths with three chorales; the first and last are always Hans Leo Hassler's "O Haupt voll Blut und Wunden" ("O Sacred Head Now Wounded") and the second is one of ten chorales chosen according to whether the deceased was a married man or woman, widow or widower, unmarried man or woman, older boy or girl, or younger boy or girl.

---

[15] Hall, "Early Sounds," 117–18.
[16] Ibid., 119.
[17] Maurer, 3–5.

Salem

A third group of Moravian settlements in America began with the
establishment of Bethabara, North Carolina in 1753. Trombones
first arrived there in 1765.[18] As in Bethlehem, the trombones led the
singing and performed at funerals and festivals. In 1766, the town of
Salem was founded, and the instruments at Bethabara were divided
in 1771 so that Salem, too, could have a trombone choir. Unlike the
Bethlehem choir, which soon became exclusively a trombone choir,
the Salem band (and most of the more recent Moravian ensembles)
was a mixed wind ensemble. And also unlike the Bethlehem trombone choir, the Salem band played secular music as well as chorales.[19]

A recording of Moravian music by the Los Angeles Philharmonic
Trombone Ensemble includes music by one native American
composer, John Antes (1740–1811). Born in Bethlehem, Antes
received his musical education in Herrnhut and never returned to
this country.[20] None of the articles on the Moravian trombone
choirs examined for this book mentions any American composers.
None of the other articles I have seen about Moravian composers in
America mentions the trombone. It would seem odd if none of the
resident composers wrote for the trombone choir, but given the
importance of tradition and the leadership of Herrnhut, it is not
impossible.

AUSTRIA AND BOHEMIA

Austria and Bohemia are ethnically separate, but were politically
united under the rule of the Habsburg Holy Roman Empire. The
Emperor was also the King of Bohemia, so Vienna, cultural capital
of Austria, was political capital of both Austria and Bohemia, as
well as other districts. In contrast with other countries included in
this chapter, there is a great abundance of music from Austria and
Bohemia with parts for trombone. As mentioned in Chapter 1,

---

[18] Pfohl, 8.
[19] Hall, "Moravian Wind," 287.
[20] Jerome Leaman, Notes to "Music of the Moravian Trombone Choir."
(Los Angeles: Crystal Records, 1976.)

trombones captured the fancy of the emperors at least as early as the middle of the seventeenth century. Their importance continued unabated throughout the eighteenth century.

Since music publishing did not take root in Austria to the extent that it did in France, no music is available to me except what has been published later, which is largely limited to the larger collected editions, historical sets, or monuments of music. Church music and the works of a few great composers receive excellent coverage. Most operatic and symphonic music still awaits rediscovery.

Austria and Bohemia stand virtually alone in the eighteenth century in their use of the trombone as a solo instrument. C. Robert Wigness has already examined several pieces with soloistic trombone parts;[21] there are many more. In a session at the 1982 International Trombone Workshop in Nashville, Tennessee, Wigness described 14 works by five composers in addition to those described in his doctoral essay. None of these have yet been prepared for publication.

Vienna

Joseph I

Like many other Habsburgs, Joseph I (r. 1705–1711) was a prolific composer. Guido Adler included "Alme ingrate" (1705), for soprano, alto trombone, and continuo, in his edition of music by Habsburg emperors.[22] Both solo parts are very florid. Wigness has described this piece in detail,[23] and modern performance is not uncommon.

Other pieces by various Habsburgs stretching back to Ferdinand III (r. 1637–1657) likewise require trombones, although not necessarily as a solo instrument. Such appreciation for the trombone in high places no doubt goes a long way to explain why Austrian composers used it so much at the same time it fell into disuse in most of the rest of the world.

---

[21] C. Robert Wigness, *The Soloistic Use of the Trombone in Eighteenth-Century Vienna* (D.M.A. Essay: University of Iowa, 1970; Nashville, TN: Brass Press, 1978).

[22] Guido Adler, *Musikalische Werke der Kaiser Ferdinand III., Leopold I. und Joseph I.*, 2 vols. (Vienna: Artaria, [1892–93]), vol. 2, 227–30.

[23] Wigness, 27–28.

Near the end of his reign, Joseph decided that his musical establishment was too expensive and ordered his *Kapellmeister*, Marc'
Antonio Ziani, to reduce its size. Ziani fired nearly a third of the
court musicians. Two trombonists survived the purge, along with 46
other instrumentalists and 17 singers.[24]

Ziani, in his own compositions, made extensive use of wind
instruments, often in soloistic roles.[25] Wigness describes "Alma
redemptoris mater" (1707) for alto, two trombones, bassoon, and
continuo.[26]

Johann Joseph Fux

One of the most prolific and influential composers of the eighteenth
century, Fux became court composer in 1698 and *Kapellmeister* in
1715. When scholars began to compile thematic catalogs of great
composers, Fux was among the earliest to attract such detailed
study. Köchel's catalog lists 405 works in 11 categories. A sup-
plemental catalog by Andreas Liess lists 55 additional works.[27]
Another 151 of Fux's works are identified by "E" (for *Ergänzung*)
numbers. The various listings describe the instrumentation for most
of Fux's music, but not, unfortunately, for his operas and oratorios.
In all, it is possible to identify about 190 works with trombone parts.
These include nearly every genre of sacred music as well as some
purely instrumental music.

The pattern of alto, tenor, and bass trombones doubling the alto,
tenor, and bass lines of the chorus, so familiar from the later works
of Mozart and Beethoven, rarely occurs in Fux's writing. Most of his
choral music calls for only two trombones, alto and tenor. The bass
line, usually doubled by bassoon, cello, and violone, has more than

---

[24] Ludwig Köchel, *Johann Josef Fux, Hofcompositor und Hofkapellmeister
der Kaiser Leopold I., Josef I. und Karl VI. von 1698 bis 1740* (Vienna:
Alfred Hölder, 1872), 221.

[25] Theophil Antonicek, "Ziani, Marc'Antonio," *The New Grove Dictionary of Music and Musicians*, ed. Stanley Sadie, 20 vols. (London:
Macmillan, 1980), vol. 20, 674.

[26] Wigness, 26.

[27] Liess, Andreas, *Johann Joseph Fux: ein steirischer Meister des Barock*
(Vienna: Doblinger, 1948), 61–71.

adequate support without the bass trombone, although Fux does use it occasionally.[28]

In common with other Austrian composers, Fux either uses trombones throughout a given movement or not at all. The practice of writing intermittent parts for any instrument, separated by long rests, belongs to a later time.

Fux did not by any means limit the trombones to doubling the choral parts. Köchel lists nine works (K. 21, 24, 25, 26, 120, 121, 175, 248, 252) and Liess lists two works (L. 18, 28) for trombones "in concerto." Unfortunately, the publication of Fux's collected works does not yet include any of these pieces. *Missa Corporis Christi* (K. 10), however, includes some passages where the trombones are independent of the chorus. See Chapter 5 for a detailed description.

Smaller pieces in which the trombone is a solo instrument reveal that Fux could write spectacularly difficult and virtuosic trombone parts. In "Alma redemptorist mater" (K. 186), an alto trombone plays as equal partner with a soprano and two violins. Wigness has described this piece in detail.[29] Liess lists a "Beatus vir" for the same instrumentation (L. 48), but gives no incipit.

Fux also used the trombone as a soloist in at least three instrumental sonatas. One, for violin, cornett, trombone, bassoon, and continuo (K. 347), was included in the nineteenth volume of *Denkmäler der Tonkunst in Oesterreich*. Wigness describes it in detail.[30] Two more pieces, for two violins, trombone, and continuo (K. 365 and E. 68) still await publication, although Liess reproduces a portion of the former.

Even some pieces in which the trombones merely double the chorus require excellent players. For example, in the motet "Plaudite Deo nostro" (K. 167), the trombones appear only in the final chorus, which is only ten measures long. The first two measures, comparable in difficulty to more soloistic parts, require not only the agility of lip and the slide technique required to play the notes, but also a delicate sound in order to support and not cover the chorus. Add to this the fact that the players had to wait until the end of the motet to play, and were thus no longer truly warmed up, and clearly

---

[28] Köchel, 58.
[29] Wigness, 28—30.
[30] Ibid., 13—16.

they must have been very good. The best were Leopold Christian, father and son. Court records show clearly Fux's respect for their unequaled prowess and virtuosity.[31] Judging from the salaries paid to trombonists, other very good trombonists available to Fux were Andreas Boog, Hans Georg Christian, Leopold Ferdinand Christian, Andreas Steinbruckner, Ignaz Steinbruckner, and Stephen Tepser.[32]

Fux's contemporaries

Contemporaries or near contemporaries of Fux in Vienna who wrote for trombone include Matthais Sigismund Biechtler, Antonio Caldara, and Georg Reinhard. Biechtler's "Ad cantus, ad chorus" requires three trombones, alto, tenor, and bass, which double the chorus throughout. Caldara's "Stabat mater" alternates between choral and solo sections. In the choral sections, all instruments double the voices. In one 24-measure alto solo, the trombone have soloistic parts. Caldara's "Te Deum," for double chorus, requires two alto trombones to double the choral altos. One of them also plays a four-measure solo. At the 1982 International Trombone Workshop, Wigness mentioned Caldara's *Le profezie evangeliche* (1725) and *La passione di Gesù Christo* (1730), and Reinhard's *Cantus pastoritius (Hirtenkantate)*, all of which use solo trombone. Reinhard's cantata includes an aria for soprano, alto trombone, two violins, and continuo.

George Reutter, Jr.

Reutter, court Kapellmeister from 1751 until his death in 1772, was apparently more concerned with courtly politics than with fulfilling his duties. He managed to gain appointment as both first and second *Kapellmeister* at both the court and cathedral, the only time in history that one man held all four positions. Yet he presided over the decline of court music in Vienna. Where there had been more than 100 musicians in the *Kapelle* under Fux, there were only 20

---

[31] Köchel, 380, 389.
[32] Ibid., 41–42.

when Reutter died. These did not include even a single bassist, cellist, or organist.[33] There were always trombones, however, and no lack of music for them.

The quality of Reutter's own compositions is uneven, even within one piece. His *Missa Sancti Caroli* (1734), for example, is extremely dull in most of the choral movements. The orchestra consists of two violins, two trumpets, two trombones, and continuo. The use of brass instruments, a hallmark of Reutter's style, does nothing to relieve the tedium of so much of the music. In fact, it adds to it. The tenor trombone plays in only two movements. In most of the rest of the movements with brass, the alto trombone merely acts like a third trumpet, playing only tonic and dominant!

The solo movements, however, are much more interesting. One, "Gratias agimus tibi," for alto solo, also calls for a virtuoso alto trombonist. Both soloists have several passages of up to five consecutive trilled half notes in an ascending scale. If the trills are interpreted literally, the movement is overly sequential and also unreasonably difficult for both the trombonist and the singer. Whoever takes the trills as an invitation to free embellishment and seeks a variety of realizations will find this movement well worth performing.

A *Requiem* in c minor (1753) appears, on the whole, to be a better piece. Alto and tenor trombones routinely double the chorus. In addition, one movement includes an extended alto trombone solo, and two others include soloistic writing for both trombones. Except for frequent trills in the alto trombone solo, these passages are not especially difficult. It would not be feasible to take any of these movements out of context and perform them on a recital. Only in "Oro supplex" do the trombones play as soloists past the opening of the movement, and that movement requires either full chorus or, with some editing, four vocal soloists.

The "Tuba mirum" of an apparently earlier *Requiem* is described by Wigness.[34] No modern edition of this piece has been made. Scored for two trombones and four solo voices, it, too, would probably present more rehearsal problems than it would be worth for performance on a recital.

At the workshop, Wigness mentioned four additional works by

---

[33] Eva Badura-Skoda, "Reutter, (Johann Adam Joseph Karl) Georg (von) (ii)," *The New Grove*, vol. 15, 744.

[34] Wigness, 30.

Reutter with soloistic trombone parts: *Missa Sancti Placidi* (n.d.), *Missa Lauretana* (n.d.), "Alma redemptoris" (n.d.), and *Te Deum* (1741). All of these use one solo trombone except the first, which requires two.

When Reutter took over the Kapelle, Andreas Boog, Leopold Christian Jr., Leopold Ferdinand Christian, Ignaz Steinbruckner, and Stephan Tepser remained as court trombonists. Except for Leopold Ferdinand Christian, all of them died during Reutter's tenure, and only one new trombonist, Wenzel Thomas, was hired.[35]

Reutter's contemporaries

Five pieces by Florian Gaßmann with trombone parts appear in *Denkmäller der Tonkunst in Oesterreich*: *Missa in C*, *Regina coeli*, *Tui sunt caeli*, *Viderunt omnes*, and a fragment of a *Requiem*. Although there is some independent counterpoint for the trombones (in each case alto and tenor) in these pieces, they mostly double the chorus. Gaßmann did not hesitate to write sixteenth notes, or even occasional pairs of thirty-second notes, for the trombones in slow movements. The disjunct motion in some of these passages requires trombonists of great agility, flexibility, and sensitivity.

Of 176 extant choral compositions of Franz Ignaz Tuma, 102 require trombones.[36] Tuma, a student of Fux, lived in Vienna from 1722 until his death in 1774. His tenure as Kapellmeister to Empress Elizabeth Christine, widow of Karl VI (1741–1751) was the most productive period of his life. There, he had 17 musicians under his direction, including trombonists Wenzel Thomas and Anton Ulbrich.[37] Like Fux, Tuma used alto and tenor trombones to double the alto and tenor choral parts. In addition, the alto trombone ranks with the violin as the instrument Tuma most often featured as soloist in concertato passages.[38] Tuma wrote instrumental as well as choral music. Wigness describes his *Sonata in e minor* for two violins, two trombones, and continuo.[39]

[35] Ibid., 41–42.
[36] Theodore Klinka, *The Choral Music of Franz Ignaz Tuma, with a Practical Edition of Selected Choral Works*, (Ph.D. dissertation: University of Iowa, 1975), 224ff.
[37] Ibid., 21.
[38] Ibid., 116.
[39] Wigness, 16–19.

At the workshop, Wigness described four masses by Christoph Sonnleither that call for one or two solo trombones.

Two Viennese concertos for trombone date from the end of Reutter's life. The first, written some time before 1763 by Georg Christoph Wagenseil, consists of only two movements, both in E^b major. The chief technical difficulty centers around the high tessitura, the slow tempo of the first movement, and the scarcity of rests. The problems of endurance are therefore formidable. Nonetheless, Wagenseil's is the less difficult of the two concertos.

The other, by Johann Georg Albrechtsberger (1769), in B^b major, contains the standard three movements, with the middle movement in the subdominant. Once again, the high tessitura and long phrases present a great challenge to endurance. Albrechtsberger provides somewhat longer and more frequent rests than Wagenseil, but his lines are more disjunct and his rhythms more intricate. His concerto, therefore, provides a more spectacular display of technique, as well as more different kinds of potential pitfalls. Modern trombonists who attempt to play either concerto on a large-bore symphonic trombone merely invite embarrassment. Wigness has described both concertos in detail.[40]

Also during Reutter's tenure in Vienna, the trombone joined the operatic orchestra. Christoph Willibald Gluck's *Orfeo ed Euridice* (1762) appears to be the first eighteenth-century opera to require trombones, although possibly one or more lesser-known operas called for them earlier. A detailed description of *Orfeo* can be found in Chapter 6. Gluck also included trombones in *Alceste* (1767). He revived both of these operas for performance in Paris, where he produced nearly all of his greatest works. His French works are described in Chapter 4.

Gluck's earliest work with trombone is his ballet *Don Juan* (1761), which consists of a sinfonia and 31 movements, the last two of which require a single alto trombone. As in Mozart's *Don Giovanni*, (see Chapter 6) the trombone represents the statue that the Don invites to supper. In the thirtieth movement, it plays a knocking motive. Except for one measure, no other wind instrument plays during this movement, so the trombone part is very prominent. In both movements, its pitch material is best described as "autonomous doubling."

---

[40] Ibid., 19–24.

That is, all of its notes occur in one or another of the string parts, but it does not follow any one part for more than a measure or two at a time before jumping to another part. As a result, the trombone's motion in the thirtieth movement is mostly disjunct, while the string parts are largely conjunct. In the final movement, the trombone is more closely associated with the viola than with any other instrument, although still autonomous. *Don Juan* requires a confident player with good basic technique, a strong high register, and exceptional breath control.

Although Gluck is most important as a composer for the theater, he wrote some religious music. His very last composition, "De profundis" (1787), requires three trombones.

Franz Joseph Haydn and after

Shortly after Reutter's death, Viennese music entered a golden age, leb by the music of Mozart, Haydn, and Beethoven. (Since nearly all of Mozart's works with trombone parts were written during his Salzburg years, they will not be considered here with Viennese music, but later with Salzburg music.)

Haydn spent most of his creative life not in Vienna, but in Eszterháza, where there were apparently no trombones available to him. He did not use them in a single one of his masses, making him unique among important eighteenth-century composers of Catholic church music.

Very little of Haydn's vast output includes trombone parts, but Hoboken lists the following pieces.:

1. *Il ritorno di Tobia*, oratorio, two trombones (Hob. XXI: 1, 1774–75).
2. "Ad aras convolate," offertory, two trombones (Hob. XXIIIa:5*, 1780).
3. *L'anima del filosofo, ossia Orfeo ed Euridice*, opera, two trombones (Hob. XXVIII:3, 1791).
4. *Der Sturm*, secular cantata, two trombones (Hob. XXIVa:8, 1792).
5. *Die sieben letzten Worte unsers Erlösers am Kreuze (The Seven Last Words of Our Savior on the Cross)*, oratorio, two trombones, (Hob. XX:2, 1798).
6. *Die Schöpfung (The Creation)*, oratorio, three trombones, (Hob. XXI:2, 1798).

7. "Te Deum," three trombones (Hob. XXIIIc:2, 1800).
8. *Die Jahreszeiten (The Seasons)*, oratorio, three trombones, (Hob XXI:3, 1801).

All of these works except *L'anima del filosofo* were first performed in Vienna. The opera, written for London's Haymarket Theatre, was never performed in Haydn's lifetime. Haydn's debt to Handel in his late choral works is well known. He is also adopted Handel's manner of writing for trombone instead of the traditional Austrian practice. For a detailed description of *The Seven Last Words*, see Chapter 5.

The music of Beethoven marks a turning point in the history of the trombone. His sacred music represents the culmination of Austrian religious music of the classical period. After his death, it was largely left in the hands of lesser composers.

Beethoven often receives credit for introducing the trombone into the symphony orchestra. Actually, a symphony by Salzburg composer Joseph Krottendorfer anticipated Beethoven's first symphonic use of the trombone by almost 40 years. None of the symphonies with trombone before Beethoven remain in the repertoire, however, and probably none were ever widely performed even during the lifetime of their composers. Beethoven's Fifth Symphony (op. 67, 1807—08) therefore marks the arrival of the trombone in a major symphonic work. He also used them in his Sixth Symphony (op. 68, 1808), *Fidelio* (op. 72, 1804—14) and the last three of its overtures (1805, 1806, 1814), *Christus am Oelberge*, (op. 85, 1811), *Wellington's Victory* (op. 91, 1813), a march from *Die Ruinen von Athen* (op. 114, 1811), *Missa solemnis*, (op. 123, 1819—23), the overture to *Die Weihe des Hauses* (op. 124, 1822), and the Ninth Symphony (op. 125, 1822—24). As a result of Beethoven's use of trombones in these pieces, they became permanent members of the symphony orchestra. (See Chapter 5 for a description of *Christus am Oelberg* and Chapter 7 for the Fifth and Sixth Symphonies.)

Oddly enough, Beethoven's trombone parts have less in common with the traditional Viennese manner of writing for trombones than with the new style from France. As the next chapter will demonstrate, French composers were severely limited in what they could expect of trombones because of the lack of expert players. French trombone parts therefore consist exclusively of the least interesting of the instrument's capabilities: doubling, rhythmic punctuation, harmonic filler, and making loud sounds. In his choral works, Beethoven follows the practice of Handel and Haydn.

Beethoven's trombone parts are much more difficult than any French part, largely because of their extreme range (to f' for alto trombone in the Fifth Symphony), but not necessarily any more interesting. In fact, the trombone parts in *Fidelio* are less imaginative and satisfying than those in Gaveaux's *Léonore*.

Not even in sacred music did Beethoven use the trombone as a solo instrument. Such was Beethoven's influence on nineteenth-century orchestration that the trombone's role continued to be limited to the same functions he allowed it. Solos for trombone were largely limited to flashy, but musically empty concertos by very minor composers. No other instrument in Beethoven's orchestra was so consistently mistreated for so long.

In addition to the orchestral and choral works already mentioned, Beethoven used trombones in two smaller works: a march for military band (WoO 18, 1809) and "Three Equali" for four trombones (WoO 30, 1812). The "Equali" seem to betray a lack of interest in the trombone, or at least in the commission for the piece. Each one is shorter, less fully developed, and less carefully provided with dynamic markings than the previous one.

Minor Viennese composers who wrote for trombone at the close of the eighteenth century include Mozart's friend Joseph Eybler, who largely confined his activities to church music. His works include 44 pieces with parts for trombone, many of which were written after the terminal date of this book.[41] Owing to the surpassing greatness of Mozart, Haydn, and Beethoven, the minor composers have received much less attention than similar composers from other times and places. Unless evidence to the contrary turns up, it can be assumed that others of these minor composers besides Eybler wrote for the trombone.

Other Musical Centers

Salzburg

Throughout most of the history of the Holy Roman Empire, the city of Salzburg was ruled by a prince-archbishop. Therefore, it enjoyed a certain political and cultural autonomy. The archbishops and

---

[41] Hildegard Herrman, *Thematisches Verzeichnis der Werke von Joseph Eybler* (Munich: Katzbichler, 1976).

emperors were both allies and rivals, and the rivalry manifested itself in the splendor and prestige of the two courts. Not surprisingly, then, Salzburg rivaled Vienna as a center of excellent trombone playing. Unlike the Viennese, who usually wrote for only two trombones, Salzburg composers usually require three: alto, tenor, and bass. Heinrich Biber's *Missa Sti. Henrici* (1701) includes instrumental writing described by Paul Steinmetz as "exceptionally resourceful and idiomatic.[42] The three trombones, however, merely double the voices. An earlier "Sonata a tre" for two violins, trombone, and continuo uses the trombone as a virtuoso solo instrument. Biber's son Carl Heinrich also wrote at least one mass in which three trombones double the voices: *Missa brevis sanctorum septum dolorum B.V.M.* (1731).

Trombone parts by Johann Ernst Eberlin are more demanding. His oratorio *Der blutschwitzende Jesus* (1755) uses two trombones in the sinfonia and one in each of three areas. In each case, the trombone parts are soloistic. While the sinfonia is not especially difficult, the arias abound in trills and florid passagework. *Der verurteilte Jesus* (n.d.) and *Der verlorene Sohn* (n.d.) make similar demands. In two motets, "Quae est ista" (n.d.) and "Universi qui te expectant" (n.d.), Eberlin uses three trombones to double the voices.

Anton Adlgasser, a student of Eberlin's, used three trombones to double the chorus in two of his motets: "Ave Maria" and "Dicte in gentibus." These trombone parts are easier than those in Eberlin's motets.

Alexander Weinmann has edited a "concerto" for alto trombone in D major taken from a divertimento by Leopold Mozart.[43] The concerto movements are the eighth, sixth, and seventh movements of the divertimento. This order is needed in order to provide an effective first movement and keep the outer movements in the same key. As a result, the concerto ends with a minuet in which the trombone participates only in the trio. For this reason, the piece does not work very well as a concerto out of its original context.

---

[42] Paul Steinmetz, "German Church Music," *The New Oxford History of Music* vol. 5 *Opera and Church Music*, ed. Anthony Lewis and Nigel Fortune (London: Oxford University Press, 1975), 589.

[43] Leopold Mozart, "Concerto für Trombone oder Viola und Orchester." Klavierauszug, ed. Alexander Weinmann (Zurich: Eulenberg, 1977).

The tessitura is extremely high, creating endurance problems more formidable than those in Wagenseil's or Albrechtberger's concertos.

The soloist Mozart intended was probably Thomas Gschlatt of Stockerau, whom he esteemed greatly.[44]

Wolfgang Amadeus Mozart

Mozart began his career in Salzburg and finished it in Vienna. All but the last six of the 22 works with trombone parts appeared during his Salzburg years:

1. K.V. 35. *Die Schuldigkeit des ersten Gebots* (1767).
2. K.V. 41a. At least one of six divertimentos, now lost (1767 or 1768).
3. K.V. 47a (139). *Missa solemnis: "Waisenhauskirche Mass"* (1768).
4. K.V. 61a (65). *Missa brevis* (1769).
5. K.V. 74e (109). *Litaniae de B.M.V. (Lauretanae)* (1771).
6. K.V. 125. *Litaniae de venerabili altaris sacramento* (1772).
7. K.V. 186d (195). *Litaniae Lauretanae* (1774).
8. K.V. 186g (193). *Dixit und Magnificat* (1774).
9. K.V. 243. *Litaniae de venerabili altaris sacramento* (1776).
10. K.V. 257. *"Credo" Mass* (1776).
11. K.V. 317. *"Coronation" Mass* (1779).
12. K.V. 321. *Vesperae de Dominica* 1779.
13. K.V. 336a (345). Incidental music to *Thämos, König von Aegypten* (1779).
14. K.V. 337. *Missa solemnis* (1780).
15. K.V. 339. *Vesperae solennes de confessore* (1780).
16. K.V. 366. *Idomeneo, Re di Creta* (1780−81).
17. K.V. 417a (427). *Mass in c minor* (1782−83, not completed).
18. K.V. 469. *Davidde penitente* (1785, using music from K.V. 417a).
19. K.V. 527. *Don Giovanni* (1787).
20. K.V. 572. Orchestration of Handel's *Messiah* (1789).
21. K.V. 620. *Die Zauberflöte* (1791).
22. K.V. 626. *Requiem* (1791, completed by Franz Xaver Süßmayr).

---

[44] T. Donley Thomas, "Michael Haydn's 'Trombone' Symphony." *Brass Quarterly* 6 (1962), 8.

All of this music requires three trombones except for the first piece, which uses only alto trombone. In most of the religious music, Mozart used trombones only to double the voices. In the *Waisenhauskirsche Mass*, however, the "Agnus Dei" opens with an unaccompanied trombone trio. The trombones are also independent of the chorus in the "Kyrie" and "Crucifixus." (See Chapter 5 for a detailed description.)

Perhaps the most interesting of Mozart's Salzburg works, to the trombonist, is *Die Schuldigkeit des ersten Gebots*, which he wrote when the skeptical Archbishop locked him in a room by himself to see if he could really compose music without help from his father. This cantata uses solo alto trombone in two movements. In the first, an accompanied recitative, the trombone plays only two measures. The second, Christ's aria "Jener Donnerworte Kraft," may be suitable for recital, although it requires six string players as well as the soloists. Wigness describes this movement in detail.[45]

After Mozart moved to Vienna, his production of sacred music slowed to a trickle, but he continued to use three trombones in it. His *Mass in c minor* uses trombones not only as doubling instruments, but also in accompanimental figures in the "Sanctus."

The *Requiem* includes probably the best known of all orchestral trombone solos at the beginning of the "Tuba mirum." Since Mozart did not live to complete the *Requiem*, there has been some question over the years whether the trombone solo was composed by Mozart or Süßmayr, who finished what Mozart left undone. The *Neue Mozart Ausgabe* prints separately that portion of the *Requiem* actually composed by Mozart; the first 18 measures of the trombone solo are Mozart's and the less interesting portion that accompanies the tenor solo at "Mors stupebit" is Süßmayr's.

The three operas are at the same time Mozart's only operas with trombone parts and the only ones with supernatural elements. Trombones participate only in those portions of the opera that are supernatural in character.

In *Idomeneo*, Mozart calls for trombones in only one arioso. At the time when it appears that Idomeneo will have to make a human sacrifice to Neptune, the god speaks, accompanied only by two horns and three trombones. His message is one of reconciliation and peace, so the harmony is full and lushly beautiful. Trombones appear

---

[45] Wigness, 34.

twice in *Don Giovanni*, both times representing the statue of the slain Commendatore. The second and longest of these numbers accompanies a speech full of divine wrath and judgment. The trombones do not play full triads, which would be inappropriately beautiful, but instead, open intervals that reinforce the starkness of the words. (See Chapter 6 for a detailed description.)

Supernatural and religious elements, infrequent in *Idomeneo* and *Don Giovanni*, pervade *Die Zauberflöte*. As a consequence, the latter makes much more extensive use of trombones, which accompany genies, priests, various ceremonies, and the appearance of daylight at the end of the opera. *Die Zauberflöte* is Mozart's only opera with trombones in the overture.

Late eighteenth- and early nineteenth-century writers credited Mozart with the revival of the trombone. (See articles by Koch, Schubart, and Fröhlich in Chapter 2.) Although they thus fail to acknowledge the earlier contributions of Gluck, there can be no doubt that Mozart's music, especially *Don Giovanni*, *Die Zauberflöte*, and *Requiem* played a key role.

Johann Michael Haydn

Haydn used the trombone extensively in both choral and instrumental music. Anton Klafksy's catalog of his church music lists 17 works with trombone.[46] Lothar Perger's catalog of Haydn's instrumental music lists two works; an incomplete and untitled work the third movement of which is identified as "Larghetto à Trombone Conc[to]" (P. 34, ca. 1763) and a *Divertimento in D* (P. 87, 1764).[47] Both of these are described by Wigness.[48] The untitled work is the subject of an article by T. Donley Thomas, who writes that it seems to be a "symphonic movement among a group of identifiable symphonies from the years 1763–64."[49] Haydn also composed "Adagio

[46] Anton Maria Klafsky, "Thematischer Katalog der Kirchenmusik von Michael Haydn," *Denkmäler der Tonkunst in Oesterreich* vol. 62 (Vienna: Universal-Edition, 1925), v–xiii.

[47] Lothar Herbert Perger, "Thematisches Verzeichnis der Instrumentalwerke von Michael Haydn," *Denkmäler der Tonkunst in Osterreich* vol. 29 (Vienna: Artaria; Leipzig: Brietkopf & Härtel, 1907), xv–xxix.

[48] Wigness, 24–25.

[49] Thomas, 6.

e Allegro molto" for horn and alto trombone, which was edited by Kurt Janetzky and published by Billaudot in 1976, and designated a trombone as an alternative to the third horn in a *Symphony in C Major* (P. 10, 1773).

Thomas's description of the "Larghetto" hardly sounds like a symphonic movement in the modern sense. If it is, then Haydn appears to be among the first composers of a symphony that uses trombone. Another early composer who used trombones in a symphony is Joseph Krottendorfer, whose symphony (1768) is found in the same archive as Haydn's "Larghetto." Thomas writes,

> This piece is scored for two oboes, eight trumpets, two trombones and strings. Krottendorfer's writing is more akin [than Haydn's] to the Beethoven finale [of the fifth symphony] and the trombones are never handled in true concertato fashion.[50]

As early as Krottendorfer's symphony is, it appears that one by Franz Beck used trombone perhaps eight years earlier. See p.267.

Provincial centers

Charles Burney wrote:

> I had frequently been told, that the Bohemians were the most musical people of Germany, or, perhaps, of all Europe; and an eminent German composer, now in London, had declared to me, that if they enjoyed the same advantages as the Italians, they would excel them. . . .
>
> I crossed the whole kingdom of Bohemia from south to north; and being very assiduous in my inquiries, how common people learned music, I found out at length, that, not only in every large town, but in all villages, where there is a reading and writing school, children of both sexes are taught music.[51]

Burney mentioned the music of several small towns where, any place else in Europe, he could not have expected to find much musical proficiency. In Melk, he took note of the large Benedictine monastery.[52] If he had had time to stop there, he would have met some very prominent musicians, including organist and composer Franz Schneider.

---

[50] Ibid., 7.

[51] Charles Burney, *An Eighteenth-Century Musical Tour in Central Europe and the Netherlands; Being Dr. Charles Burney's Account of His Musical Experiences*, ed. Percy Scholes (London: Oxford University Press, 1959), 131–32.

[52] Ibid., 69.

Schneider was a skilled and widely respected composer working in one of the smaller musical centers of Austria and Bohemia whose music is entirely unknown today. He stands out among surely dozens of similar composers only because Robert Freeman has lately compiled a thematic catalog of his works.[53] The catalog includes 48 works, in nearly all categories of Schneider's output, that include parts for trombones, usually alto and tenor. Occasionally, manuscripts exist with added parts for bass trombone.

Surely the trombones doubled the voice parts. Whether they also took a more soloistic role is impossible to say without examining the music. One of Schneider's masses (no. 2 in Freeman's catalog) exists in three versions, which reflect the varying fortunes of church music under the reforms of Joseph II. The first, completed in 1782, calls for chorus and an orchestra without trombones. Shortly afterward, Joseph's reforms resulted in the closing of the abbey's theological seminary, cloister school, and the choirboys' institute. These losses stripped the abbey of its normal sources of performers and forced Schneider and his colleagues to retrench. The second version of the mass, therefore, replaces the orchestra with organ and augments the chorus with alto and tenor trombones.[54] Only in Austria or Bohemia would a composer add trombones in response to a cutback in available musical forces.

Until more thematic catalogs of composers like Schneider become available, or until a significant quantity of their music sees publication, it will be impossible to discern the importance, or even the availability of the trombone in the provincial musical centers.

We do know, however, that trombones were available in Prague; Mozart's *Don Giovanni* received its first performance there, with trombones in the orchestra. Prague actually seems to have been less well supplied with local musicians than many smaller towns. Burney says that music formed no part of the school curriculum, so musicians had to be brought in from elsewhere in the country.[55]

In the late seventeenth century, much trombone music was composed in the town of Olmütz (now Olomouc), the seat of a Prince-Bishop, as well as in the neighbouring town of Kremsier (now Kroměříž). The trombone continued to be important into the

---

[53] Robert Freeman, *Franz Schneider (1737–1812): A Thematic Catalogue of His Works* (New York: Pendragon, 1978).

[54] Ibid., xxvii.

[55] Burney, *Musical Tour*, 134.

eighteenth century; the musical inventory of Prince-Bishop Leopold Egk (1760) includes three anonymous trombone concertos (in D major, G major, and B^b major), now apparently lost.[56]

England

Throughout the middle ages and well into the seventeenth century, English musicians called waits played wind instruments, including trombones, in settings comparable to the German *Stadtpfeifer*. At that time, the trombone was known as the sackbut. Trombones, along with other wind instruments, enjoyed favor at the court up until the end of the seventeenth century. Towards the end of the reign of Charles II (1660–1685), the bassoon took over much of the trombone's earlier role.[57] From that time until the very end of the eighteenth century, the trombone makes only sporadic appearances in English music. That it was not well known as late as 1784 can be seen from a note that one listener wrote in his program for the Handel Festival, that trombones "are something like bassoons with an end like a large speaking trumpet."[58]

It fares somewhat better in reference works, although it is clear that none of the authors had much first-hand knowledge of it. The article entitled "Sacbut" in Ephraim Chambers's *Cyclopaedia: or an Universal Dictionary of Arts and Sciences* (1728) relies heavily on Brossard, who had little if any first-hand knowledge himself, and, apparently, Mersenne. James Grassineau's *A Musical Dictionary* (1740) copies Chambers's article, and William Tans'ur's *The Elements of Musick Displayed* (1772) relies on it. The *Encyclopaedia Britannica*, which has come a long way from its humble beginnings in depth and breadth of coverage, defined the trombone in a mere 52 uninformative words. The third edition, which represented the first

---

[56] Jiří Sehnal, "Das Musikinventar des Olmützer Bischofs Leopold Egk aus dem Jahre 1760 als Quelle vorklassischer Instrumentalmusik," *Archiv für Musikwissenschaft*, 29 (1972), 315; Robert Melvin Miller, *The Concerto and Related Works for Low Brass: A Catalogue of Compositions from c. 1700 to the Present* (Ph.D. dissertation: Washington University, 1974), xxi.

[57] Anthony Baines, "James Talbot's Manuscript (Christ Church Library Music MS 1187) I. Wind Instruments," *The Galpin Society Journal* 1 (March 1949), 19.

[58] Trevor Herbert, *The Trombone in Britain before 1800* (Ph.D. dissertation; Open University, 1984), 474.

great expansion of the encyclopedia, did not include a new article on the sacbut. Abraham Rees's *Cyclopaedia* broke new ground. Charles Burney wrote most of the musical articles. Although the article on trombone did not appear in print until 1819, Burney probably wrote it in about 1805.[59] Perhaps the most important work is John Marsh's *Hints to Young Composers of Instrumental Music*, with its up-to-date information on performance practice. See Chapter 2 for the complete texts.

Theater Music

By far the most important use of the trombone in English theater music occurred in 1738, when George Frederick Handel used trombones in two oratorios, *Saul* and *Israel in Egypt*. Anthony Baines has called the trombone parts in *Saul* the finest in the eighteenth century.[60] Except for one march in *Samson* (1741), Handel never called for trombones again, surely only for the lack of adequate players.

Burney relates that organizers of the Handel Festival of May and June 1784 had trouble finding either players or instruments:

> In order to render the band as powerful and complete as possible, it was determined to employ every species of instrument that was capable of producing grand effects in a great orchestra. Among these, the SACBUT, or DOUBLE TRUMPET, was sought; but so many years had elapsed since it had been used in this kingdom, that, neither the instrument, nor a performer upon it, could easily be found. It was, however, discovered, after much useless enquiry, not only here, but by letter, on the continent, that in his Majesty's military band there were six musicians who played the three several species of sacbut, tenor, base, and double base.* The names of these performers will be found in the general list of the band.

---

*The most common sacbut, which the Italians call *trombone*, and the Germans *Posaune*, is an octave below the common trumpet; its length eight feet, when folded, and sixteen, strait. There is a manual,

---

[59] Percy Scholes, *The Great Dr. Burney*, 2 vols. (London: Oxford University Press, 1948), vol. 2, 186.

[60] Anthony Baines, "Trombone," *Grove's Dictionary of Music and Musicians*, 5th ed., ed. Eric Blom, 9 vols. (London: Macmillan, 1954), vol. 8, 557.

Plate 14. Plan of the Orchestra from *Account of the Musical Performances...in Commemoration of Handel.*

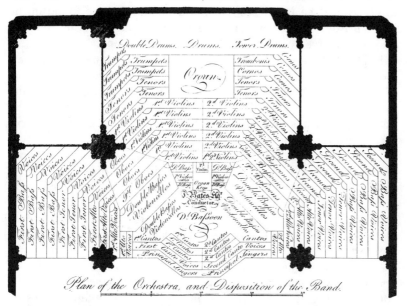

by which a note can be acquired a fourth lower than the usual lowest sound on the trumpet, and all the tones and semitones of the common scale. [By manual, Burney means the slide, not a crook.][61]

Although Burney's comments have been quoted extensively, the difficulties have been more noticed than the fact that the committee eventually found six players on English soil to play three parts. Burney gives their names as Karst, Kneller, Moeller, Neibour, Pick, and Zink. With the exception of Pick, these men were all Germans. Burney adds, "These performers played on other instruments when the sacbuts were not wanted."[62] If, as seems likely, they were trained in the *Stadtpfeifer* tradition, they played a variety of wind instruments.

Burney's comments are not entirely reliable. Other reviews and descriptions of this festival name only three trombonists: Zink,

[61] Charles Burney, *An Account of the Musical Performances ... in Commemoration of Handel* (London: T. Payne and G. Robinson, 1785), 7.
[62] Ibid., 19.

Miller, and Niebuher (or Nerbuher). Burney may have spelled their names better, but no one else seems to have mentioned the other three. And if he is correct that the trombonists were found in the king's private band, then that band was unlike any other in England; no other source corroborates Burney on this point.[63]

England's king at the time was George III, whose grandfather, George I, became the first of the Hanoverian kings of England in 1714. Although the trombone became obsolete and rare in England by about 1685, it was still widely used in Germany when George I became English king. His antipathy towards the English people extended even to his refusal to learn the English language.

His court musicians were German, and although none of the cities of Hanover seem to have ranked among the most important centers of German trombone playing, his musicians probably included trombonists. In all likelihood, trombonists remained in the royal household throughout the rest of the century, but had little influence elsewhere in England. Francis Galpin claimed as much, but Trevor Herbert found no documentary evidence.[64] If Handel had access to the king's trombonists for his oratorios, it remains a mystery why he could use them in 1738 and not before, or for all practical purposes, since. Possibly, he used itinerant players from Germany or Austria who, for whatever reason, did not remain in London very long.

That trombones remained rare even after Handel introduced them is clear from an announcement for a concert to benefit trumpeter Valentine Snow in 1741, which included a performance of "the Dead March in Saul to be performed with Sackbuts."[65] If performance of this march normally included trombones, there would seem little point in mentioning them in an advertisement.

After the 1784 Handel Festival, the use of trombones, and mention of them in reviews and advertisements, became more frequent. A festival in Liverpool in September 1784 featured a concert of music from the Handel Festival by the same performers, including the trombonists, who had played in London. A military concert in

---

[63] Herbert, 303, 305, 473.

[64] Francis William Galpin, "The Sackbut, Its Evolution and History," *Proceedings of the Royal Musical Association* 33 (1906—07), 20; Herbert, 467.

[65] Herbert, 291.

Edinburgh in 1786 included trombones. Samuel Arnold used four trombones in two of his oratorios, which he compiled from Handel's music: *Redemption* (1787) and *The Triumph of Truth* (1789). John Marsh wrote that "composers seldom insert parts for them in their scores, but leave them to be added afterwards," a practice that makes it impossible to compile an accurate list of pieces with trombone parts. See Chapter 2 for the full text.

In 1798, Michael Kelly used a trombone in his opera *Blue Beard*, or perhaps more accurately, Ferdinando Mazzanti did. By the late eighteenth century, English theater music had reached a low point. Kelly, resident composer at the Drury Lane Theatre, had a nice sense of melody, but virtually no knowledge of harmony or notation or orchestration. He merely hummed his tunes and Mazzanti, a very minor Italian composer, did the rest.[66]

Roger Fiske reports that long-held single notes in the trombone (or trombones?) were intended to have a spine-chilling effect.[67] It is not clear from his description just how many trombones *Blue Beard* calls for. One trombone joins the oboes at the end of the final lamentation in Kelly's incidental music to *Pizzaro*, a play by Richard Brinsley Sheridan (1799).[68]

It is hard to believe that such a team of semicompetent musicians as Kelly and Mazzanti deserves credit as the first resident composers to use trombones in an opera, but it may be impossible to prove otherwise. Covent Garden burned to the ground in 1808 and Drury Lane burned the following year. The fires destroyed not only the theatres, but all scores, manuscripts, and personnel records. Unlike French publishers, English publishers did not bring out full scores of operas. Victorian librarians threw out whatever scores survived the fires.[69]

If we do not know what music required trombones in England, we at least know who some of the trombonists were and where they played. Lyndesay G. Langwill has written of a 1794 musical directory compiled by J. Doane of London, which includes the names of six trombonists:

---

[66] Roger Fiske, *English Theatre Music in the Eighteenth Century* (London: Oxford University Press, 1973), 572.
[67] Ibid., 283.
[68] Ibid., 575.
[69] Ibid., 581–82.

Dressler, John: double-bass and trombone, Drury Lane Theatre, the Abbey, & c.
Franks: trombone at the Abbey and Ranelagh.
Mariotti: trombone at the Oxford Meeting, 1793.
Schubert, Geo. Fredk.: trombone and bassoon, Drury Lane Oratorios and at the Abbey.
Zinck: trombone in the Queen's Band, and at the Abbey.
Zwingman, John: violin and trombone, of the Guards Second Regiment.[70]

Of these, Mariotti seems the most prominent. He is also noteworthy for his performances in France. Zinck is probably the same man, otherwise spelled "Zink," who performed at the Handel Festival. An additional name is mentioned in the program of a music festival held in Liverpool in 1805, which lists trombonists Mariotti, Zwingman, and Flack.[71]

None of these men were virtuosos. Evidence comes in the form of manuscript notes on the ranges of various instruments by Samuel Wesley, who gives G to c' for the bass trombone, c to g' for the tenor, and g to c'' for the alto. These ranges match or exceed the timidity of Vandenbroek's (see p. 76). Wesley also noted "sackbut or double trumpet, the scale of which is wanting."[72] Apparently, he was unaware that the sackbut and trombone are the same instrument.

Even before the decline of English theater music that enabled a man like Kelly to become resident composer at a major theater, it appears that the bulk of operas performed in England were imported. By 1790, most operas composed for Paris, and probably many composed elsewhere, included trombone parts. English productions of these operas must be responsible for the reintroduction of the trombone to the English theater.

Whatever was the first operatic production in London with trombones, it could not have been earlier than 1784, when, as Burney reported, organizers of the Handel Festival had so much trouble finding either instruments or players. It probably predated 1791, when Haydn composed his opera *L'anima del filosfo* for performance

---

[70] Lyndesay G. Langwill, "Two Rare Eighteenth-Century London Directories," *Music & Letters* 30 (1949), 41.
[71] Herbert, 315.
[72] Ibid., 717.

at the Haymarket Theatre. No performance of this opera took place until 1951, but Haydn would not have written trombone parts if trombonists were not readily available. He did not call for trombones in any of his other operas.

Near the end of 1791, Ignace Pleyel went to London as Haydn's rival. Part of his contract was to provide new symphonies. Fétis says that he wrote three and neglected to keep copies for himself; when the Professional Concerts went out of business, their library was dispersed, and Pleyel's symphonies were lost.[73] But not lost forever, as Fétis lamented. Rita Benton found autograph manuscripts of three symphonies, Ben 150A, 152, and 155, at both the British Library and the Bibliothèque nationale in Paris.[74] When she lent me the microfilms, she said she had dated them incorrectly in her catalog, for if these are the ones Fétis mentioned, they cannot have been written later than 1791.

These symphonies all require one trombone, used in the French style, which will be explained in the next chapter. For a detailed discussion of these symphonies, see Chapter 7. Whether these symphonies were ever performed in London or not, Pleyel's *Sinfonia concertante in F Major* (Ben 113), which includes a trombone in the orchestra, received excellent reviews following its London premiere in 1792.[75]

Whatever work was responsible for the introduction of the trombone to London, it must have opened the floodgates. By 1805, Burney was complaining that they were "so frequently used at the opera, oratorios, and in symphonies, that they are become a nuisance." (See Chapter 2 for the full text.)

Military Music

The trombone's debut in military bands remains as mysterious as its first use on stage. We know from Burney's account of the Handel

---

[73] François Fétis, "Pleyel, Ignace," *Biographie universelle des musiciens et bibliographie général de la musique*, 2d ed. 8 vols. (Paris: Firmin-Didot Frères, 1866–70; facs. ed., Brussels: Editions Culture et Civilization, 1972), vol 7, 75.

[74] Rita Benton, *Ignace Pleyel: A Thematic Catalogue of His Compositions* (New York: Pendragon, 1977), 64–66.

[75] Ibid., 19.

Festival that the king's band included trombones. Although much
has been written about British military music, most reports lack
dates and solid documentation. W. T. Parke recalled trombones in
the Coldstream Guards band as early as 1783, but official records do
not mention them.[76]

The Royal Artillery Band had eight musicians up until 1792, when
a ninth was added.[77] These were probably the pairs of oboes,
clarinets, horns, and bassoons that had formed the standard military
bands all over Europe. Henry George Farmer found nothing about
the exact composition of the band before 1810, but it appears that
there was no trombone as late as 1801.[78]

Harold C. Hind reports a work by Henry Pick (1805) for two
flutes, four clarinets, two horns, two bassoons, serpent *or* trombone,
bugle, trumpet, and drum.[79] (Could this be the same Pick mentioned
by Burney?) The fact that the trombone was merely an alternative
to the serpent hints that it was not yet, even at this fairly late date, a
regular member of whatever unit Pick wrote it for, but he wrote it at
about the same time Burney wrote his complaint about trombones
overrunning operas and symphonies. Judging from events in France,
it seems unlikely that the trombone would be so extensively played
with a coarse and grating sound without first having picked up bad
habits from the military bands. Of course, if English musicians took
Pleyel's symphonies and French opera as their point of departure
for composing for and playing the trombone, they were emulating a
style already corrupted by the French national guard band.

The trombone seems not to have been used at all in English
church music until the 1790s. Three of the trombonists in Doane's
directory are identified with the Abbey, which is probably Westminster
Abbey. Even so, it does not mean that they performed for services
if oratorio performances were given there. The only other references
to any church found by Trevor Herbert are two inventories of the

---

[76] Harold C. Hind, "Military Band," *Grove's Dictionary*, 5th ed., vol. 5,
770.

[77] Henry George Farmer, *The Rise & Development of Military Music*
(London: Wm. Reeves, [1912]), 85.

[78] Henry George Farmer, *Memoirs of the Royal Artillery Band* (London:
Boosey & Co., 1904), 57.

[79] Harold C. Hind, "The British Wind Band: A Brief Survey of Its Rise
and Progress During Three Centuries," *Music Book* 7 (1952), 187.

Canterbury Cathedral (1752, 1761) that mention "two brass Sack-buts not used for a great number of years past,"[80] probably meaning not used since the 1680s.

GERMANY

In the eighteenth century, Germany was not a politically unified country. Certain German states were, culturally speaking, more important than others. For the history of the trombone, the Elector-ate of Saxony, which included Leipzig and Dresden, is by far the most important, although the trombone was used elsewhere. Zedler's encyclopedia, for example, says that trombones were used "by the *Stadtpfeifer* of Thuringia," which includes Weimar and Eisenach. (See Chapter 2.)

Trombones held a special place in the German musical imagination because of Luther's translation of the Bible. Most instances of "trumpet" in the King James Version translate two Hebrew words, *chatsotserah* and *shophar*, and one Greek word, *salpigx*.[81] Luther used *Dromet* for *chatsotserah* and *Posaune* for *shophar* and *salpigx*.

Luther himself probably did not have the modern trombone in mind in his use of *Posaune*. The word is derived from *busine*, or *buisine*, or *busûn*, a medieval military trumpet. That term, in turn, is related to the Latin *buccina*. By the eighteenth century, however, these words and the instruments they described were long obsolete. The author of the articles in Zedler's *Universal Lexikon* recognized that the ancient instruments were somehow different from the modern trombone. But although modern scholars consider the ancient instru-ments as varieties of trumpet or horn, he considered them somehow trombone-like.

Other authors were less careful in their scholarship. Eisel wrote that Moses invented the trombone, with no recognition that the biblical "trombone" differed from the modern one. Schubart, think-ing of the slide mechanism, asserted that parts of the Old Testament

---

[80] Herbert, 293.

[81] Robert Young, *Analytical Concordance to the Bible*, 22d American ed., rev. William B. Stevenson (Grand Rapids, MI: Eerdmans, [1951]), 1003–04.

were unthinkable apart from the trombone. And so although Luther did not mean to imply that the ancient Hebrews played slide trombones, only the most diligent eighteenth-century scholars inferred anything else.

In Luther's translation, Joshua 6:4 reads, "Am siebenden tage aber, las die Priester sieben Posaunen des Halliars nemen, für der Laden her, vnd gehet desselben siebenden tages, siebenden mal vmb die stad, vnd las die Priester die Posaunen blasen."[82] In the King James Version, substituting "trombone" for "trumpet," that verse reads, "and seven priests shall bear before the ark seven trombones of rams' horns; and the seventh day ye shall compass the city seven times, and the priests shall blow with the trombones." As a result, of course, the walls of Jericho collapsed and the children of Israel easily conquered the city.

Luther rendered St. Paul's description of the last days: "Sjhe, Jch sage euch ein Geheimnis. Wir werden nicht alle entschlaffen, Wir werden aber alle verwandelt werden, vnd dasselb plötzlich in einem Augenblick zur zeit der letzten Posaunen. Den es wird die Posaune schallen, vnd die Todten werden aufferstehen vnuerweslich, Vnd wir werden verwandelt werden." (I Corinthians 15:52)[83] or, "Behold, I show you a mystery; we shall not all sleep, but we shall all be changed, in a moment, in the twinkling of an eye, at the last trombone; for the trombone shall sound and the dead shall be raised incorruptible, and we shall be changed." To the German mind, therefore, the trombone was like the voice of God himself.

More German authors wrote about the trombone than those of any other nationality. Nearly half, 12 of 26, of the treatises and other works mentioned in Chapter 2 are by Germans. Also, the great majority of the trombone makers mentioned earlier were German. Given the symbolic importance of the trombone in the German language and the worldwide dominance of German trombone makers, it is ironic that the instrument nearly passed out of use in Germany, yet writers from Mattheson (1713) to Koch (1802) mentioned its rarity.

---

[82] Martin Luther, *Die gantze Heilige Schrifft Deudsch*, ed. *Friedrich Kur* (Munich: Rogner & Bernhard, 1972), 412.

[83] Ibid., 2324.

Town Bands

Well into the eighteenth century, the trombone was associated not only with church music, but with royal spendor and processions. Stringed instruments were associated with dancing. Therefore, wind music and musicians had more prestige than string music and musicians.[84]

In the early eighteenth century, German towns, continuing a centuries-old tradition, hired bands to perform for various civic and ceremonial occasions, including worship in the town's leading churches. Zedler lays great stress on the New Year celebration, which, he implies, had its origin with the ancient Hebrews. (See his article "Posaunen-Fest" in Chapter 2.) There were two divisions of town musicians. The *Stadtpfeifer*, the more prestigious of the two, specialized in wind instruments, although they played stringed instruments whenever the occasion demanded. The *Kunstgeiger*, string players, played wind instruments publicly only when substituting for *Stadtpfeifer*.[85]

It was the ambition of every *Kunstgeiger* to gain promotion to the rank of *Stadtpfeifer*. Indeed, of 25 Leipzig *Stadtpfeifer* listed by Arnold Schering, 15 had previously been *Kunstgeiger*.[86] The official musicians attempted to hold a monopoly of music making, but did not succeed. Early on, they faced competition from unlicensed, untrained string players, whom they dismissed as *Bierfiedler*. These musicians played at parties and weddings for less money than the *Stadtpfeifer* would have received, an economic threat that was a source of constant litigation.[87] Eventually, the numbers of unlicensed musicians overwhelmed the *Stadtpfeifer*.

The eighteenth century brought other powerful rivals: traveling operatic troups and concert organizations like the Collegium Musicum and *Dreischwanenkonzerte*, which got around the *Stadtpfeifer's* monopoly by holding concerts outside the city limits.[88]

The *Stadtpfeifer* played all instruments; they did not specialize. A

---

[84] James Albert Wattenbarger, *The Turmmusik of Johann Pezel* (Ph.D. dissertation: Northwestern University, 1957), 56, n.2.

[85] Ibid., 56.

[86] Arnold Schering, "Die Leipziger Ratsmusik von 1650 bis 1775," *Archiv für Musikwissenschaft* 3 (1921), 53.

[87] Wattenbarger, 41.

[88] Ibid., 69.

footnote in the German edition of Burney's travel diary (1772) complained:

> The variety of instruments with which an apprentice *Kunstpfeifer* is plagued keeps many a musical genius from achieving real excellence on *one*. When we know that in many parts of Germany the town musicians have the exclusive right of all public music-making, we have found one of the factors which prevent music in Germany, in spite of German abilities, from being everywhere as good as it might be.[89]

For example, when a position as *Stadtpfeifer* opened in Leipzig in 1769, two *Kunstgeiger* auditioned before Johann Friedrich Doles, the cantor at Thomaskirche. They were required to play a horn, oboe, or flute concerto, the violin part of a trio, a concerted chorale on the slide trumpet and bass viol, and a simple chorale on soprano, alto, tenor, and bass trombones.[90] As late as 1850, an advertisement for a bassist requested an applicant "who also plays trombone or tuba, and perhaps cello."[91]

While none of the *Stadtpfeifer* limited themselves to the trombone, no one else seems to have played it at all. It was wholly absent from most of the new concert orchestras,[92] even where it is known to have been available, as in Mannheim.[93] Therefore, when the *Stadtpfeifer* movement declined, the trombone nearly disappeared from Germany.

At least two German orchestras are known to have included trombones. Both Otthmar Schreiber and Adam Carse list orchestras according to instrumentation, relying on contemporary almanacs, journals, and diaries. Carse shows three trombones in the *Königliche Kapelle* in Berlin in 1787.[94] Schreiber gives instrumentation for this orchestra for 1782, 1792, and 1811, mentioning trombones only 1811.[95] He also shows three trombones in the *Kurfürstliche Hofkapelle* of Mainz in 1782, but not 1790.[96] He fails to list trombones among the

---

[89] Burney, *Musical Tour*, 184, n.3.

[90] Schering, 45.

[91] Ottmar Schreiber, *Orchester und Orchesterpraxis in Deutschland zwischen 1780 und 1850* (Berlin: Junker und Dünnhaupt, 1938), 26–27.

[92] Schering, 51.

[93] Louis Adolph Coerne, *The Evolution of Modern Orchestration* (New York: Macmillan, 1908), 45.

[94] Adam Carse, *The Orchestra in the XVIIIth Century* (Cambridge: Heffer, 1940), 19.

[95] Schreiber, 101.

[96] Ibid., 107.

personnel of the Paris Opéra until 1810, by which time they had been present for more than 20 years, so the absence of trombones from his list (or Carse's) does not necessarily mean that none were used. Nonetheless, the trombone was clearly not a normal member of German orchestras.

The Decline of the Trombone

Schubart, writing in about 1784, lamented the wretched state to which the trombone had fallen, but commented that there were still excellent trombonists in Bohemia and Saxony. (See Chapter 2 for the full text.) At about the same time, Christoph Friedrich Nicolai determined that trombones were hardly ever used any more in northern Germany, but still took part in church music in Bavaria and Austria.[97] From this disagreement, it appears that trombonists, and especially good ones, were few and far between, and that it would have entailed more diligent searching than either Schubart or Nicolai undertook in order to find them. Since both noted trombonists in districts where the other believed the instrument had disappeared, it may be that the situation was less bleak than they believed.

In Berlin, six trombones took part in a performance of Handel's *Messiah* in 1786, and Mozart's *Requiem* was given there with all three trombone parts covered in 1800.[98] But another performance of the *Requiem* in Berlin near the turn of the century had to be given without trombones, with a horn taking the trombone solo in the "Tuba mirum"; at about the same time, Mozart's *Zauberflöte* was performed in Berlin without trombones.[99]

But if the *Stadtpfeifer* movement was in decline, it still fought for its life. Town musicians, after generations of attempting to monopolize all public music performance by playing all of the instruments, began to specialize in wind instruments, especially the trombone.[100] Therefore, they became, probably for the first time in generations, a dependable source of good trombonists.

---

[97] Cited ibid., 139.
[98] Ibid., 112.
[99] Ibid., 139−40.
[100] Ibid., 28.

In Leipzig, trombones were first used in Mozart's *Requiem* in 1805. The *Allgemeine musikalische Zeitung* commented:

Man hatte früher die Instrumente nicht zu besetzen wagen können, weil sie von Mozart sehr schwer (zuweilen über die Gebühr) geschreiben worden sind, wir aber keine Posaunisten besaßen, die das alles sicher und gut hätten ausführen können. Jetzt aber hat sich unter den jungen Männern, die nach der verbesserten Einrichtung mit den Stadtmusikern hier Instrumentalmusik studieren, ein Chor Posaunen gebildet, daß schon jetzt verzüglich genannt werden darf, und sich bei dieser, sowie bey anderen Productionen des Konzerts und des Theaters, sehr vorteilhaft zeigte.[101]

Earlier, one could not risk using these instruments, because Mozart wrote very difficult parts (sometimes unreasonably so), and we had no trombonists who could perform them reliably. But now a trombone section that can already be called excellent has been trained among the young men, who study instrumental music according to the improved arrangement of the town musicians, and showed themselves to advantage in this and other concert and theatrical productions.

At about the same time, some conductors began to add trombone parts to classical works, such as Mozart's symphonies. Schreiber mentions one Friedrich Schneider, who also composed 12 "Tower Sonatas" for two trumpets and three trombones in 1803 and 1804.[102] The popularity of French opera may be one reason. Beethoven's use of trombones in his Fifth Symphony must also have been influential.

Music with Trombone Parts

After Gottfried Reiche's *24 neue Quatricinia* (1697) for cornett and three trombones, I have no reference to any works by or for the *Stadtpfeifer*. Possibly none was written or published; possibly scholars have not been interested enough in the period of the *Stadtpfeifer's* decline to bring any later music to light. In any event, very little German music of any kind for trombones is available for examination.

---

[101] Quoted ibid., 29.
[102] Ibid. 145—6.

If the Moravian trombone choirs in America reflect German practice at all, then the trombonists' repertoire must have consisted largely of chorales.

Johann Sebastian Bach

Bach used trombones in 15 of his cantatas. The letters following the titles in the list below show which trombones Bach included.

BWV 2   Ach Gott vom Himmel sieh' darein (satb)
BWV 3   Ach Gott, wie manches Herzeleid (b)
BWV 4   Christ lag in Todesbanden (atb)
BWV 21   Ich hatte viel Bekümernis (satb)
BWV 23   Du wahrer Gott und Davids Sohn (atb)
BWV 25   Es ist nichts Gesundes an meinem Leib (atb)
BWV 28   Gottlob! Nun geht das Jahr zu Ende (atb)
BWV 38   Aus tiefer Not schrei' ich zu dir (satb)
BWV 64   Sehet, welch eine Liebe hat uns der Vater erzeigt (atb)
BWV 68   Also hat Gott die Welt geliebt (atb)
BWV 96   Herr Christ, der ein'ge Gottes-Sohn (a)
BWV 101 Nimm von uns, Herr, du treuer Gott (atb)
BWV 118 O Jesu Christ, mein's Lebens Licht (atb)
BWV 121 Christum wir sollen loben schon (atb)
BWV 135 Ach Herr, mich armen Sünder (b)

All but one (BWV 21) belong to Bach's tenure as cantor of Leipzig's Thomaskirche. The exception was composed for Halle, which, like Leipzig, had an active local *Stadtpfeifer* guild. Apparently *Stadtpfeifer* intruments were not available in other places where Bach worked. Bach made less use of the trombone than almost any other instrument he wrote for. In 13 of the 15 cantatas, the trombones merely double the chorus. In the case of BWV 4, they seem to have been added years after the first performance in order to help out an inadequate chorus.[103] Even when Bach conceived trombone parts from the very beginning, he seems to have had vocal deficiencies in mind rather than any coloristic or textual associations.[104]

---

[103] Johann Sebastian Bach, *Cantata No. 4, "Christ lag in Todesbanden"* ed. Gerhard Herz (New York: Norton, 1967), 74.
[104] Charles Sanford Terry, *Bach's Orchestra* (London: Oxford University Press, 1932), 41.

The trombone seems not to have had the same association with
the voice of God for Bach as it did for so many Germans. Otherwise,
he would have used solo trombone rather than trumpet in BWV 70
("Wachet, betet, seid bereit allezeit") when the bass sings "the
trombone shall sound" to announce the second coming of Christ.

Two of Bach's cantatas use trombones independent of the voices.
In BWV 25, three trombones supply the harmonization to a chorale
played on cornett. This chorale, part of the orchestral accompaniment,
is not sung. In BWV 118, a wind band including three trombones
supplies the entire accompaniment. (See Chapter 5 for a more
detailed description of BWV 118.) Parts of the other cantatas, when
the trombones double some of Bach's more intricate vocal parts, are
actually more difficult to play than these cantatas where they are
more prominent.

Considering that Bach pushed other instruments to their technical
limits, his use of trombones seems timid indeed. Part of the explanation probably lies in the sorry state of both the performers and
instruments available to him. In 1704, his predecessor, Johann
Kuhnau, complained that the church's trombones were so battered
as to be useless.[105] Neither he nor Bach achieved much success in
getting the city council to upgrade the instrument collection, so even
though the instrument inventory of 1723 is lost, it appears likely that
Bach inherited those same woefully inadequate instruments.

As for performers, the Leipzig *Stadtpfeifer* included Gottfried
Reiche, who must have been a very good trumpet player. He and
his colleagues also played the horn and trombone, but perhaps only
barely adequately. In 1730, Bach wrote to the city council about the
professional musicians: "Discretion forbids me to offer an opinion
on their competence and musicianship. I merely observe that some
of them are *emeriti*, and others not in such good *exercitium* as
formerly.[106]

Yet Leipzig's trombones and trombonists were not alone in being
inadequate. Hardly any of Bach's performers were consistently reliable, and many instruments were in deplorable condition, but he
demanded more from all of the others than from the trombones.
Charles Sanford Terry speculates that, having spent most of his

---

[105] Ibid., 18.
[106] Quoted ibid.

career in places where the trombone was not available to him, Bach had no interest either in the traditional, old-fashioned role of the trombone or in developing a new one.[107]

One new feature of Bach's writing for trombone deserves mention, however, for in three cantatas (2, 21, and 38) he calls for soprano trombone. Before the eighteenth century, the alto trombone had been the highest member of the family. According to Anthony Baines, the earliest extant specimen of a soprano trombone was made in 1733 in Leipzig by J. H. Eichentopf.[108] There must have been earlier ones, because Bach asked for one in Cantata BWV 21, which he wrote in 1714. Indeed, Langwill's index mentions a descant trombone made in Nürnberg by Johann Karl Kodisch in 1697.[109] There is not necessarily a conflict between Langwill and Baines on this point; before the earliest soprano trombones were made, the highest alto trombones (a fifth rather than the more usual fourth higher than the tenor) were called descant trombones. If soprano trombones existed in 1697, they cannot have been widespread.

Other music

Helmut Banning's thematic catalog of the works of Johann Friedrich Doles[110] lists 31 pieces with trombone parts. Doles, a student of J. S. Bach and Cantor at Leipzig's Thomaskirche from 1755 to 1789, was one of the most important late eighteenth-century composers of Lutheran church music, according to *The New Grove*.[111] Even so, he is apparently not important enough for anyone to have published his music either in modern edition or facsimile. According to Banning's catalog, Doles used four trombones, presumably soprano, alto, tenor, and bass, in most of his works with trombones. Surely they doubled the choral parts. Whether they were independent at any time is impossible to guess.

---

[107] Ibid., 41.

[108] Anthony Bains, *Brass Instruments*, 179.

[109] Langwill, *Index*, 93.

[110] Helmut Banning, *Johann Friedrich Doles, Leben und Werke* (Leipzig: Kistner & Siegel, 1939).

[111] Bradford Robinson, "Doles, Johann Friedrich," *The New Grove* vol. 5, 526.

Johann Adolph Hasse used trombones in at least one mass (in D) for the royal chapel in Dresden. Alto and tenor trombones are solo instruments in the "Agnus Dei." They always play antiphonally with the other instruments and choir, accompanied only by continuo. Both parts contain many trills, and the trombones play the only sixteenth notes in the entire section. (The trombones take no part in the "Dona nobis pacem".) This mass, which has not been published, shows that Hasse knew how to write well for trombones. Perhaps other of his masses likewise include them either as solo or doubling instruments.

Operatic composition was infrequent in most of Germany for most of the eighteenth century. Nevertheless, at least one opera includes trombone parts. Viennese composer Carl Ditters von Dittersdorf produced his *Ugolino* in Dresden in 1796. The three trombones in a trio in the second act mark his only operatic use of the trombone.[112]

The unknown writer Haider, whose description of the trombone caused Schubart to desist from writing his own, also lived in Dresden. (See under Schubart in Chapter 2.) Surely the two pieces mentioned here merely scratch the surface of music with trombone parts that was composed and performed there. Considering the conditions that Bach faced in Leipzig, Dresden seems a more likely place to find the excellent trombonists that Schubart claimed for Saxony. Herrnhut, worldwide headquarters of the Moravians, boasted numerous amateur trombonists, who played much the same music as their brethren in America.

I have found no references to purely orchestral music with trombone parts. Regarding military music, I find only the barest hints. Henry Farmer wrote that Prussian and Austrian bands around 1800 included trombones.[113] Unfortunately, he neglected to mention specific bands or provide any other detail or documentation. If there were indeed trombones in Prussian bands, they joined some time after the death of Frederick the Great in 1786. For a music lover and military commander, Frederick took remarkably little interest

---

[112] Lothar Riedinger, "Karl von Dittersdorf als Opernkomponist," *Studien zur Musikwissenschaft: Beihefte der Denkmäler der Tonkunst in Oesterreich* (Leipzig: Breitkopf & Härtel; Vienna: Artaria, 1914), vol. 2, 303.
[113] Farmer, *The Rise & Development of Military Music*, 84–85.

in military music. At his death, the bands were the same as those of his father's time.[114]

ITALY

The trombone figures prominently in Italian instrumental music of the early seventeenth century. After 1640, however, new works requiring trombone became infrequent. San Marco in Venice kept a trombonist (Lodovico Vazzio, hired in 1685) on its payroll until 1732.[115] In 1714, there were two trombonists. The maestro di capella, Antinio Biffi, wanted to expand the orchestra, but complaining that it was impossible to find more bassoonists, trombonists, and theorbo players, asked permission of the Procurators to substitute other instruments. When Vazzio died, his place was taken by a trumpeter, and the trombone disappeared from San Marco for most, if not all, of the rest of the century.[116] In all likelihood, smaller churches had long since abandoned the instrument by that time, although Filippo Bonanni included a description of it in his *Gabinetto armonico* of 1722. (See Chapter 2 for the full text.)

No Italian music of the eighteenth century that includes trombone has yet been identified. Adam Carse asserts that there are traces of the trombone in Italian church music, but gives no examples.[117] Through the early years of the eighteenth century, at least, trombones were "seldom" used in the theater, according to Eleanor Selfridge-Field, who mentions no occasions on which they were used.[118] Henri Lavoix asserts that they were used many times in Italy before Gluck introduced them to Paris in the 1760s (!), but, like Carse, gives no details.[119]

---

[114] Peter Panoff, *Militärmusik in Geschichte und Gegenwart* (Berlin: Karl Siegismund, 1938), 87.

[115] Eleanor Selfridge-Field, *Venetian Instrumental Music from Gabrieli to Vivaldi* (New York: Praeger, 1975), 21.

[116] Denis Arnold, "Orchestras in Eighteenth-Century Venice," *The Galpin Society Journal* 19 (April 1966), 5–6.

[117] Carse, 43.

[118] Selfridge-Field, 38.

[119] Henri Lavoix, *Histoire d'instrumentation depuis le seizième siècle jusqu'à nos jours* (Paris: Firmin-Didot, 1878), 312.

There are a few facts to indicate that Carse and Lavoix may be correct, although even taken together, they do not make very strong evidence. Eitner records that a "Miserere a 4v. (2T. 2B.) V. Vlc. e 2 Tromboni in concerto" by Franz Tuma was found in Bologna.[120] He also reports that it is actually for mixed chorus (SATB) and that only string parts were found. It is unlikely that a piece with concerted trombone parts would find its way to Italy if there were no trombonists there. But since the trombone parts are not with the rest of the music, and since the cover is inaccurate about the makeup of the chorus, this piece constitutes no proof of the trombone in Italy, only a vague hint.

At least one opera with trombone parts, Gluck's *Orfeo ed Euridice*, was produced in various Italian cities, beginning with the 1769 production in Parma. According to Alfred Loewenberg, it was given twice in Naples in 1774, once with additional music by J. C. Bach, but the first time "in its original form."[121] By this comment, Loewenberg means that no additional music by other composers was used for this production. It cannot be taken to mean that the production adhered to the original instrumentation. The composition of operatic orchestras has not received the attention it deserves, and so while the Italian productions of *Orfeo* may have given the Italians a chance to hear trombones in an operatic orchestra, a definitive answer cannot be given at this time.

Italian composers Piccinni, Sacchini, and Paisiello composed operas for presentation in Naples before they moved to Paris. In Paris, all of them used trombones. Piccinni's very first opera in French, *Roland*, shows great confidence in its use of the trombone, as if he were already familiar with its technical capabilities and dramatic possibilities. (See Chapter 6 for a detailed description.)

In about 1789, the name Mariotti begins to appear on personnel lists in Paris as a trombonist. The *Almanach général* of 1791 observed, "Trombone: M. Mariotti, étonnant pout sa précision sur cet instrument, dont le bel effect était inconnu en France." ([The trombonist

---

[120] Robert Eitner, *Biographisch-bibliographisches Quellen-Lexikon der Musiker und Musikgelehrten der christlichen Zeitrechnung bis zur Mitte des neunzenten Jahrhunderts* 11 vols. (Leipzig: Breitkopf & Härtel, 1898–1904; facs., Graz: Akademische Druck, 1959), vol. 9, 472.

[121] Alfred Loewenberg, *Annals of Opera, 1597–1940*, 3rd., revised and corrected (Totowa, NJ: Rowman and Littlefield, 1978), col. 261.

is] M. Mariotti, astonishing for his precision on this instrument, of which the pleasing effect was formerly unknown in France.)[122] And so not only was an Italian playing trombone in France, but he was enough better that the other trombonists in Paris to be singled out by name. His earliest positions were the Concert Spirituel and the orchestra of the Théâtre de Monsieur, a company founded by Giovanni Battista Viotti. David Charlton speculates that Mariotti moved to Paris at Viotti's invitation.[123] Of all the hints that the trombone was known and used in eighteenth-century Italy, the activity of Mariotti in Paris seems the strongest. Until more work is done to identify the personnel in Italian theaters, churches, and other musical organizations, it will be impossible to know Mariotti's whereabouts before he joined Viotti in Paris, but he must have played trombone somewhere in Italy.

Perhaps because of familiarity with Mariotti's work, Alexandre Choron, writing in 1813, declared that:

Le trombone est un Instrument qui a été inventé en Italie, il y a enviorn quarante ans, et qui s'est introduit en France il y a trene ans: son nom est l'augmentatif du mot *tromba* qui, en Italien, signifie trompette indique assez le genre auquel appartient cet Instruement.[124]	The trombone is an instrument that was invented in Italy about 40 years ago [1773!] and that was introduced to France about thirty years ago; its name, the augmentation of the word *tromba*, which means trumpet in Italian, sufficiently indicates the genre to which this instrument belongs.

Surely, Choron had never bothered to look even at the index of the *Encyclopédie*, which contains a reference to "Trompette des italiens appellée trombone." The index, published in 1780, refers to an article published in 1765.

---

[122] Quoted by David Charlton, *Orchestration and Orchestral Practice in Paris, 1789–1810*, (Ph.D. dissertation: King's College, University of Cambridge, 1973), 124.

[123] Ibid.

[124] Louis Joseph Francoeur, *Traité général des voix et des instruments d'orchestre*, new ed. by Alexandre Choron (Paris: Aux adresses ordinaires de musique, [1813]), 72.

164 David M. Guion

RUSSIA

The trombone's role in Russian music is very shadowy, but there is
no doubt that the instrument was available. Proof comes in the form
of an opera printed in St. Petersburg in 1791, *Nachal'noe upravlenie
Olega*, jointly composed by Giuseppe Sarti, Carlo Canobbio, and
Vasily Pashkeevich, on a libretto by the Empress Catherine the
Great. This, the first opera published in full score in Russia,[125]
contains parts for flute, piccolo, oboe, clarinet, piccolo clarinet,
bassoon, trumpet, horn, trombone, and serpent. The trombones
participate in only one movement, a 36-measure march for four
horns, two trombones, two serpents, and triangle. As in French
military music, the trombones play a simplification of the serpent
part.

Since *Nachal'noe upravlenie Olega* requires such a large orchestra,
presumably the numerous foreign operas given in St. Petersburg
could have been given with their original instrumentation. Several
composers who included trombone parts in operas they composed
for Paris subsequently spent some time in Russia and mounted
productions of their own works.

Boieldieu, for example, produced *Ma tante Aurore* in Paris in
1803 and in St. Petersburg in 1804.[126] He conducted the first performance of his *La jeune femme colère* in St. Petersburg in 1805.[127]
Both works include trombone parts according to scores published in
Paris.

Even as late as the middle of the nineteenth century, most orchestral musicians were foreigners attached to the court.[128] Therefore, it
seems unlikely that trombonists or trombone music could be found
outside the capital, with the possible exception of some operatic
performances in Moscow. Undoubtedly, if the court orchestra in St.
Petersburg was mostly foreign, Moscow's orchestra must have been
as well. If enough foreign trombonists moved to Russia, some may
have found their way to Moscow.

According to Peter Panoff, the trombone entered the Russian

[125] Lowenberg, col. 484.
[126] Ibid., col. 571.
[127] Ibid., col. 587.
[128] Gerald Abraham, "Union of Soviet Socialist Republics, §IX, 1, ii,"
The New Grove, vol. 19, 382.

military band in the second half of the eighteenth century, but he offers neither detail nor documentation.[129] A march by Canobbio for four trumpets, trombone, and triangle (1791) may have been intended for military use.[130]

SWEDEN

As in the case in Russia, very little, if any, research has yet been done to document the use of the trombone in eighteenth-century Sweden. I am indebeted to Bertil van Boer, who called my attention to the following music with trombone parts: *Cora och Alonzo* (1782), an opera by Johann Gottlieb Naumann, *Electra* (1787), an opera by Johann Christian Friedrich Haeffner, *Begravningskantat över Gustav III* (1792) by Jospeh Martin Kraus, Jakob Bernhard Struve's *Overture in c minor* (1805), and Johann Nikolas Eggert's Third Symphony (1807). Van Boer characterizes the trombone parts in Struve's overture as intricate.[131] See Chapter 7 for a detailed description of Eggert's symphony.

In addition, the thematic catalog in van Boer's edition of Swedish symphonies[132] shows trombone parts in overtures by Haeffner (in E^b major, before 1808) and Pehr Frigel (in f minor, 1804).

The identity of the musicians who played these parts remains a mystery. Van Boer reports that the standard lists of musicians do not identify trombonists.[133] By analogy with Paris, it seems possible that they were primarily performers on other instruments and played trombone only on exceptional occasions. Or perhaps they were members of the king's private household and lent to the public theaters and orchestras by special permission. In any case, the royal chapel included three trombonists in 1790.[134]

---

[129] Panoff, 94.

[130] Otto Kade, *Die Musikalien-Sammlung des Grossherzoglich Mecklinburg-Schweriner Fürstenhauses aus den letzten zwei Jahrhunderten* 2 vols. (Wismar: Hirnstoff'sche Hofbuchhandlung, 1893) vol. 1, 200–01.

[131] Bertil van Boer, personal correspondence February 24, 1983.

[132] *The Symphony, 1720–1840*, Barry S. Brook, ed. in chief, Series F, Vol. III, *The Symphony in Sweden* ed. Bertil van Boer, Jr., Pt. 2 (New York: Garland, 1983),

[133] van Boer, personal correspondence, December 9, 1983.

[134] Schreiber, 110.

Surely information exists in Stockholm that would settle the issue, and it appears that some lovely music awaits anyone who will look for it.

I have said nothing about Spanish, Belgian, Dutch, Danish, Swiss, or Polish musical centers. None has been mentioned in connection with the trombone in any book or article I have consulted, except for two brief references. In trying to account for Gossec's introduction of the trombone to France, Cucuel speculates that he may have heard them in the cathedral at Antwerp.[135] As mentioned earlier in this chapter, Langwill's *Index of Musical Wind Instrument Makers* lists a Swiss trombone maker and one in Breslau, then a Prussian city and now in Poland. The trombone can be placed in at least most of these countries before the eighteenth century. Only the archives and libraries can tell if it remained or reappeared during the eighteenth century.

---

[135] Georges Cucuel, *Etudes sur un orchestre au 18me siècle* (Paris: Fischbacher, 1913), 34.

CHAPTER 4

THE TROMBONE AND TROMBONE MUSIC IN FRANCE

The trombone appears to have been largely unknown in France during the early eighteenth century. Except for a brief article in Sébastien de Brossard's *Dictionnaire de musique* (1703), no French author mentioned it; no French composer called for it, and no French instrument maker built it. Adam Carse writes, "There were traces of trombones in Italian and French church music,"[1] but gives no clue of when or where. It is known that trombones were used at the court of Louis XIV.[2] (See plate 15.)

After Brossard, the next published reference to the trombone, in France, is in the *Encyclopédie, ou Dictionnaire raisonné des sciences, des arts et des métiers* (1751−72). Jean-Jacques Rousseau, who wrote the articles on music, was apparently not familiar with the trombone. The article entitled "Trombone" is lifted from Brossard, omitting the first paragraph. Another article, "Sacquebute," again merely describes the appearance and measurements. Except for a

---

[1] Adam Carse, *The Orchestra in the XVIIIth Century* (Cambridge: Heffer, 1940), 43.
[2] Margaret M. McGowan and Frank Dobbins, "Louis XIV," *The New Grove Dictionary of Music and Musicians*, 20 vols. ed., Stanley Sadie (London: Macmillan, 1980), vol. 11, 254.

comment that it served as a bass, like the serpent and bassoon, in combinations of wind instruments, it says nothing about the use of the trombone. (Both of these articles were published in 1765.)

At the time the *Encyclopédie* appeared, the trombone had hardly ever been used in France in living memory. The earliest clearly documented use in the eighteenth century came in 1760; the next was either 1771 or 1773, depending on the reliability of one document. After this time, two more treatises appeared that described the trombone in more detail, albeit briefly: Jean-Benjamin de la Borde's *Essai sur la musique ancienne et moderne* (1780) and Othon Vandenbroek's *Traité général de tous les instruments à vent à l'usage des compositeurs* (c. 1794). See Chapter 2 for the texts of all of these treatises.

PREREVOLUTIONARY MUSIC

The earliest record of the use of trombones in a French orchestra is a letter from the Comte de Clermont to the Comte de Billy dated February 11, 1749, in which he lists the trombone (as trombone, not

Plate 15. Coronation of Louis XIV: Les douze grands hautbois.

saquebute) among 28 instruments in his orchestra.[3] This letter was cited at least twice in the nineteenth century, according to Georges Cucuel, but Clermont's orchestra was not well documented and seems not to have influenced anyone else.

Another more important private orchestra, that of La Riche de Pouplinière, probably had trombones, although here again documentation is lacking. Unlike Clermont's orchestra, Pouplinière's had a great influence on French music, particularly in the introduction of wind instruments from Germany. The clarinet, for example, made its first French appearance there and rapidly became a regular member of French orchestras. Likewise, horns were first heard in Pouplinière's orchestra and were quickly adopted by others.

François-Joseph Gossec wrote that Pouplinière imported three trombonists from Germany,[4] but the trombone was not at all common in French orchestras until the mid-1770s. It did not become a regular and expected member of the orchestra until the 1790s. Furthermore, Pouplinière's surviving records do not mention the trombonists. For these reasons, Cucuel, among others, chose not to believe Gossec's testimony.[5] It cannot be lightly set aside, however. Gossec became a member of that orchestra in 1751 and served as its music director from 1756 until Pouplinière's death in 1762. And Gossec wrote the earliest French piece so far known that calls for trombones.

François-Joseph Gossec

In 1760, Gossec produced his *Messe des morts*. (The date often given, 1762, appears to be an error.)[6] Trombones appear in the *Tuba mirum* as part of an offstage band comprised of one clarinet, two trumpets or horns, and three trombones. On stage, a baritone soloist is accompanied by an orchestra of strings, horns, and oboes.

---

[3] Quoted in Georges Cucuel, *Etudes sur un orchestre au 18me siècle* (Paris: Fischbacher, 1913), 15.

[4] François-Joseph Gossec, "Notice sur l'introduction des cors, des clarinettes et des trombones dans les orchestres français, extraite des manuscrits autographes de Gossec" *Revue musicale* 5 (1829), 219.

[5] Cucuel, 15, 34.

[6] Louis Dufrane, *Gossec: sa vie, ses oeuvres* (Paris: Fischbacher, 1929), 39.

The onstage and offstage musicians play antiphonally. The band rarely plays more than four measures at a time, or at any time when the soloist is singing. Gossec's writing for trombones seems tentative. The range is very narrow, and most of the note values are moderate to long. Much of the time, the trombones are in unison. Otherwise, they play simple triads in open spacing.

The antiphonal structure of the movement guarantees that the color of the trombone will be noticeable. It also lends the movement a certain dignity and solemnity that is dramatically effective. Gossec was quite pleased with his work. Much later, he wrote:

En 1762 [sic], M. Gossec donna pour la première fois sa messe des Morts, où il fit connaître l'effet des trombones dans un orchestre de deux cents musiciens. Ces instrumens inconnus, et cette rèunion de deux cents artistes d'élite, étaient alors une double nouveauté pour Paris. Dans des deux strophes *Tuba mirum* et *Mors stupebit et naturae* de la prose des morts, on fut effrayé de l'effet terrible et sinistre de trois trombones réunis à quatre clarinettes, quatre trompettes, quatre cors et huit bassons cachés dans l'éloignement, et dans un endroit élevé de l'église, pour annoncer le jugement dernier, pendant que l'orchestre exprimait la frayeur par un frémissement sourd de tous les instrumens à cordes.[7]

In 1762 [sic], Mr. Gossec gave for the first time his *Messe des morts*, where he made known the effect of the trombones in an orchestra of two hundred musicians. These unknown instruments and this gathering of two hundred elite artists was thus a double novelty for Paris. In the two strophes *Tuba mirum* and *Mors stupebit et natura* of the *Dies irae*, people were frightened by the terrible effect of three trombones with four clarinets, four trumpets, four horns, and eight bassoons hidden in the distance and in an elevated place in the church to announce the last judgment, while the orchestra expressed fright by a muted tremolo of all the string instruments.

(The score, published by Henry, contains no trombone parts in *Mors stupebit*. Either the engraver left them out or Gossec's memory failed him.) The requiem had over a dozen performances in Paris before the Revolution.[8] Presumably, composers could have heard

---

[7] Gossec, 221.

[8] Robert James MacDonald, *François-Joseph Gossec and French Instrumental Music in the Second Half of the Eighteenth Century*, 3 vols. (Ph.D. dissertation: University of Michigan, 1968), vol. 1, 346.

trombones. But for more than ten years, it appears that no one else used them. The next use of the trombone is unclear. Gossec claimed the honor for himself:

En 1771, M. Gossec fit répéter son opéra de *Sabinus* en cinq actes, au théâtre de l'Académie royale de Musique. En 1773, cet ouvrage fut représenté sur le grand théâtre de la Cour, à Versailles, pour le mariage du comte d'Artois, et de suite sur le théâtre de l'Opéra à Paris: ce fut pour la première fois qu'on entendit à ce théâtre les trombones, et pour la second fois les clarinettes réunis aux cors et trompettes. Mais comme il n'existait alors à l'Opéra qu'une grande trompette de cavalerie, sonnée par un homme que n'était pas musicien, il fallut, pour l'exécution de *Sabinus*, faire fabriquer des trompettes dans différens tons, et, pour sonner, appeler deux musiciens allemands (les deux frères Braun). Les mêmes y embouchaient aussi les trombones, avec le transylvain Lowitz.[9]

In 1771, Mr. Gossec had his five-act opera *Sabinus* rehearsed at the theater of the Royal Academy of Music. In 1773, this work was given in the large theater at the court of Versailles for the marriage of the Comte d'Artois, and then at the Opéra in Paris. For the first time, trombones were heard in this theater, and for the second time, clarinets were heard there, along with horns and trumpets. But since the Opéra had only one large cavalry trumpet, and that played by a non-musician, it was necessary, in order to perform *Sabinus*, to have trumpets made in different keys and to hire two Germans (the Braun brothers) them. These men, along with the Transylvanian Lowitz, played the trombones.

But, as in the case of Gossec's comment that Pouplinière's orchestra employed trombonists, there is neither literary nor musical corroboration. The holograph score does not mention trombones.[10] Musicological literature contains numerous theories regarding the discrepancy between Gossec's score and his memory. Cucuel, citing Gossec's jealousy of Gluck, asserts that Gossec's claim was false; he claimed to have used trombones in *Sabinus* in order to attribute an innovation to himself that was actually Gluck's.[11]

Robert J. MacDonald speculates that trombones were used only in the overture, which is lost.[12] While there are several printed

---

[9] Gossec, 222–23.
[10] MacDonald, vol. 1, 348.
[11] Cucuel, 35.
[12] MacDonald, vol. 1, 348.

operas with trombones only in the overture, it is difficult to believe that trombones did not participate in the rest of the opera. Many operas require trombone parts that are not included in the score. (For a more detailed discussion of this point, see Chapter 6.) A more reasonable explanation for the discrepancy is either that Gossec added the trombones for the Paris performance, after he had already made his copy of the score,[13] or he left them out of the score to save space. John Marsh described just such a practice a few years later in England. See Chapter 2 for the full text.

Jean-Joseph Rodolphe

If Gossec's claim is false, the distinction of being the first composer of a French opera to use trombones belongs to Jean-Joseph Rodolphe, whose *Isaménor* was presented at Versailles in 1773. Rodolphe was a renowned horn player. As such, he was perhaps more likely to introduce a new wind instruments than a string or keyboard player, all else being equal. His use of trombones appears to be the only interesting feature of *Isaménor*, however. Lavoix called the trombone parts timid.[14] Neither *Isaménor* nor *Sabinus* was performed many times. Probably neither made much of an impression on other composers.

Christoph Willibald Gluck

Therefore, even though Gluck was not the first composer to use trombones for the French stage, it was his operas that served as an inspiration and model for other composers in France. While it is not clear when or where Gossec or Rodolphe first heard trombones, Gluck mastered their use in Vienna, where the eighteenth century's best trombonists worked. Lajarte shows one example of the impact Gluck had on French music; François-André Danican Philidor wrote a three-act opera *Ernelinde* in 1767. In 1777, after three of Gluck's

---

[13] Dufrane, 36.

[14] Henri Lavoix, *Histoire de l'instrumentation depuis le seizième siècle jusqu'à nos jours* (Paris: Firmin-Didot, 1878), 312.

masterpieces had been produced in Paris, Philidor mounted a five-act revision of *Ernelinde*; he added three trombones to the orchestra.[15]

Five of Gluck's Parisian operas call for trombones. The first, *Iphigénie en Aulide* (1774), presents problems. The earliest printed score (Le Marchand, 1774), does not contain trombone parts. Neither does the critical edition of Gluck's works published in 1873. (At this writing, *Iphigénie en Aulide* has not yet been issued in Bärenreiter's current critical edition.) Yet both Cucuel and Lajarte identify the trombonist (Braun) who was hired to play the trombone part.[16] It appears, therefore, that the orchestra included only one trombone instead of the more normal three.

Besides *Iphigénie en Aulide*, Gluck's French operas with trombones are *Orphée et Euridice* (1774). *Alceste*, (1776), *Iphigénie en Tauride* (1779), and *Echo et Narcisse* (1779). All of these use three trombones and are available in modern editions. The discussion that follows is necessarily based on these four works. (See Chapter 6 for a more detailed description of *Orphée*.)

Gluck nearly always uses trombones to signify the supernatural or funereal aspects of the drama. The opening of *Orphée* is the funeral of Euridice; trombones accompany the chorus. The first scene of Act II takes place at the gates of hell. Once again the trombones' color is an important dramatic element. No other scenes in the opera have supernatural character, thoughts of death, or trombones. Similarly, trombones participate in the supernatural scenes of the first and third acts of *Alceste*, but not in the more domestic and worldly second act. In *Iphigénie en Tauride*, trombones join the Eumenides in chasing Orestes. Their only other appearance is during a funeral ceremony Iphigenia conducts in honor of her family. Gluck uses trombones in *Echo et Narcisse* only for one scene in Hades and another to accompany a chorus of evil spirits.

Trombones in Gluck's orchestra function chiefly as doubling instruments. Gluck was the only composer of French operas who consistently used trombones to double the chorus in the manner of Austrian church music. When there is no chorus, trombones most often double other orchestra parts, although not necessarily strictly.

---

[15] Théodore de Lajarte, "Introduction du trombone dans l'orchestre de l'Opera," *La chronique musicale* 6 (Oct.–Dec. 1874), 77.

[16] Cucuel, 35; Lajarte, 76.

Rhythmically, Gluck's trombone parts are generally uncomplicated. The trombones usually have the longest sounding note in the texture. Frequently, they have no notes shorter than quarter notes. Pairs of eighth notes are not uncommon, but pairs of sixteenth notes occur in only one movement (*Alceste*, Act I, scene 3).

Gluck seldom if ever uses his entire orchestral forces all at once. But whenever the trombones play, all or nearly all of the other instruments called for in the movement play at the same time. Trombones are used in a light texture very rarely. Not surprisingly, therefore, the dynamic level is usually loud whenever the trombones play, but Gluck's dramatic instincts were too good for him to neglect the possibilities of trombones playing softly.

Except for the range, Gluck's trombone parts must have been easy to play. In the alto trombone parts, c'', or even d'', is not uncommon. Tenor trombone parts go as high as a'. Once, in *Alceste*, the bass trombone is required to play b'. While not every movement is so high, each has a narrow range. Therefore, the high movements demand great endurance. Only one opera, *Echo et Narcisse*, has a moderate tessitura. Even there, the tenor trombone needs a secure $a^{b'}$.

Although these ranges, except perhaps for the unreasonable b' in the bass trombone, present no problems for modern trombonists, they must have been difficult indeed for the trombonists in Gluck's Paris, who can hardly have been as good as the ones he knew in Vienna.

Other Prerevolutionary Operas

Not until the 1790s did trombone parts become commonplace in French operas and ballets, but they are included in a significant number from the 1770s and 1780s. Lajarte lists 13.[17] My own survey[18] includes 21 besides those already mentioned. In the following list, an asterisk (*) indicates operas listed by Lajarte that I have not seen.

---

[17] Lajarte, 78.

[18] David Guion, "The Instrumentation of Operas Published in France in the 18th Century," *Journal of Musicological Research* 4 (1982), 134–41.

Cherubini, Luigi
*Dezède, Nicolas

Edelmann,
   Johann Friedrich

Grétry, André
   Ernest Modeste
*LeFroid de Méreaux, Nicolas-Jean
Lemoyne, Jean
   Baptise

——

——

Piccinni, Niccolò

——

——

——

* Rodolphe, Jean-
   Joseph
Sacchini, Antonio

——

——

Salieri, Antonio

——

Vogel, Johann
   Christoph

——

Demophoon (1788)
Alcindor (1787)
Peronne sauvée (1785)
Arianne dans l'isle de Naxos
(1782)

Andromaque (1780)
Alexandre aux Indes (1783)

Electre (1782)
Nephté (1786)
Phèdre (1786)
Didon (1783)
Iphigénie en Tauride (1781)
Pénélope (1785)
Roland (1778)

Apelles et Campaspe (1776)
Dardanus (1784)
Evelina (1788)
Oedipe à Colonne (1786)
Les danaïdes (1785)
Tarare (1787)

Demophon (1789)
Le toison d'or (1786)

Trombones were used also in ballets, but it is not possible at this time to compare operas with ballets; no ballet scores were published until Catel's *Alexandre chez Appelles* in 1808.[19]

The Newberry Library has scores of 84 operas from the 1770s and 1780s, of which 17 have trombone parts. (Its score of Sacchini's *Oedipe à Colonne*, published by Imbault, does not include trombone parts. This opera is included in the above list on the authority of Lajarte.) The following comments are based on 9 of these 17

---

[19] David Charlton, *Orchestration and Orchestral Practice in Paris, 1789–1810* (Ph.D. dissertation: King's College, University of Cambridge, 1973), 5.

operas. Gluck's influence can be seen in a number of ways. The trombones are basically used for harmonic filler or rhythmic punctuation, with no thematic significance of their own. The parts can therefore be described in terms of various kinds of doublings.

Like Gluck, the other prerevolutionary composers used three trombones, the only exception being his rival Piccinni, who used three trombones in *Didon*, but only two in *Iphigénie en Tauride* and only one in *Roland*. Likewise, most prerevolutionary operas that use trombones are based on mythological subjects. The use of trombones usually coincides with the supernatural or with death. No such association is apparent in *Roland*, however.

Note values are usually a quarter note or longer. As was the case in Gluck's trombone parts, pairs of eighth notes are not uncommon, but pairs of sixteenth notes are exceedingly rare, occurring only in a single measure of Grétry's *Andromaque*, on a repeated-note figure. The trombones nearly always have the longest-sounding note in the texture. Passages in which the entire orchestra has the same rhythm are common, but passages where the trombones have moving parts against any other sustained instrument are rare. Most of these are in Piccinni's *Roland*, where in one movement, it is the horns that most often have the longest notes.

Scoring is usually full. There might be one or two instruments that drop out of the texture briefly while the trombones are playing. Generally speaking, however, the trombone parts occur in tutti or near tutti passages. There are some important exceptions. For two measures in Edelmann's *Ariane dans l'isle de Naxos*, a single trombone is the only instrument accompanying the chorus. (It doubles the tenor part.) At the opening of one number in Grétry's *Andromaque*, the trombones and bassoons are the only wind instruments that play. Pairs of oboes, clarinets, trumpets, and horns join them after nineteen measures. The orchestra for one number of Sacchini's *Dardanus* is very small, consisting only of oboes, horns, trombones, and strings. While the trombone parts are important, the horn parts are almost inconsequential. The movement is very chromatic, and so the trombones take on the normal horn functions.

In such normally heavy scoring, it is not surprising that the dynamic levels are generally loud. In one movement of Lemoyne's *Electre*, the entire orchestra keeps blasting at full volume even after the chorus enters. But in all the works examined here, even *Electre*, the trombones are expected to play softly at times. A few movements with trombone are soft throughout.

As I have mentioned, other composers, on the whole, did not follow Gluck's lead in writing high parts. Of the works examined, the composite ranges, with a couple of exceptions, are e^b to $b^{b\prime}$ for the alto trombone, A to $a^{b\prime}$ for the tenor, and G to f' for the bass. The exceptions are a $d^{b\prime\prime}$ in *Ariane* ... and an e'' in *Andromaque* in the alto trombone, and E^bs in the bass trombone in *Tarare* and Vogel's *Demophon*. It is not clear from the score whether Salieri really intended E^b in *Tarare*, but there can be no doubt about *Demophon*, which even requires C. (See Chapter 6 for descriptions of *Tarare* and *Roland*.)

As late as 1781, trombones were still sufficiently novel that a writer in the *Almanach musical* felt the need to make special mention of them in an article devoted to new oddities in musical instruments. After his description of a new kind of flute, a contrabass oboe, and something called a "violon-vielle," he concludes:

M. Gluk a employé avec succès dans l'Orchestre, des Instruments qui produisent un effet très-imposant. On appelle ces Instruments *Tromboni*; ils fournissent des sons nourris & pleins.[20]	Mr. Gluck has successfully used in the orchestra some instruments that produce a very imposing effect. These instruments are called "trombones"; they furnish sustained and full sounds.

The year 1789 is significant in the history of the trombone. In that year, the Opéra hired its first full-time trombonist.[21] (Before then, trombonists had been hired as freelancers for specific pieces.) The Concert Spirituel and the Théâtre de la rue Feydeau likewise hired a full-time trombonist in the same year.[22] (Of course, 1789 also marks the beginning of the French Revolution, an event of critical important for the trombone. Discussion of the Revolution will come later.) After 1789, therefore, the trombone became a regular member, not merely an exceptional member, of the orchestra: and not only of the operatic orchestra, but also of the concert orchestra.

Just as the Opéra hired trombonists for special occasions before

---

[20] *Almanach musical* 6 (1781), 62 (reprint ed. Paris: Minkoff, n.d.), 1214.
[21] Jan La Rue and Howard Brofsky, "Parisian Brass Players, 1751–1793," *Brass Quarterly* 3 (1960), 135.
[22] Ibid.

1789, it is possible that the Concert Spirituel did likewise. Constant Pierre lists the programs of the Concert Spirituel,[23] but unfortunately in a way that makes it very difficult to identify particular pieces. Even the programs given for 1789 and 1790 contain no music that I can positively identify as requiring the trombone.

John Marsh observed that composers seldom included trombone parts in their scores, but that trombonists played from the contra-bass part. (See Chapter 2 for the full text.) If this was the practice of French composers, as well as English composers, the trombone may have been played in any or all of the music on these concerts.

The "Dies irae" from Gossec's *Messe des morts* was performed in four different years on the Concert Spirituel (1761, 1762, 1773, 1780).[24] If, as seems likely, the entire text of the "Dies irae" was performed, and not merely the opening section, Parisian audiences-- and composers--had ample opportunity to hear the effect trombone made in religious music. It would be surprising if other composers of sacred music did not attempt to follow Gossec's lead.

One other piece by Gossec performed in the Concert Spirituel may have included trombones: a *Te Deum* written in 1779. Some writers believe that Gossec reworked this *Te Deum* for the festival on the anniversary of the fall of the Bastille.[25] In any case, the 1790 *Te Deum* calls for trombones, but none of the citations I have found for the 1779 *Te Deum* mentions what forces were required to perform it.

Players and Playing Conditions

It is possible to identify at least some of the trombonists in Paris by name. The *Almanach des spectacles* (1751–1794 and irregularly to 1815) lists the musicians active in Paris. Jan La Rue and Howard Brofsky have extracted the names of the brass players listed there.[26] Those identified as trombonists are Braun l'aîné, Jacobi (Jacobé),

---

[23] Constant Pierre, *Histoire du Concert spirituel: 1725–1790* (Paris: Société Française de Musicologie, 1975).

[24] Ibid., 668 (1761); 674 (1762); 904, 908 (1773); 1035 (1780). Numbers refer to concert listings, not pages.

[25] MacDonald, vol. 1, 350.

[26] La Rue and Brofsky, 138–40.

Lagrange, Louis, Marillac (Marsillac), Mariotti, Mozer (Mozet) [Moser], Nau, Sieber, and Witterker (Widerkehr). David Charlton adds the names of Guthmann and Sturme; Guthmann played horn, trombone, trumpet, harp and viol.[27] According to Lajarte, Braun was hired to play trombone for Gluck's *Iphigénie en Aulide* in 1774; later that year, he was joined by Moser and Sieber for Gluck's *Orphée*.[28] Nau's name appeared in the Opéra's archives in 1775.

The list in La Rue and Brofsky includes French, German, and Italian names. The Italian Mariotti first appeared in the *Almanach* only in 1789. As mentioned in the section on Italian music in Chapter 3, Mariotti appears to have played better than the trombonists already established in Paris before he arrived; one critic called him "astonishing for his precision." He was trombonist for the Concert Spirituel and the Théatre de la rue Feydeau. Jacobi, or Jacobé, is not listed as a trombonist before 1789, although he played horn in 1787. Marsillac does not appear in the listings until 1792, well after the Revolution was under way. Therefore, of those who can be identified as trombonists before the Revolution, only Louis, a bass player who doubled on trombone at the Opéra in 1780 and 1781 was not German. Even he may have been Alsatian, and therefore influenced by German culture as he was growing up.

These men cannot have been especially good players. The parts written for them are extremely simple, as the chapters on opera and band music (6 and 8) will show. The ranges of the parts are very narrow, usually well within the timid limits proposed by Vandenbroek, and there are no rhythmic complexities whatsoever. The lack of technical difficulty in Parisian trombone parts is all the more striking considering the low reputation of the French as technicians. For example, Mozart wrote to his father:

Ich habe eine *sinfonie*, um das *Concert Spirituel* zu eröfnen, machen müssen .... bey der Prob war es mir sehr bange, deñ ich habe meins lebe-Tag nichts schlechters gehört; sie köñen sich nicht vorstellen, wie sie die *sinfonie* 2	I have had to compose a symphony for the opening of the Concert Spirituel .... I was very nervous at the rehearsal, for never in my life have I heard a worse performance. You have no idea how they twice scraped and scrambled through it. I

---

[27] Charlton, 110, 119.
[28] Lajarte, 76.

mahl nacheinander herunter gehudeld, und herunter gekrazet haben. -- mir war wahrlich ganz bang -- ich hätte sie gern noch einmahl *Probirt*, aber weil man allzeit so viell sachen *Probirt*, so war keine zeit mehr; ich muste also mit bangen herzen, und mit unzufriedenen und zornigen gemüth ins bette gehen. Den andern tage hatte ich mich entschlossen gar nicht ins *Concert* zu gehen; es wurde aber abends gut wetter, und ich entschlosse mich endlich mit dem vorsaz, daß weñ es so schlecht gieng, wie bey der *Prob*, ich gewis aufs *orchstre* gehen werde, und den *H: Lahousè Ersten violin* die *violin* aus der hand nehmen, und selbst *dirigen* werde.[29]

was really in a terrible way and would gladly have rehearsed it again, but as there was so much else to rehearse, there was no time left. So I had to go to bed with an aching and in a discontented and angry frame of mind. I decided next morning not to go to the concert at all; but in the evening, the weather being fine, I at last made up my mind to go, determined that if my symphony went as badly as it did at the rehearsal, I would certainly make my way into the orchestra, snatch the fiddle from out of the hands of Lahoussaye, the first violin, and conduct myself![30]

French composers consistently wrote difficult parts for strings and woodwinds. A few occasionally wrote "impossible" notes for trombone, too. (See Othon Vandenbroek's treatise in Chapter 2.) But on the whole, the extreme caution of most trombone parts indicates that most composers did not greatly trust the available players.

There is one crucial difference between working conditions in Paris and in the various German cities from which the trombonists probably came. The *Stadtpfeifer* were hired by the town government and played instruments owned by their employers. In Paris, however, they seem to have been freelancers playing in opera orchestras during the opera season and in concert orchestras during Lent. More important, they provided their own instruments.[31] Under the circumstances, the true bass and alto trombones quickly fell by the

---

[29] Wolfgang Amadeus Mozart, *Briefe Wolfgang Amadeus Mozarts* 2 vols., ed. Erich H. Müller von Asow (Berlin: Alfred Metzner Verlag, 1942), vol. 1, 482−83.

[30] Mozart, *The Letters of Mozart & His Family*, trans. and ed. Emily Anderson, 3 vols. (London; Macmillan, 1938), vol. 2, 825.

[31] Anthony Baines, *Brass Instruments: Their History and Development* (New York: Scribner, 1978), 242.

wayside, although a handful of operas scattered throughout the period require the former. The tenor trombone, which could adequately cope with the ranges of the other parts in most cases, became the standard instrument.

THE REVOLUTION AND AFTER

At the same time that the trombone was being introduced into French music, political, economic, military, and intellectual events were set in motion that resulted in the French Revolution. The progress of the Revolution had a decisive impact on French music and contributed significantly to a new role for the trombone. Millions of words have been written about the causes and progress of the Revolution. Only minimal background needs to be given here.[32]

Neither eighteenth-century French king, Louis XV or Louis XVI, was a strong, able administrator or an inspiring person. After decades of indecisive mismanagement and courtly extravagance, the court ran out of money. By this time, Louis XVI was so unpopular that he was incapable of any action that would please anyone. Unable to raise money by any of the normal means, he convened the Estates General in 1788 for the first time since 1614. French society was traditionally divided into three estates: the clergy, the nobility, and everyone else. The king had no support from any estate. The Estates General was in no mood to give him the money he wanted without exacting concessions that he was unwilling to make. But the estates could not agree among themselves on how to proceed. Drastic change was unavoidable, but no one was able to exert the leadership needed to keep the fabric of society from unraveling completely.

The Third Estate demanded that all decisions be made by the assembly as a whole rather than each estate voting separately. This demand, if granted, would have effectively destroyed the special privileges of the first two estates. Otherwise, the commoners would have been effectively silenced. For a while, they seemed to have the upper hand. On June 17, 1789, the Third Estate proclaimed itself the National Assembly. The king failed in his attempt to annul their

---

[32] The following three paragraphs are based on *The New Encyclopaedia Britannica: Macropaedia*, 1975 ed., "France, History of: IV. France, 1715–1789" by Patrice Louis-René Higonnet and Albert M. Soubel.

decisions and appeared to accept their idea of a constitutional monarchy. At his invitation, the clergy and nobility joined the Third Estate in a body that called itself the National Constituent Assembly. Then, as he had done too often in the past, Louis changed his mind and tried to force the assembly back to obedience using Swiss and German mercenaries.

On July 13, 1789, a civic militia was formed to protect the interests of the assembly against both the king and any lower class threats to "public safety." (One of the captains in the militia, Bernard Sarrette, soon began to play a decisive role in the development of French military music and music education.) The next day, July 14, 1789, members of the militia, in need of arms, pillaged the armory at the Invalides and then stormed the Bastille. Thus, the Revolution entered its first violent stage.

A pivotal festival took place on the first anniversary of the fall of the Bastille. On this occasion, there was a procession from the Bastille to an amphitheater that had been built largely with volunteer help at the Champ de Mars. After the celebration of a Mass, the commander-in-chief of the new French army (Lafayette), members of the Constituent Assembly, and, unwillingly, even the king, swore an oath of allegiance to the new order.

The ceremony concluded with a *Te Deum* by Gossec that had been composed especially for the occasion,[33] although it may have been a reworking of the 1779 *Te Deum* already mentioned. Throughout the ceremony, a huge military band played, including 300 drums and 50 serpents. All told, 1,200 musicians participated.[34] Naturally, with such large forces, probably few of whom were professional musicians, the style of the *Te Deum* is mostly very simple. The chorus is often in unison. Trombones play in one movement, "Judex crederis," which David Whitwell calls the work's most exciting moment.[35]

The Festival of Federation was so successful that even its planners were surprised. Its popularity was noticed by political leaders of all persuasion, so there were many more festivals.

As the optimism of 1789–90 degenerated into anarchy and terror,

---

[33] David Whitwell, *Band Music of the French Revolution* (Tutzing: Hans Schneider, 1979), 20.

[34] Ibid., 22.

[35] Ibid., 154.

the various ruling factions that came and went used the arts for mass indoctrination. The more radical of the revolutionaries, not content with new political structures, wished to destroy the old order and everything associated with it. Their program included the abolition of Christianity in favor of new, man-made religions. They even adopted a new calendar that replaced weeks of seven days with decades of ten days.

Revolutionary music

Music has always been used to reinforce social beliefs. Philosophers and music theorists dating back to the ancient Greeks have written of music's conditioning power. In prerevolutionary France, leading intellectuals, such as Voltaire, Montesquieu, and Rousseau, commented on it. Rousseau expressed the political usefulness of festivals in stirring terms:

Quoi! ne faut-il donc aucun spectacle dans une république? Au contraire, il en faut beaucoup. C'est dans les républiques qu'ils sont nés, c'est dans leurs seins qu'on les voit briller avec un véritable air de fête. A quels peuples convient-il mieux de s'assembler souvent et de former entre eux les doux liens du plaisir et de joie, qu'à ceux qui ont tant de raisons de s'aimer et de rester à jamais unis? Nous avons déjà plusieurs de ces fêtes publiques; ayons-en davantage encore, je n'en serai que plus charmé. Mais n'adoptons point ces spectacles exclusifs qui renferment tristement un petit nombre des gens dans un antre obscur; qui les tiennent craintifs et immobiles dans le silence et l'inaction; qui n'offrent aux yeux que cloisons, que pointes de fer, que soldats, qu'affligeantes images de la servitude et de l'inégalité. Non, peuples heureux, ce ne sont

What! Must there be no spectacles in a republic? On the contrary, there must be many. It is in republics that they are born. It is in their bosoms that one sees them blaze with a veritable air of festival. To what people is it more suitable to gather together often and to form among themselves the sweet bonds of pleasure and joy, those who have so much reason to love each other and remain forever united? We have already had several public festivals; let's have still more. It will only make me happier. But let us not adopt the exclusive spectacles that sadly confine a small number of people in a dark cell, who remain fearful and immovable in silence and inaction, spectacles that offer nothing to the eyes but walls, spears, soldiers, afflicting images of servitude and inequality. No, happy peoples, these are not your festivals. It is in the open air, under the

pas là vos fêtes. C'est en plein air, c'est sous le ciel qu'il faut vous rassembler et vous livrer aux doux sentimes de votre bonheur. Que vox plaisirs ne soient efféminés ni mercenaires, que rien de ce qui sent la contrainte et l'intérêt ne les empoisonne, qu'ils soient libres et généreux comme vous, que le soleil éclaire vos innocents spectacles; vous en formerez un vous-même, le plus digne qu'il puisse éclairer.

heavens where you must gather and indulge yourselves in the sweet sentiments of your happiness. May your pleasures be neither effeminate nor mercenary. May nothing that feels constraint and interest poison them. May they be as free and generous as you. May the sun shine on your innocent spectacles. You yourselves make one, the most worthy that can shine.

Mais quels seront enfin les objets de ces spectacles? qu'y montera-t-on? Rien, s'il l'on veut. Avec la liberté, partout où regne l'affluence, le bien-être y règne aussi. Plantez au milieu d'un place un piquet couronn'e de fleurs, rassemblez-y le peuple, et vous aurez une fête. Faites mieux encore: donnez les spectateurs en spectacle; rendez-les acteurs eux-mêmes; faites que chacun se voie et s'aime dans les autres, afin que tous en soient mieux unis.[36]

But what will be the objects of these spectacles? What will one demonstrate there? Anything one wants. With liberty, everywhere where affluence reigns, well-being reigns there, too. Plant in the middle of a broad place a post crowned with flowers, gather the people, and you will have a feast. Better still, give the spectators to the spectacle. Make them actors themselves. Make each one see and love himself in the others, so that all will be better united.

The constitution of 1791 contained provision for major festivals each year to commemorate such events as the fall of the Bastille, the overthrow of the monarchy, and the execution of the king. By 1794, there were also plans for lesser ceremonies every ten days in honor of such ideas as nature, agriculture, youth, old age, martyrs, the "Supreme Being," etc.-- sort of a mock church service.

Many of the peculiar characteristics of the music of these festivals can be traced to the vision of one man, Bernard Sarrette. A captain in the national guard, he was given the responsibility of training military musicians. Since he was not himself a musician, he served

---

[36] Jean-Jacques Rousseau, "A M. D'Alembert" (1758), *Œuvres complètes de J. J. Rousseau*, 25 vols., ed. V. D. Musset-Pathay (Paris: P. Dupont, 1824), vol. 2, 175−176.

only as an administrator, leaving musical direction to Gossec and Charles Simon Catel, one of Gossec's students.

In building a suitable military musical organization, Sarrette had to start almost from nothing. At the beginning of the Revolution, French military bands were not of good quality. They were small ensembles of oboes, clarinets, bassoons, and horns, with a repertoire largely limited to traditional marches and arrangements of popular songs.[37] In an abrupt departure from tradition, Sarrette formed a 45-piece band. The size of the band fluctuated widely, reaching 78 members before the end of 1789, and then being reduced to 54 members in 1792.[38]

Sarrette's reasons for forming such a large band were both ideological and practical. An orchestra based on stringed instruments had aristocratic connotations that he and his fellow revolutionaries wanted to avoid.[39] In addition, they believed, along with Rousseau, that the festivals should be outdoors under the heavens. Practically speaking, a string orchestra could neither produce a suitable volume of sound nor stay in tune. Therefore, only a large wind ensemble was suitable for their purposes.[40]

For a while, Sarrette bore the expense of maintaining the band himself, although he was not wealthy. In May 1790, he persuaded the city of Paris to support the band. The city withdrew its support in January 1792, but the following June, Sarrette won the approval for the establishment of a school for military music, which eventually became the Conservatoire Nationale. A concert given by the school's pupils was instrumental in gaining official support from the national government.

Because of the political chaos that engulfed France, not all of the festivals that were mandated by the government actually took place. But between 1790 and 1799, new music was composed for at least 40 festivals and earlier music was reused at others.

---

[37] Walter Sherwood Dudley, *Orchestration in the Musique d'harmonie of the French Revolution*, 2 vols. (Ph.D. dissertation: University of California, Berkeley, 1968), vol. 1, 5.

[38] Constant Pierre, *Le Conservatoire Nationale de Musique et de Déclamation: documents historiques et administratifs, recueillis ou reconstitués* (Paris: Imprimérie National, 1900), 103.

[39] Dudley, vol. 1, 3–4.

[40] Whitwell, 63.

David Whitwell describes 158 pieces of revolutionary band music,[41] some of which also require a chorus. Of these, at least 71 call for one to three trombones. Several more are either lost or exist only in later arrangements. The original instrumentation of many of these may have included trombones. When both the original work and later arrangements are known, trombones are nearly always deleted from the latter. Trombones were played in Paris by professional freelancers and military musicians, but not by amateurs. So far as surviving records are concerned, no ensemble could ever have used more than three trombones at a time; serpents were far more numerous.[42] Outside of Paris, trombones were even more scarce.

Besides the band music, a considerable body of patriotic songs, operas (which will be discussed later), and orchestral music was written. The songs, originally for piano and voice were often arranged for various instrumental combinations, including military band. Operatic overtures and arias were arranged for the same combinations. Dozens of band arrangements are listed in publishers catalogs, but without instrumentation given. RISM lists arrangements of two pieces by Rouget de Lisle that include trombone parts: "Marche des Marseillois," R2867, and "Hymne dythyrambique sur la conjuration de Robbespierre," R2884.

Rita Benton's catalogs of the publications of Imbault and Pleyel, alas unfinished at her death, contain several arrangements for which the instrumentation has been identified. Since the catalogs were not completed, I cannot date the arrangements with certainty. (Imbault sold his business in 1803; Pleyel did not establish his until 1795.) Imbault's publications with trombone parts include arrangements of the overture and airs from Dalayrac's *Maison à vendre*, the overture to Paer's *Numa Pompilio* and *Pirro*, and Steibelt's *La bataille d'Austerlitz* and *La journée d'Ulm*. Dalayrac's music was arranged by Frédéric Blasius, Steibelt's by Georg Fuchs. (The arranger of Paer's overtures is not identified.) Most often, the trombone parts are *ad lib*. The obligatory parts are for the instruments of the older military band: pairs of oboes, clarinets, bassoons, and horns. Pleyel's publications include arrangements of the overtures and airs of Berton's *Le grand deuil* (arranged by Amand Vanderhagen) and two anonymously arranged suites from Haydn's *Creation*.

---

[41] Ibid., 105–202.
[42] Charlton, 140, 150, 207.

Although the vast bulk of revolutionary music was written or arranged for wind band, there were some orchestral pieces. Most of them require a chorus, and sometimes also vocal soloists. Pierre lists several that require trombone. The numbers below are Pierre's.[43]

27. Pleyel. La Révolution du 10 août 1792, ou Le tocsin allégorique (1793).
58. Adrien l'aîné. Invocation á l'être suprême (1794).
83. Lemière. Hymne funébre en l'honneur de nos frères morts en combattant pour la liberté (1794).
84. Anonymous. Hymne à la victoire (1794).
89. Chant patriotique (1794).
107. Gossec. Serment républicaine (1795).
111. Gossec. Hymne guerrier (1796).
138. Lesueur. Chant nationale pour l'anniversaire du 21 janvier (1798).
142. Lesueur. Chant dythyrambique pour l'entrée triomphale des objects de science et d'arts recueillis en Italie (1798).
161. Méhul. Chant nationale du 14 juillet 1800 (1800).

Most of the purely instrumental music was for band, but at least two revolutionary orchestral pieces include trombones: Devienne's *La bataille de Jemappes* (1792) and Cambini's *La patriote* (1796).

Composers of revolutionary music run the gamut from major figures to outright incompetents. Gossec, whom Sarrette appointed as music director, wrote more band music than any other composer: 33 of the pieces listed by Whitwell. In fact, he wrote so much that younger composers complained.[44] Other composers who contributed significant numbers of band music include Catel (20 pieces in Whitwell's catalog), Lefèvre (17), Cambini (11), Cherubini (9), Lesueur (8), Méhul (8), and Louis Jadin (6). Kreutzer, Devienne, Hyacinthe Jadin, Berton, and Pleyel also wrote revolutionary band music. The quality of their music varies widely. Some of the lesser composers provided more interesting music than some of their otherwise more noteworthy comtemporaries.

The composers so far mentioned were all important figures in

---

[43] Constant Pierre, *Les hymnes et chansons de la Révolution: Aperçu général et catalogue avec notices historiques, analytiques et bibliographiques* (Paris: Imprimérie nationale, 1904).

[44] Whitwell, 21.

French music, although some were more important as performers or teachers than as composers. At the other end of the scale, one Horix of Strasbourg submitted a march in 1798 that is known only by a memorandum signed by Cherubini and Méhul, who rejected it on grounds of faulty instrumentation and harmony.[45] Considering that much revolutionary music was trite and tedious, Horix's march must have been bad indeed. It is worth mentioning here only because it contained trombone parts. By 1798, then, the trombone, largely unknown twenty years earlier, was so commonplace that even the most deficient of composers tried to write parts for it.

Trombone parts in military music

Although revolutionary band music requires considerable virtuosity of some instruments, especially clarinet and bassoon, the trombone parts of the works available for inspection are uniformly dull. Most of the scores mention only bass trombone, which plays a simplified version of the bassoon line and drops out whenever the music becomes soft. Alto and tenor trombones, when they appear at all, provide only rhythmic punctuation, harmonic filler, and volume, without any melodic or rhythmic interest. Sherwood Dudley points out that the absence of alto and tenor trombones from the scores does not necessarily mean that they were not used in performance; the Conservatory and its predecessors had a firm rule that all of its professors had to participate in the music of the festivals, as players, singers, or overseers of students.[46] In so saying, Dudley seems to have forgotten that the trombonists all played other instruments as well, but it is entirely possible that even if no part was written for as unimportant an instrument as the trombone, one was improvised at the festival.

It may seem odd that an instrument that was used so much would have so little to do. But composers needed the trombone for outdoor music for its weight and carrying power. Perhaps many of them had never given much thought to the trombone before the Revolution and had neither the time nor the desire to learn to use it once the Revolution was underway. (Once, Gossec and Méhul were ordered

[45] Ibid., 169.
[46] Dudley, vol. 1, 38−39.

to compose marches for a funeral and have them printed on three' days notice).[47]

Considering that the trombones seemed most valued for making a loud noise, it is ironic that no trombone partbooks were made for the big outdoor festival concert given July 14, 1794 at the Tuileries, even though the program included at least one piece, Gossec's "Ronde nationale" (W. 85) that included trombone parts. Charlton, calling attention to the small number of trombones and trombonists available in Paris at the time, speculates that they were omitted from this festival on the grounds that their limited tone could not possibly make any kind of impression among the large forces engaged for the occasion.[48]

By the time of Napoleon, one other military organization, the cavalry band or *orchestre de fanfare* deserves mention. This type of band usually consisted of sixteen trumpets, six horns, three trombones, and sometimes timpani.[49] One collection of music can be mentioned: *Seize fanfares* by David Buhl. If this collection is standard fanfare music, then it appears that there were four trumpeters, three horns, and three trombones on each part. This sort of ensemble would have had a splendor, brilliance, and power unmatched since the time of Giovanni Gabrieli. Napoleon briefly attempted to suppress the cavalry bands as an economy move, but they returned with full imperial blessing by the time his expansionist wars began in earnest.

I have already mentioned that the men who played in the theaters up to the time of the Revolution were not skillful trombonists. In each case, their principal instrument was something other than trombone. The national guard band drew its trombonists from the same freelancers who worked in the theaters. These same men also taught at the Conservatory.

The Paris Conservatory

The Paris Conservatory, which had different official names as the political climate shifted, was an outgrowth of the national guard

---

[47] Whitwell, 88.

[48] Charlton, 141–42, 153.

[49] Henry George Farmer, *The Rise & Development of Military Music* (London: Wm. Reeves, [1912]), 80–81.

band. One reason for establishing it was to provide enough good French wind players to end France's dependence of foreigners.[50] This same impulse may have led the horn maker Lefèvre to start making trombones.[51]

Because the earliest documents are no longer extant, it is not possible to reconstruct the original faculty. Considering that trombones were required for so much of the earliest revolutionary band music, the school's first faculty must have included a trombonist. It was probably Philippe Widerkehr, a member of the faculty from 1789 to 1815.[52] Pierre, however, nowhere identifies him as a trombone teacher. A Widerkehr was listed as a trombonist at the Théâtre du Palais in 1792,[53] and according to *The New Grove*, Philippe Widerkehr was a trombonist in the national guard band.[54] Whitwell reproduces one document that lists Widerkehr as a trombonist and faculty member.[55] Apparently, the intent of this document was to show the instrumentation available for performances.

On November 20, 1793, Sarrette arranged a concert to demonstrate the school's accomplishments. Included on the program were two works by Catel and three by Gossec that require trombones, along with four pieces not listed in Whitwell's catalog.[56] Of these latter pieces, one is a type of piece that may have required trombones. Catel's overture requires only bass trombone. The other works for which instrumentation is known require three trombones. The performers must have been Widerkehr and two students.

The following day, the government provisionally added thirteen new faculty members, including Pierre Marciliac,[57] who remained on the faculty until 1802. Pierre lists him as a trombone teacher in two of those years.[58] He is also listed as a trombonist at the Théâtre du Palais in 1792 and the Comédie Italienne in 1793.[59]

---

[50] Whitwell, 63.

[51] Lyndesay G. Langwill, *An Index of Musical Wind-Instrument Makers* 5th ed. (Edinburgh: Langwill, 1977), 103.

[52] Pierre, *Conservatoire*, 407–14.

[53] La Rue and Brofsky, 140.

[54] Barry S. Brook and Barbara S. Kafka, "Widerkehr [Wiederkehr, Viderkehr], Jacques (-Christian-Michel)," *The New Grove*, vol. 20, 395.

[55] Whitwell, 42.

[56] Ibid., 62.

[57] Pierre, *Conservatoire*, 92.

[58] Ibid., 407–12.

[59] La Rue and Brofsky, 140.

The decree that established the Conservatory (August 3, 1795), provided for a staff of 115 artists, of whom one was designated as a trombone teacher (probably Marciliac) and three as performers on trombone.[60] Comparing the 1795 faculty list in Pierre with the trombonists listed by La Rue and Brofsky, we find one name (besides Marciliac and Widerkehr) in common: Braun.[61] But Braun was such a common name that it is not safe to identify Braun as the third trombonist on the Conservatory's staff. (La Rue and Brofsky list two Brauns.) Another, more likely, possibility is Guthmann, identified by Charlton as a respected trombonist, although not identified as such by La Rue and Brofsky.[62]

After Marciliac's departure from the Conservatory in 1802, Pierre identifies no trombonist until Antoine Dieppo joined the faculty in 1836. It is not clear, however, that the trombone was not taught there in the interval. Widerkehr remained on the faculty until 1815. Although he is not identified as a trombonist on any of the faculty lists, neither is Marciliac more often than not.

REVOLUTIONARY AND POSTREVOLUTIONARY OPERA

Given the emotional and ideological upheaval of the Revolution, it was inevitable that opera would be profoundly affected. Operas largely shed their mythological trappings for more contemporary settings. Particularly during the Reign of Terror, composers were careful to chose politically safe plot ideas. The so-called rescue opera, although its roots predate the Revolution, is very characteristic of what Parisian audiences expected during this time.

According to Lajarte and Cucuel, nearly all operas written after 1791 included trombone parts; ballets used the trombone even more heavily.[63] If so, most of them were omitted from the published scores. My own survey shows trombones in only 40 of 86 operas written between 1790 and 1806.[64] These are listed in Table I, along

---

[60] Pierre, *Conservatoire*, 124–25.
[61] Ibid., 407; La Rue and Brofsky, 138.
[62] Charlton, 150; La Rue and Brofsky, 138.
[63] Lajarte, 78; Cucuel, 35.
[64] Guion, "Instrumentation," 143.

TABLE I. Operas during and after the French Revolution with trombone parts.

Composer	Opera	Date	Theater	Trombones
Berton	Le délire	1799	Favart	1
Berton	Montano et Stephanie	1799	Favart	1
Berton	La romance	1804	Favart	1
Berton	*Le vaisseau amiral	1805	Op. Com.	1
Boieldieu	Bieniowsky	1800	Favart	2
Boieldieu	La dot de Suzette	1798	Favart	2
Boieldieu	La famille suisse	1797	Feydeau	2
Boieldieu	*Ma tante Aurore	1803	Feydeau	1
Boieldieu	Zoraïme et Zulnar	1798	Favart	2
Candeille	*La patrie reconnaissante	1793	Opéra	3
Catel	Sémiramis	1802	Opéra	3
Cherubini	*Achille à Scyros	1804	Opéra	3
Cherubini	Anacréon	1803	Opéra	3
Cherubini	Les deux journées	1800	Feydeau	1
Cherubini	*L'hotêllerie portugaise	1798	Feydeau	1
Cherubini	Lodoïska	1791	Feydeau	1
Cherubini/ Méhul	*Epicure	1800	Favart	1
Dalayrac	Adèle et Dorsan	1795	Favart	1
Dalayrac	Alexis	1798	Feydeau	1
Dalayrac	La boucle des cheveux	1802	Op. Com.	1
Dalayrac	Camille	1791	Com. Ital.	1
Dalayrac	Gulnare	1798	Favart	1
Dalayrac	Léhéman	1801	Op. Com.	1
Dalayrac	Léon, ou Le chateau de Monténéro	1798	Favart	1
Dalayrac	La maison isolée	1797	Favart	1
Dalayrac	Maison à vendre	1800	Favart	1
Dalayrac	Philippe et Georgette	1791	Com. Ital.	1
Dalayrac	Picaros et Diego	1803	Op. Com.	1
Fioravanti	I virtuosi ambulante	1807	Th. Ital.	2
Gaveaux	Léonore	1798	Op. Com.	2
Gaveaux	Le petit matelot	1796	Feydeau	1
Gaveaux	Sophie et Moncars	1797	Feydeau	2
Gaveaux	Le traité nul	1797	Feydeau	2
Gossec	*La triomphe de la république	1793	Opéra	3
Grétry	Anacréon chez Polycrate	1797	Opéra	3
Jadin, L. E.	*Le siège de Thionville	1793	Opéra	3
Kreutzer	Lodoïska	1791	Com. Ital.	1
Langlé	*Corisandre	1791	Opéra	3
Langlé	*Solimon et Eronime	not given		3
Lefroid de Méreaux	*Fabius	1793	Opéra	3

TABLE I. continued.

Composer	Opera	Date	Theater	Trombones
Lefroid de Méreaux	*Jocaste	1791	Opéra	3
Lemoyne	*Louis IX en Egypte	1791	Opéra	3
Lemoyne	*Militiade à Marathon	1793	Opéra	3
Lemoyne	*Toute la Grèce	1794	Opéra	3
Lesueur	*La mort d'Adam et son apothéose	1809	Opéra	3
Lesueur	Ossian	1804	Opéra	3
Lesueur	Télémaque dans l'isle de Calypso	1796	Feydeau	3
Méhul	*Adrien (composed 1791−92)	1799	Opéra	3
Méhul	Adriodant	1799	Op. Com.	1
Méhul	Bion	1800	Op. Com.	1
Méhul	*Cora et Alonzo	1791	Opéra	3
Méhul	*Daphnis et Pandrose	1803	Opéra	3
Méhul	*Henry IV	1797	Favart	1
Méhul	L'irato	1801	Op. Com.	1
Méhul	Le jeune sage et le vieux fou	1793	Op. Com.	1
Méhul	*Le jugement de Paris	1793	Opéra	3
Méhul	Mélidore et Phrosine	1794	Favart	1
Méhul	Stratonice	1792	Op. Com.	1
Méhul	*Timoléon	1794	Th. Repub.	3
Müller	*Psyche et l'amour	1790	Opéra	3
Paisiello	*Proserpine	1803	Opéra	3
Plantade	*Palma	1798	Feydeau	2
Rochefort	*Bacchus et Ariane	1791	Opéra	3
Rochefort	*Toulon soumis	1794	Opéra	3
Steibelt	Roméo et Juliette	1793	Feydeau	3
Tarchi	*Le trente et quarante	1799	Feydeau	2
Winter	Tamerlan	1802	Opéra	3

(N.B): I have not seen any of the scores marked with an asterisk. I have found two errors in my earlier survey: Dalayrac's *Léhèman* uses one trombone, not two; Lesueur's *Télémaque* uses three trombones, not one.)

with the date of performance, the theater, and the number of trombones required. Because ballet scores were not published, I have not seen any and cannot comment on Lajarte's and Cucuel's findings on the use of the trombone in ballets.

The following comments on the use of the trombone in revolutionary and postrevolutionary opera are based on an examination of 17 scores. In some ways, these trombone parts are similar to those in prerevolutionary operas. They are rhythmically uncomplicated and make few technical demands. The trombones function

only to provide some combination of harmonic filler, rhythmic punctuation, weight, and volume. Trombones usually appear only in
loud tutti passages. Only the lesser composers limited trombone to
such passages, but more of them were writing trombone parts. As
trombone parts became more numerous, they also became less
interesting.

A new symbolism occurs occasionally to replace the trombone's
old association with religion and the supernatural. In Cherubini's
Les deux journées (1800) and Dalayrac's *Léhéman* (1801), the trombone nearly always coincides with the appearance of soldiers.

All of the prerevolutionary operas with trombone parts were
given at the Opéra, but most of those given in 1790 and after were
produced elsewhere. While all operas produced at the Opéra require
three trombones, most of the rest require only one. A handful call
for two.

Steibelt's *Roméo et Juliette* calls for three trombones in the overture. Six scenes in the opera have parts for two trombones. Three
more need only one. Lesueur's *Télémaque dans l'isle de Calypso*
uses three trombones in such a short passage that I missed it entirely
the first time I looked at the score. Assuming that the score is
accurate, not necessarily a safe assumption, only one trombone is
needed throughout most of the opera. These last two operas were
written for the Opéra, which rejected them. Both were produced at
the Théâtre de la rue Feydeau, which, at the time, had only one
trombonist on its regular payroll. It probably did not hire extra
trombonists for these works, but rather performed them with only a
bass trombone. The upper parts are so inconsequential that nothing
at all would be lost in such a performance.

When only one trombone is required, it was invariably a bass
trombone, in function if not in fact. In operas with more than one
trombone part, the lowest never goes higher then e'. Only two
works with one trombone part require higher notes: Dalayrac's
Léhéman calls for f' and Méhul's *Bion* requires $f\#'$. In both cases,
the lowest note in B, which is higher than the usual lowest notes.
Only Cherubini's *Lodoïska*, with a range from c to e', has a higher
lowest note.

The lowest notes are most often A, G, or F. Nearly all of the
parts, then, including the third trombone parts in works produced at
the Opéra, fall entirely within the range given by Vandenbroek for
the tenor trombone. At least one, however, goes below the lowest
note he gives for the bass trombone (F): Boieldieu's *Béniowski*

requires a *C*. Only two of these operas require notes higher than *g'*, even for the highest of three trombone parts. Grétry's *Anacréon chez Polycrate* calls for *b'*, and Catel's *Sémiramis* demands *c''*, which is not approached by step!

When more than one trombone is required for an opera, the lowest often plays more than the others. For example, in the overture to Steibelt's *Roméo et Juliette*, the third trombone plays in 128 measures. The first plays in 71 and the second in 90. In Lesueur's *Ossian*, the top two trombones have only isolated notes, while the third trombone has a much more extensive part, not to say a more interesting part: it merely plays in unison with the cellos or an octave higher, avoiding the octave leaps at cadences. (For a detailed description of *Roméo et Juliette* and *Léhéman*, see Chapter 6.)

The vast bulk of French music with parts for trombone was either theater music or military music. Some of the revolutionary orchestra music, with and without voices, has already been mentioned. I have found references to a few other works with trombone parts, although in most cases I have not seen them. A complete list is given in Chapter 7. By all accounts, these parts do not differ significantly from those in operas.

In less than half a century, the trombone changed from an instrument unknown in France to one used, some complained overused, in all types of music. The quality of music written for trombones in France was vastly inferior to most of that written elsewhere, but it had its own special power and influence:

> Critics in many parts of Europe in the first third of the nineteenth century were remarking that it seemed to be an age of trombones. The trombone craze apparently began in France around the turn of the century and spread throughout most of Europe in the wake of Napoleon's armies. A report from Paris about 1802 wailed, "Trombones, trombones, these are for our latest composers the most splendid, just like drums for children."[65]

---

[65] Mary Rasmussen, "Two Early Nineteenth-Century Trombone Virtuosi: Carl Traugott Queisser and Friedrich August Belcke," *Brass Quarterly* 5 (1961), 15.

CHAPTER 5

THE TROMBONE IN CHORAL MUSIC

The trombone participated more in choral music than in any other medium in the eighteenth century. The vast majority of trombone parts was written for the church. In addition, three of Handel's oratorios, *Israel in Egypt*, *Saul*, and *Samson*, use the trombone. Most of this music has not yet been published; much probably remains undiscovered.

Many little-known composers wrote church music in small or medium sized towns. That one of them, Franz Schneider of Melk, Austria, wrote extensively for trombone can be seen in the thematic catalog of his works.[1] Other similarly obscure but gifted composers probably used the trombone, too. Many composers who were prominent in their own day, such as Telemann, have since languished in the shadows of greater masters, and their works have not been collected or adequately cataloged. Some of these, at least, must have used the trombone in their church music.

Although the greatest amount of unknown trombone music can probably be found in Austria and Bohemia, and to a lesser extent in

---

[1] Robert Freeman, *Franz Schneider (1737–1812): A Thematic Catalogue of His Works* (New York: Pendragon, 1979).

Germany, it is possible that some French church music with trombone parts exists, written under the influence of Gossec's *Messe des morts* (1760). Probably some Swedish composers, and possibly some Italians, used trombones in their church music.

Even though only a small portion of the eighteenth-century choral music with trombone parts has been published in modern times, the wealth of easily available music made it difficult to choose what to describe in this chapter. In order to keep it to a reasonable length. I have decided to include only the music of great masters and to discuss only one work of each.

JOHANN JOSEPH FUX

Missa Corporis Christi (K. 10)

Johann Joseph Fux wrote about 80 masses, of which 43 include trombone parts. Five of these have been published so far in the twentieth century: *Missa brevis solennitatis* (K. 5), *Missa Corporis Christi* (K. 10), *Missa Purificationis* (K. 28), *Missa Lachrymantis Virginis* (E. 12), and *Missa Sanctissimae Trinitas octo vocum* (E. 113). In the first four named of these, Fux uses alto and tenor trombones to double the altos and tenors of the chorus. The fifth also includes the bass trombone, and the trombones double only the second of two choruses. Two of these masses (K. 5, 10) use trumpets, and cornett and bassoon to double the sopranos and basses. In the others, trombones are the only wind instruments used. Regrettably, none of the eleven works identified by Köchel and Liess as including trombones "in concerto" (K. 21, 24, 25, 26, 120, 121, 175, 248, 252; L. 18, 28) have yet been published. *Missa Sanctissimae Trinitas* includes a few brief passages of independent counterpoint for trombone. *Missa Corporis Christi* includes more and longer such passages.

Throughout the entire mass, the trombones double the alto and tenor voices. At no point are these parts are not doubled by the trombones and at no point does Fux simplify the rhythmic or melodic material for the trombones. Unlike so much of the music described in later chapters, the trombone parts in choral music are not modified to omit melodic embellishment or otherwise simplify the line. I reiterate this point because it describes not only *Missa Corporis Christi*, but nearly all the choral music with trombone parts written in the eighteenth century.

In addition to the doubling, Fux uses the trombones independently in four passages. The ranges are *e* to *b'* for the alto trombone and *c* to *g'* for the tenor. The alto trombone plays no note lower than *a*, except in the "Christe," where it is a solo instrument, and one *g* in the *Agnus Dei*.

The mass begins with a sonatina for clarino trumpets, trombones, and continuo in 6/4 time, editorially marked Allegro moderato. The trombones have a more important role than the trumpets, participating in 14 of the 15 measures. In contrast, the two trumpets play together only in the last five and a half measures, and two and half measures have no trumpet parts at all. The alto trombone has trills on *f#* and *b'*. See Ex. 16.

Example 16. Fux: *Missa Corporis Christi*, "Sonatina," measures 1–8.

In the *Kyrie*, the trombones accompany a four-measure tenor
solo, using the same musical material as the sonatina. In the "Christe,"
which is scored for soprano and alto solo without chorus, two violins
and alto trombone play an introduction, two interludes, and a
concluding phrase. Only the continuo plays while the soloists sing.
Each of the four instrumental passages is in imitative style, with the
first violin playing first and the trombone entering last. The trombone
plays every kind of rhythmic figure the violins do, except that it has
no trills. All of its phrases are shorter, though, and it plays fewer
sixteenth notes. In the second interlude, for example, the first violin
plays sixteenth notes on four consecutive beats, and the trombone
plays them on only two. See Ex. 17.

Example 17. Fux: *Missa Corporis Christi*, "Kyrie," measures 64–66.

The two trombones, supported only by continuo, play a four-
measure introduction to the "Crucifixus" section of the *Credo*. In
keeping with the text, the tempo is slow. Both trombones play
disjunct lines with sixteenth notes (which move stepwise). The alto
trombone has lip trills on b'.

It is not any of these soloistic passages that appear to be the most
difficult, but the "Amen" that concludes the *Gloria*, which is in 6/8
time, with an editorial tempo marking of 72 for the dotted quarter.
The choral parts, and therefore the trombone parts, contain many
sixteenth notes, which sometimes extend through an entire beat.
Although they are mostly in stepwise motion, they frequently include
changes of direction and skips of a third.

JOHANN SEBASTIAN BACH

O Jesu Christ, mein's Lebens Licht (BWV 118)

This work, known as Cantata 118, is an anomaly in Bach's output, being the only cantata accompanied by wind band, the only one based on a single hymn stanza, and the only one with a single movement. Bach himself did not call it a cantata, but a motet,[2] so it is considered as a seventh motet instead of a cantata in the *Neue Bach Ausgabe*. Even there, it does not entirely fit, being the only motet conceived with full instrumental accompaniment. (Of the other six motets, B.W.V. 226 has an orchestra accompaniment, known as B.W.V. 226a, that appears to have been added later, and B.W.V. 230 includes continuo.)

It was written for the funeral of count Joachim Friedrich von Fleming, governor and therefore highest military official of the city of Leipzig. The first performance was at the grave site on October 11, 1740, which explains the wind accompaniment. Bach specified two litui, one cornett, and three trombones. (Bach's lituus was probably a horn in high B♭.[3]) Nine days later, the motet was performed indoors, this time with a standard string orchestra replacing the cornett and trombones.

O Jesu Christ, mein's Lebens Licht consists of one movement of 108 measures. The trombones and cornett play throughout. The litui, on the other hand, drop out for two of the choral sections. Because the trombones are not tied to the vocal parts, they can have a wider range (alto, *f* to *c″*; tenor, *d* to *g′*; bass *D* to *c′*) than most of eighteenth-century trombone parts. They are also more disjunct than most others, probably at least in part for the same reason.

During the choral sections, the cornett and upper trombones double the voices, but in a most unusual way. The cornett doubles the soprano in a conventional fashion, but the trombones sometimes actually embellish the alto and tenor parts. The bass trombone doubles the choral bass less than half the time. Often, the basses sing an independent line between the tenors and the bass trombone, or even cross above the tenors. See Ex. 18. The repeated quarter-note figure in the example, as the following chapters will show, is

---

[2] Thomas Andrew Miller, *An Investigation of Johann Sebastian Bach's Cantata 118 "O Jesu Christ meins* [sic] *Lebens Licht"* (D.M.A. essay: University of Missouri, Kansas City, 1971), 10.

[3] Miller, 25.

common for cello and bassoon, but rare for trombone, which more often sustains a note than repeats it.

Only in *O Jesu Christ, mein's Lebens Licht* does Bach approach the level of difficulty and interest for trombone that characterizes his writing for nearly all other instruments. It is a sample of how well he understood the trombone and how well he could have written for it in other pieces if he had had any interest or incentive. Perhaps some of the lesser composers who worked more closely with *Stadtpfeifer*, and who had more success than Bach in getting good instruments and personnel, wrote music of similar interest.

Example 18. Bach: *O Jesu Christ, mein's Lebens Licht*, measures 70–84.

Example 18, continued.

Example 18, continued.

Example 18, continued.

GEORGE FREDERICK HANDEL

Saul

George Frederick Handel spent his entire career in musical centers where trombones were little used. His Hamburg colleague Mattheson commented on the rarity of the trombone in Germany. During the time Handel was in Italy, one old man was on the payroll of San Marco in Venice as a trombonist; otherwise, I cannot document the use of the trombone there at all.

In England, where Handel wrote his greatest works, there were likewise apparently no trombones available to him except for a very brief period. Handel called for trombones in *Israel in Egypt* and *Saul*, both composed in 1738. Except for a short march in *Samson* (1741), he never used trombones again. Although Handel's acquaintance with the trombone was brief, he demonstrated a masterful understanding of its potential.

Anthony Baines has called the trombone parts in *Saul* the finest in the eighteenth century.[4] Leaving aside works with soloistic parts for trombone, it is difficult to disagree with him. So many other trombone parts can be summarized merely in terms of doubling some other instrument or voice. Handel, in not clinging to any stereotypes, introduced an entirely new manner of using the trombone.

Saul consists of 87 musical numbers plus an opening symphony which, in the *Hallische Händel-Ausgabe* is unnumbered. Eight numbers require trombones, four choruses and four instrumental interludes. It is possibly the first dramatic work to use trombones since Cesti's *Il pomo d'oro* (1660) and the last until Gluck's *Don Juan* (1761). (*Israel in Egypt* is contemplative and descriptive in character, not dramatic.) In seventeenth-century operas with trombone, and in the earliest ones of the eighteenth century, trombones depict death, gloom, and infernal spirits. In *Saul*, they participate in choruses of victory and rejoicing, although the famous Dead March (no. 77) puts their more funereal capabilities to good use.

In most eighteenth-century choral music, trombones doubled the choral parts and usually did not play when the chorus did not sing.

---

[4] Anthony Baines, "Trombone," *Grove's Dictionary of Music and Musicians*, 5th ed., ed. Eric Blom, 9 vols. (London: Macmillan, 1954), vol. 8, 557.

Almost the only important exceptions to this practice were the soloistic passages in Austrian church music. In *Saul*, trombones play with and without the chorus and occasionally rest during choral sections. Strict doubling hardly ever occurs for more that a few measures at a time. Modified doubling does not necessarily mean that the rhythm is simplified for the trombones. Most of the time, it consists not of any rhythmic alteration, but different notes, which fill out the texture and harmony. At one point, the bass trombone plays an embellishment of the bass part. See Ex. 19. This example is less notable than that from the Bach motet; it is shorter, and the trombones here doubles the other bass instruments.

Example 19. Handel: *Saul*, number 24, measures 1–4.

Text: David his ten thousand slew, ten thousand praises are his due.

Even when the trombone parts essentially double the chorus, the trombones do not necessarily stay with the same part. In a typical choral fugue, for example, alto, tenor, and bass trombones double the altos, tenors, and basses of the chorus, respectively, while the soprano part is either doubled by a cornett or, late in the century, left on its own. Handel's flexibility enables him to achieve a much more satisfying result, in effect doubling all four choral parts with three trombones. See Ex. 20.

Example 20. Handel: *Saul*, number 1, measures 61—66.

Example 20, continued.

Example 20, continued.

In the final chorus, the alto trombone at one time or another doubles the sopranos, altos, tenors, first and second violins, violas, and second oboes. The tenor trombone doubles all of the same parts plus the basses and second trumpet. Not all of this doubling is at the unison. Through use of octave doubling, Handel creates nearly independent trombone parts. Often, the upper trombones' notes do not duplicate any other part in unison. In this way, Handel's trombone parts are more important to the overall effect than any others throughout the eighteenth century except those with solo passages and those of Joseph Haydn, whose treatment of trombones owes much to Handel's example.

The bass trombone parts double the choral and instrumental bass lines more consistently, but frequently an octave lower. The bass trombone almost invariably has the lowest written notes in the texture, although the violone occasionally sounds lower, being written an octave higher than it sounds. Characteristic of Handel's writing for trombones is the wide gap between the bass and tenor trombones and the close spacing between the tenor and the alto, which can be seen in the ranges for each part: alto, *b* to *d"*; tenor, *d* to *g'*; and bass, *C* to *a*.

In the first of the instrumental interludes (no. 58), marked Largo, the wind section consists only of two oboes, two bassoons, and three trombones. The oboes, second bassoon, and bass trombone double string parts. The alto and tenor trombones, along with the first bassoon, are entirely independent. The texture is very full through-out, broken only by one measure in which most of the orchestra has a single eighth rest. Rhythmically, a dotted quarter, eighth-note figure dominates the movement. All of the shorter notes are in the strings, and most of the long, sustained notes are in the trombones.

The next symphony (no. 65), marked Allegro, has a wind section of two oboes, bassoon, two trumpets, and three trombones. The wind parts can be described entirely as modified doublings of the string parts, with generally longer note values. On the whole, the trombones have longer note values than the other winds, but the upper trombones have occasional pairs of sixteenth notes or dotted eighth, sixteenth-note figures. The trombone parts are usually an octave lower than the string parts they double; the bass trombone doubles at the unison more often than the other trombones. Even so, the bass and tenor trombones are so far apart that their ranges do not even overlap. The bass trombone plays frequent *C*s and no note higher than *d*. The tenor trombone plays no note lower than *g*.

Innovative though he was, Handel did not invent the orchestral trombone choir, or indeed, separately functioning string, woodwind, and brass choirs, but he came close to this latter device in one of the symphonies (no. 74). The three groups play antiphonally for the first twelve measures and together for the last four, although the bassoon plays throughout the string sections. In the closing tutti, the alto trombone doubles the violas and the bass trombone doubles the cellos and bassoons (but not exactly). The tenor trombone is entirely independent.

Perhaps the best-known excerpt from *Saul* is the Dead March (no. 77). The trombones double the strings with only slight modifi-cations. Besides a bassoon doubling the bass line, the only other winds are a pair of flutes, which usually play antiphonally to the rest

Plate 16. Weigl: Posaune.

POSAUNE

Ich suche fast den Ruhm   an allen Ort und Enden
so wohl den Alterthum   als auch der Würkung nach.
man sehe was ich kan   in beeden Testamenten
ich warff die Mauren ein   als man mich recht besprach
kein Opffer oder Fest wurd recht ohn mich vollführet
und heunt zu Tag bin ich was große Chör bezieret.

Reprinted from *The Trumpet & Trombone in Graphic Arts: 1500–1800* by
Tom L. Naylor © 1979 The Brass Press. Used by permission.

of the orchestra. Unlike most music with trombone parts, this march is soft throughout. Although the trombones exhibit less independence from the strings in this movement than any other in *Saul*, it is this movement that Charles Burney singled out as an example of good writing for trombone. (See Chapter 2 for the full text.) It would be very effective and solemn played as a trombone trio doubled, with some embellishment, by strings. In other words, the trombones can be allowed to dominate, and, in this movement, it will heighten the effect and not merely destroy the balance.

WOLFGANG AMADEUS MOZART

Waisenhauskirche Mass (K. V. 47a [139])

In most of Mozart's choral music, trombones merely double the alto, tenor, and bass lines of the chorus if they are used at all. Such parts are technically simple or difficult depending on the nature of the vocal writing, and there is little more to say about them.

Mozart wrote independent passages for trombones in three of his masses. The most famous is the tenor trombone solo in the "Tuba mirum" of the *Requiem* (K. V. 626), a required work on many orchestral auditions. Trombones also take part in the orchestral accompaniment in the *Sanctus* of the *Mass in c minor* (K. V. 417a [427]).

Mozart's most extensive use of independent trombones comes in his first large-scale work, a mass written for the consecration of an orphanage church (*Waisenhauskirche*) in Vienna in 1768 (K. V. 47a [139]), about a month before his thirteenth birthday. The conception and execution of this mass are so mature that generations of scholars were persuaded that not even Mozart could write such music at age 12; only recently has the evidence become overwhelming enough to outweigh this assumption.[5]

The autograph score includes three trombone parts only where the trombones are independent of the chorus: the introduction to the *Kyrie*, the "Crucifixus," and the opening section of the *Agnus*

---

[5] Edward Olleson, "Church Music and Oratorio," *The New Oxford History of Music*, vol. 7, *The Age of Enlightenment, 1745–1790*, ed. Egon Wellesz and Frederick Sternfeld (London: Oxford University Press, 1973), 307.

Dei. The score gives no indication that the bass trombones was intended to double the chorus during the rest of the mass.[6] As noted in Chapter 3, the normal practice in Salzburg, where Mozart lived when he composed the mass, was to double the chorus with three trombones. Viennese composers usually used only alto and tenor trombones. Mozart wrote his mass for Vienna, but it would seem odd to require a bass trombone to play only in the independent sections and not while the other trombones were doubling the chorus. Accordingly, the *Neue Mozart Ausgabe* includes a bass trombone part throughout the mass, but prints most of it in smaller noteheads.

In the first six measures of *Kyrie*, the bass trombone functions as the primary bass instrument, and the alto and tenor trombones double the violas. See Ex. 21. In the following six measures, all the trombones double the chorus; the bass trombone does not drop out, a significant clue of Mozart's intentions for the whole mass.

The very operatic "Crucifixus" opens with muted trumpets and timpani antiphonal with trombones and strings. With some modifications, the upper trombones double a divided viola section and the bass trombone doubles the cellos and basses. The chorus enters after a five-measure introduction, but the trombones continue to be more closely identified with the strings than with the singers.

---

[6] Walter Senn, "Zum vorliegenden Band," *Neue Mozart Ausgabe* Serie I: *Geistliche Gesangwerke*, Werkgruppe 1: Messen und Requiem; Abteilung 1: Messen, Band 1 (Kassel: Bärenreiter, 1968), xi.

Example 21. Mozart: *Waisenhauskirche Mass*, "Kyrie," measures 1–6.

Example 21, continued.

By far the more important of the independent passages for trombones is *Agnus Dei*, which opens with a twelve-measure trombone
trio, unaccompanied except for the continuo. See Ex. 22. In the
next fifteen measures, during an alto solo, the trombones are joined
by the strings. The bass trombone doubles the cellos and basses

Example 22. Mozart: *Waisenhauskirche Mass*, "Agnus Dei," measures 1–12.

rather strictly, except that it plays half notes or whole notes in place of repeated quarter notes. The alto and tenor trombones sometimes double string parts and sometimes have entirely independent parts. When the chorus enters, the trombones double it exactly, and then continue for one measure after the chorus's final cadence.

For the rest of the mass, the trombones double the chorus in every movement except "Benedictus." Their silence in this movement makes their solo appearance in the following *Agnus Dei* fresher in color than it would have been otherwise. The ranges are *a* to *c″* for the alto trombone, *d* to *g′* for the tenor, and *E* to *d′* for the bass.

Although the trombone parts are less important to the overall effect of the mass when they double the chorus than when they are independent, they are no less musically rewarding or technically challenging. See Ex. 23.

Example 23. Mozart: *Waisenhauskirche Mass*, "Credo." measures 244–53.

FRANZ JOSEPH HAYDN

Die sieben letzten Worte (Hob. XX:2)

That Joseph Haydn thought very highly of his music for the seven last words of Christ can be seen from the number of versions of it that he wrote. In about 1785, he was commissioned by the Cathedral of Cádiz to write orchestral meditations for the Good Friday services. He wrote seven adagio sonatas, one for each word, and a finale, *Il Terremoto* (the earthquake), to depict the immediate aftermath of Jesus's death.[7]

Of all the qualities of this music, one can be pointed out to justify Haydn's high regard for his work: he succeeded in writing more than an hour's worth of slow music that is not tedious from lack of variety. Wishing to give it the widest circulation possible, Haydn arranged it for string quartet and collaborated with his publishers on a piano reduction. All three versions were published in 1787, although the original orchestral version was published in parts only. No score was issued until the 1950s, so this version languished in obscurity for a century and a half.[8]

In 1795, Haydn stopped to visit a long-time friend, Karl Frieberth, in Passau. Frieberth had made a choral arrangement of the *Seven Last Words* and had it performed for Haydn, who liked it, but thought he could do a better job. Some of Frieberth's *a capella* additions survive in Haydn's own choral version.[9] Haydn added not only a four-part chorus and five soloists, but clarinets, trombones, and contrabassoon. He composed a new introduction to the fifth word for winds alone, but otherwise, the music remained essentially unchanged. The difficult task of fitting words to preexisting music fell to Baron Gottfried van Swieten, who later wrote the texts of *The Creation* and *The Seasons*. The choral version was first performed in 1796.[10]

---

[7] Lydia Hailparn, "Haydn: The Seven Last Words. A New Look at an Old Masterpiece," *The Music Review* 34 (1973), 2.

[8] H. C. Robbins Landon, *Haydn; Chronicle and Works* Vol. 4, *Haydn: The Years of "The Creation," 1796–1800* (London: Thames and Hudson, 1977), 181.

[9] Hailparn, 4; Landon, 97. (Landon gives the name as Joseph Friebert.)

[10] Landon, 97.

The well-known influence of Handel on Haydn's oratorios is no less true of *The Seven Last Words* than of those conceived and written after Haydn's visit to England. Haydn does not use his trombones in the traditional Viennese manner of doubling the chorus with occasional soloistic passages. The influence of Handel's *Saul* can be seen clearly in *The Seven Last Words*, although it does follow the traditional Viennese practice of including only two trombone parts, alto and tenor. (The later works have three trombone parts.)

Haydn omits the trombones from the introduction. The first choral movement, a commentary on "Father, forgive them. They know not what they do," uses the trombones to provide sustained harmonic filler. They consistently have the longest notes in the texture and play in the close spacing of Handel's upper trombone parts. They are usually a third apart, sometimes in unison, seldom as much as an octave, and never more. The trombones do not double the chorus at any time. Their parts consist of a modified doubling of various parts, including clarinets, bassoons, violas, and cellos, usually in unison, but sometimes in octaves. Although the orchestration is usually very full while the trombones play, there are a few brief passages of less than a measure each, where almost all the rest of the orchestra stops playing. At these places, the trombones' timbre can come out clearly and reinforce the solemn character of the text. Otherwise, they will probably be more felt than heard.

The foregoing comments adequately describe most of the choral movements, but the details change. The third movement includes no trombones at all. Otherwise, the doubling of other parts ranges from strict doubling to autonomous doubling, that is, where the trombones' notes are played at the unison somewhere else in the orchestration, but where their lines do not duplicate any other instrument for more than a few notes at a time. A few times, notably in the fifth movement, the trombones are the only wind instruments heard. In Ex. 24, the trombones are mostly in unison with the violas and an octave higher than the cellos and choral basses, although there is some deviation. For some brief moments, the trombones have independent counterpoint, lines that cannot be explained in terms of any kind of doubling. Several movements have long stretches of trombone parts in octaves, which contribute to a very cold, bleak mood that exactly suits the text. These passages still have the character of harmonic filler. There is no soloistic writing at all in the choral movements.

Example 24. Haydn: *Die sieben letzten Worte*, number 5, measures 19−25.

In the introduction to the fifth movement, scored for winds only, the trombone parts are much more prominent and thematically much more important. In several places, one or both trombones play along with only one or two other instruments. As can be seen in Ex. 25, the trombones have greater rhythmic independence from each other than in the rest of the oratorio.

Example 25. Haydn: *Die sieben letzten Worte*, Introduzione [2], measures 4–8.

Haydn marked his trombone parts with care, calling for a wide variety of both dynamics and, what is rare for the eighteenth century, articulations. Nearly every movement includes slurs and staccato. The range is much wider than Haydn could have used if he had merely used the trombones to double the chorus; the alto trombone part extends from e^b to $e^{b'''}$, and the tenor trombone from B^b to c''. Clearly both players need a strong embouchure, especially considering that Haydn saves the highest note for the last movement.

LUDWIG VAN BEETHOVEN

Christus am Oelberge (op. 86)

Sacred choral music occupies only a small place in Beethoven's output: two masses and one oratorio. Of these, two require trombones: *Christus am Oelberge* (op. 86) and *Missa solemnis* (op. 123). One secular choral work, the Ninth Symphony (op. 125), also uses trombones. Only the first named falls within the chronological limits of this study.

Beethoven offered his oratorio to the public with high hopes on the same program with his first two symphonies and third piano concerto. At first, it was the most favorably received of these works, but before long, critics began to find fault with both the text and the music. Beethoven made some important revisions between the first performance of the work (1803) and its publication (1811), but for whatever reason, he never attempted to compose another oratorio.

Christus am Oelberge depicts Christ's struggle within himself on the night that he was betrayed. He prays for deliverance from his impending execution, but the angel of God informs him that the divine plan must be carried out. Immediately after his arrest, an angel chorus sings of God's great victory, for in the moment that Christ's enemies believe they have silenced him, they have merely played into God's hands in order that sin and the forces of evil might be defeated forever.

In Beethoven's handling of the trombone, he represents the tradition that can be traced through Haydn back to Handel rather than the Austrian tradition exemplified by Fux and Mozart. Beethoven's trombone parts are largely independent. They never slavishly double the chorus as in traditional Austrian church music, but they never take on a soloistic role, either.

In common with most German-speaking composers, Beethoven uses trombones to represent the voice of God. They appear in the introduction, Jesus's opening recitative (his prayer for deliverance), an angel chorus, and the Seraph's announcement of God's will. Then they fall silent during the entire arrest scene until the final victory chorus. But although trombones would call up such images in the minds of German-speaking musicians of the eighteenth century, such images did not immediately call trombones to Beethoven's mind. Ferdinand Ries reported that he discovered Beethoven sitting in bed the morning of the premiere of *Christus am Oelberge* writing the trombone parts as an afterthought.[11]

Beethoven begins his oratorio with a note of foreboding, that is, an e^b minor arpeggio with bassoons, horns, and the lower two trombones. The brighter alto trombone does not participate in the introduction at all. Although the score is marked "Trombone Basso" for the lowest part, Beethoven clearly expected it to be played on a

---

[11] Alan Tyson, "The 1803 Version of Beethoven's Christus am Oelberge," *The Musical Quarterly* 56 (1970), 559, n. 11.

trombone in B^b; he avoids the low E^b, which he surely would
have used without hesitation if it had been available. (The ranges
Beethoven uses for the entire oratorio are g to d'' for the alto
trombone, c to a' for the tenor, and F to c' for the "bass.") see Ex.
26. For most of the rest of the movement, the bass trombone plays
mostly a modified doubling of the cello and bass parts. The tenor
trombone usually plays either an octave below the first violins or
first clarinet or an octave above the bass trombone. Rhythmically,
the trombone parts are comparable to the other wind parts when
they play at all, which is only 17 out of 54 measures.

Example. 26. Beethoven. *Christus am Oelberge*, number 1, measures 1−2.

Jesus's opening recitative follows the introduction without pause.
The alto trombone joins the others for the two short passages that
the trombones play. Both of these passages can be described in
terms of unison or octave doubling, but the rhythmic structure
guarantees that the trombones' timbre will be heard; the trombones'
attack points are different from much of the rest of the orchestra,
and occasionally they hold their notes while other instruments have
rests.

Trombones do not participate in Jesus's aria or in the recitative
and aria of the Seraph that follow. The angel chorus at the end of

the Seraph's aria is in two sections. The second includes trombones in their most extensive role so far in the oratorio: 69 of the last 92 measures. They double the opening interval of all parts of the choral fugato. Afterward, the alto and tenor trombones play largely independent parts, while the bass trombone remains closely allied to the bassoons, cellos, and basses. The most noteworthy feature of this movement, for the trombones, is their participation in a long soft passage. It is scored for full orchestra, but only the strings, flute, and trombones play throughout. The other winds instruments play only alternate measures. More common eighteenth-century practice was for the trombones to drop out during soft passages. Beethoven uses them as the only sustaining instruments, giving them a more prominent and important role than they have in most nonsoloistic movements.

The next appearance of trombones was singled out for comment by the reviewer for the *Zeitung für die Elegante Welt*: "There are a few admirable passages: an air of the Seraph with trombone accompaniment in particular makes an excellent effect."[12] Ironically, it is these trombone parts in particular that seem to have been added at the last minute. The reviewer must have meant the recitative in which Jesus asks God's will and the Seraph declares that he must go to the cross. For seven measures, she is accompanied only by oboes, clarinets, bassoons, trombones, and low strings. Apparently, the color of the trombones dominated the entire accompaniment, as indeed it should, dramatically speaking. See Ex. 27.

In the final chorus, the trombone parts are once again largely autonomous, except for the bass trombone, which stays close to the cello part. The alto and tenor trombones double various other parts, including the chorus for a few brief passages, but do not follow any one part for very long. They play in 99 of 173 measures in this movement. Rhythmically, they are comparable to the trumpets and horns, playing longer notes than the chorus, woodwinds, and strings.

In *Christus am Oelberge*, Beethoven stays closer to the Handel-Haydn model than in the *Missa solemnis* or the Ninth Symphony. In the later works, Beethoven uses the trombone to double the chorus in some sections, although not as slavishly as in earlier Austrian church music. Beethoven's use of trombones as a doubling instrument is interesting chiefly for the deviations. The trombones drop

---

[12] Quoted by Tyson, 551.

Example. 27. Beethoven: *Christus am Oelberge*, number 3, measures 7–13.

Text: Eh' nicht erfillet ist das heilige Geheimnis der Versöhnung, so lange
bleibt das menschliche Geschlecht verworfen und beraubt des ew'gen
Lebens

Example 27, continued

out during some soft passages, and the alto trombone frequently drops out for several beats when the altos sing notes higher than d''. In places where the trombones do not double the chorus in these later works, Beethoven uses them in a manner that seems based on the French operatic style of writing for trombone, which Beethoven adopted for his Fifth and Sixth Symphonies. See Chapter 7 for descriptions of these two works.

CHAPTER 6
THE TROMBONE IN OPERA

Trombones appeared in operatic orchestras as early as Monteverdi's *Orfeo* of 1607. They participated in only a handful of operas, however, and by mid-century seem to have disappeared from the theater. I have found no trace of the operatic use of trombones in the eighteenth century until Gluck used them in *Orfeo ed Euridice* in 1762, although it is quite possible that some now-forgotten composer used them earlier. In any case, *Orfeo* is not the first appearance in eighteenth-century theater music. Gluck used one in his ballet *Don Juan* in 1761 and Handel used three in each of his oratorios *Saul*, *Samson*, and *Israel in Egypt* between 1738 and 1741.

Oddly enough, given the gap of almost a century, both the seventeenth-century operas and the earliest eighteenth-century operas with trombones used the instrument to portray supernatural, and most often, infernal characters.

Aside from five Austrian operas (Gluck's *Orfeo ed Euridice*, Haydn's *L'anima del filosofo: ossia Orfeo ed Euridice*, and Mozart's *Don Giovanni*, *Idomeneo*, and *Die Zauberflöte*) and one Russian opera (*Nachal'noe upravlenie Olega* by the Italian composer Giuseppe Sarti and others, who wrote and produced it in St. Petersburg in 1790) only French operas were available to me for examination. These can be divided into three groups: those produced before the French Revolution, post-Revolutionary operas intended

229

for the Opéra, and those produced at one of the smaller theaters. In the years after the Revolution, the Opéra continued to employ three trombonists, while the smaller theaters, for the most part, had only one. (In about 1797, the Théâtre de la rue Feydeau added a second trombonist to its staff.)

The best of these French operas are, for the most part, those in the first category. Neither of the others are still represented in the repertoire. The operas most significant for later developments are those in the third category. The Opéra fell on hard times during the 1790s. It produced no new works during the 1795−96 season.[1] New works produced thereafter until the end of the century were not engraved.[2] While productions at the Opéra continued to be more pretentious than those of the smaller theaters, they were not any more significant. In fact, the trombone parts are generally duller.

The second of these categories includes two works, Steibelt's *Roméo et Juliette* and Lesueur's *Télémaque dans l'île de Calypso*, that were rejected by the Opéra and actually produced at the Théâtre de la rue Feydeau, where the top two trombone parts were almost certainly not played, yet, in both cases, the published scores show parts for three trombones.

ACCURACY OF PRINTED SCORES

My earlier skepticism about the reliability of printed scores[3] has been confirmed by later research. The analyses of specific works in this chapter are offered subject to a few additional warnings.

Scores of works produced at the Opéra were not intended to be used as the basis of performances at other theaters. The only other places that gave these works were comparably large theaters in other musical capitals. These theaters presented French *tragédie lyrique* only with substantial modifications, if at all. Therefore, publishers had little reason to be scrupulously accurate and authentic. They did have economic incentives to save time and paper. And so

---

[1] David Charlton, *Orchestration and Orchestral Practice in Paris* 1789−1810 (Ph.D. dissertation: King's College, University of Cambridge, 1973), 8.

[2] Ibid., 372.

[3] David Guion, "The Instrumentation of Operas Published in France in the 18th Century," *Journal of Musicological Research* 4 (1982), 119.

they frequently omitted whole sections of music, such as ballets, and certain parts for trombone, clarinet, and percussion.[4]

At times, the entire trombone part was left out of the score. No hint of trombone parts exists in the score of Gluck's *Orphée et Euridice* (1774), even though three trombones participated in the performance.[5] At other times, trombone parts were printed partially and haphazardly. Cherubini's *Demophoon* (1788), for example, requires three trombones in the overture and in several scenes of the opera. The score contains some trombone parts, but none in the overture.[6] Numerous other scores include trombone parts only in the overture. An examination of part books would probably reveal more extensive use of the trombone in most of these works.

Charlton reports that Cherubini's *Anacréon* (1803) and Blangini's *Nephtali* (1806) "achieve complete accuracy in the clarinet and trombone parts, and are laid out with clarity."[7] Since virtually all works given at the Opéra examined for this dissertation were engraved before these two, presumably none is completely accurate. And certainly none is laid out with clarity.

Works intended for the smaller theaters used smaller orchestras, and so the scores did not take up so much room. The printed scores are therefore generally more reliable, although the addition of trombone to these works in about 1791 caused some problems at first. In at least one case, Dalayrac's *Camille* (1791), the trombone part was omitted from the score entirely. The engraver called attention to the existence of separate parts, which Charlton was unable to locate.[8] How many other operas were engraved with neither trombone part nor engraver's note is impossible to guess. On the whole, however, if a trombone part is given at all, it can usually be trusted to be complete. Some of the earliest works, however, such as Cherubini's *Lodoïska* (1791) include trombones only in the overture. Here again, it makes little sense dramatically, and therefore the likelihood is that, if parts are ever found, they will reveal at least some use of the trombone within the body of the opera.

---

[4] Charlton, 7.

[5] Théodore de Lajarte, "Introduction du trombone dans l'orchestre de l'Opéra," *La chronique musicale* 6 (Oct.–Dec. 1874), 76.

[6] Charlton, 8.

[7] Ibid., 9.

[8] Ibid., 11.

Plate 17. Anonymous 18th-Century Dutch Etching.

Reprinted from *The Trumpet & Trombone in Graphic Arts: 1500–1800* by
Tom L. Naylor © 1979 The Brass Press. Used by permission.

OPERA IN VIENNA

Orfeo ed Euridice

Music: Christoph Willibald Gluck
Libretto (Italian): Raniero Calzabigi
Libretto (French): Pierre Louis Moline
Premieres: Burgtheater (Vienna), October 5, 1762;
          Opéra (Paris), August 2, 1774.
First editions: Paris: Duchesne, 1764; Lemarchand, 1774.

Gluck's *Orfeo ed Euridice* appears to be the earliest opera in the eighteenth century to use trombones, although such a statement can be made only with fear and trembling. German and Austrian operas of the eighteenth century have not received much scholarly attention yet (except for acknowledged masterpieces), and hardly anyone mentions the instrumentation of operas except in passing.

Orfeo was written to celebrate the emperor's name day, and was therefore not a full-length opera.[9] Gluck arranged to have the score printed in Paris shortly after the premiere, but the opera received no further performances until 1769, when it was given under Gluck's direction at Parma. Thereafter, it became known worldwide, with performances in London, Florence, Bologna, Munich, Stockholm, Naples, and Paris. Most of these performances contained additional music in order to expand *Orfeo* to a full-length opera.[10] Many of these were pasticcios, with the new music being provided by other composers. The Paris version was Gluck's own. No scholar has yet seen fit to mention how much of the original instrumentation remained intact in the pasticcios, but comparisons can be made between Gluck's two versions.

The Vienna version is in three short acts. In the opening scene, Orpheus and the chorus are mourning the death of Euridice, Orpheus's wife. By the end of the first act, Orpheus has decided to visit the underworld to bring her back to life. At the opening of the second act, the Furies attempt to bar the living (Orpheus) from entering the realm of the dead. But his music is so beautiful and irresistible that they relent and allow him to pass. Euridice is allowed to return to life, but only if Orpheus does not look at her or explain his behavior. He does look, of course, and she dies again. But the occasion of the emperor's name-day, not to mention eighteenth-century taste, would not have permitted the opera to end there. The god of love restores Euridice to Orpheus once again, and they all live happily ever after.

---

[9] Daniel Heartz, "*Orfeo ed Euridice*: Some Criticisms, Revisions, and Stage Realizations During Gluck's Lifetime," *Chigiana* 29—30, n.s. 9—10 (1972—73), 385.

[10] Michael F. Robinson, "The 1775 S. Carlo Version of Gluck's *Orfeo*," *Chigiana* 29—30, n.s. 9—10 (1972—73), 396.

Analysis

Gluck used trombones in only two scenes, the opening funeral scene and the beginning of the second act, where Orpheus overcomes the Furies. In the latter scene, the trombones are associated with the chorus. Thus, the gloom of death hangs heavily whenever the trombones are heard. Gluck used an orchestra of pairs of flutes, clarinets, oboes, English horns, bassoons, cornetts, horns, and trumpets, in addition to three trombones, timpani, harp, harpsichord, and strings. At no point does the entire orchestra play together. In fact, the numbers with trombone parts include no other wind instruments except the cornetts. Dramatic and affective considerations demand that the timbre of the trombone dominate these numbers.

In the opening scene, for chorus, Orpheus, and orchestra, Orpheus is so overcome with grief that he can only sob Euridice's name. The trombones play throughout the number, except that the brass trombone has eight measures of rest along with the basses in the chorus. Whenever the chorus sings, the trombones and cornetts double it exactly. In purely instrumental sections, the wind instruments double the strings, but not as strictly. For example, in the fourteen-measure introduction (see Ex. 28), the alto trombone part is identical with the viola part for seven of the first eight measures. Then it switches its allegiance to the violins, but does not double either partly exactly.

The trombone's rhythms are comparable to those of other parts except that they include fewer eighth notes. So while there is no radical difference between string parts with very short notes and trombone parts with very long notes, as in much orchestral music, the trombones are still relatively more sustained. In this regard, the bass trombone's modification of the bass line is noteworthy. (See Ex. 28.)

Example 28. Gluck: *Orfeo ed Euridice*, Act I, scene i, measures 1–14.

Example 28, continued.

Example 28, continued.

Gluck uses the trombones in a predominantly open spacing in this movement. The bass trombone's tessitura is moderately low and the alto trombone part lies rather high. Unless the high tessitura of the alto trombone causes endurance problems, this movement poses no technical difficulties.

A short reprise of the opening chorus occurs after a brief arioso and ballo. Most of the foregoing comments apply to the reprise as well. The trombones are next heard in the confrontation between Orpheus and the Furies near the opening of the second act, which requires two orchestras, one to accompany Orpheus and the other for the chorus. The first 110 measures of the act alternate between instrumental and choral sections. Orpheus's harp is heard briefly before the first choral entrance, but Orpheus himself does not appear on stage until the brief ballet beginning with measure 91. The actual confrontation begins with the pickup to measure 111. Up to this point, the Furies' orchestra has included oboes and horns, but no trombones.

The confrontation itself occupies 43 measures. As in the opening scene, trombones and cornetts are the only wind instruments heard in this section. But unlike the first act, where three trombones played constantly, there are only two trombones here, playing in 13 scattered measures. Orpheus, accompanied by strings and harp, sings a beautiful arioso, which the chorus interrupts with the word "No!." It is always in octaves, and its orchestra usually doubles it exactly.

The tension between the soft, soothing harp and loud, abrasive trombones mirrors the dramatic tension on stage. Once again, therefore, the color of the trombones must predominate before ultimately losing to the harp. The trombones remain silent for the rest of the opera.

French version, 1774

When Gluck produced *Orphée et Euridice* in Paris, he demonstrated a detailed familiarity with the conventions of French opera, French text setting, and Parisian performing conditions. I have already expressed the belief that trombonists in Paris were less proficient than those in Vienna, but it would be difficult to tell from a comparison of the two versions whether Gluck in fact expected less of them. Potential problems of endurance are just as great in the Paris version as in the Vienna version. But the trombones are not so nearly alone when they play. The full orchestra is not quite the same for the Paris version; Gluck added a pair of clarinets and deleted the cornetts, English horns, and harpsichord.

The trombones appear in the same two scenes in both versions. For the Paris version of the opening scene, the cornetts are replaced by the clarinets, and two bassoons join the bass line. Other changes in the movement are minor enough not to require comment here.

The only other appearance of trombones is once again in the confrontation between Orpheus and the Furies. The brief introduction is essentially the same music as in the Vienna version. The oboes and horns are here joined by bassoons, trumpets, and trombones. The trombones play throughout; any lightening of texture is achieved by the omission of the trumpets and horns. Rhythmically, it is not the trombones but the other brasses that have the longest notes in the texture. The trombones double the strings strictly, although the alto and tenor trombones do not double the same parts throughout.

After a three-measure interlude by Orpheus's orchestra, the chorus enters, once again with an expanded orchestra, including the trombones. The trombones double the chorus. Gluck omitted the ballo that in Vienna came between this chorus and the actual confrontation. Once again, Gluck enlarged the orchestra, adding, among other instruments, the third trombone. When the chorus sings "Non!," the orchestra backs it in full harmony instead of unison.

It was after this number that the trombones ceased to play in the Vienna version, but the Furies are only beginning to relent. In Paris, the trombones double the chorus in the next number as well until the last nine measures, where the text is "Il est vainqueur" (He is the winner.) Gluck added an instrumental "Air de Furies" to finish the scene. It seems to be one of the obligatory Paris ballets that merely impede the dramatic flow. Trombones play in 55 out of 195 measures, providing rhythmic punctuation and, dramatically, continuing the identification with the Furies.

The trombones parts that Gluck added for the Paris performance generally have lower tessituras than the parts remaining from the Vienna version, although at one point, where the alto trombone doubles the sopranos, he writes c'', which is the highest note he wrote for Vienna. Dramatically, the identification of trombones and Furies is more complete in Paris, although the addition of other wind instruments dilutes the trombone timbre.

Conductors must not allow the trombones to be lost in the texture; their absence from the final measures of the last chorus must be noticeable. Berlioz later wrote that Gluck erred in adding trombones to the second act before the chorus tells first Orpheus, "Non!"[11] He believed that the introduction of the trombone's timbre before this number weakened its effect. That is perhaps an arguable point, but surely the addition of trombones to the following chorus, and their dropping out for the last nine measures, is an improvement.

Don Giovanni

Music: Wolfgang Amadeus Mozart
Libretto: Lorenzo da Ponte
Premiere: Prague, October 29, 1787
No eighteenth-century score seen.

Although the largest number of operas available for examination is French, the best are Austrian, specifically those of Mozart. Given the extensive and effective use of the trombone in the operas of Gluck and Mozart, it is inconceivable that lesser composers in Austria and Bohemia did not also use them. Unfortunately, most Austrian operas were not published, and Mozart so greatly over-shadowed his contemporaries that little interest has been shown in them since their works passed from the repertoire. It is therefore not possible even to offer a list of Austrian operas that used trombone.

Mozart used trombones in three operas: *Idomeneo* (K. 366), *Don Giovanni* (K. 527), and *Die Zauberflöte* (K. 620). Significantly, these are his only operas with strong supernatural or religious elements, and the trombones have no other function but to support those elements.

Don Giovanni concerns a dissolute nobleman whose only occupation seems to be seducing women. In the opening scene, he kills an old man in a duel. By the middle of the second act, he has given

---

[11] Hector Berlioz, *Gluck & His Operas, with an Account of Their Relation to Musical Art*, trans. Edwin Evans (London: Reeves, 1914), 7.

nearly everyone else in the cast reason to seek his death. The dead man's daughter and her lover, as well as a woman whom the Don had earlier jilted, seek vengeance. The Don's attempt to seduce a young bride stirs her husband to violence. But the Don's cunning and social position, and the ambivalence of some of his adversaries, enable him to laugh off the threats and continue his plans without serious opposition. But then, in a churchyard, the dead man's statue comes to life and denounces him. The Don merely instructs his servant Leporello to invite the statue to dinner. From then on, he refuses several opportunities to repent of his evil ways, and the statue arrives with a chorus of demons to carry him off to the underworld.

Analysis

Trombones are so closely associated with the statue that Mozart does not even use them in the overture. In the churchyard scene, an offstage band of two oboes, two clarinets, two bassoons, three trombones, cello, and bass play while the statue sings. Otherwise, the scene is entirely in recitative. The upper trombones are doubled by the bassoons and the bass trombone by the strings. The oboes and clarinets play an upper line that completes the four-part harmony. (See Ex. 29.) It would be easy to allow the other instruments to cover the sound of the trombones. It would also be a mistake. Mozart so carefully saved the trombones for this solemn occasion that their color must dominate the scene.

The scene before the statue's next appearance is full of foreshadowing. The orchestra even depicts its knocking at the door. There are no trombones, however, until it actually steps on stage. At first, they play only while the statue sings. Gradually, however, they encroach on Don Giovanni's comments, symbolizing that, little by little, he is coming under the statue's absolute power. By the time an offstage chorus replaces the statue's singing lines, the trombones play every measure until just before the end of the movement. When the Don is carried to his just reward, the trombones fall silent for a measure and a half, during which the rest of the orchestra sinks to a menacing quietness, only to return with full force to underline Leporello's scream of terror. Another six measures, and the movement is over. Trombones take no part in the final ensemble.

Example 29. Mozart: *Don Giovanni*, Act II, scene xi, measures 50—54

Besides the close association with the statue, Mozart's use of trombones underlines the dramatic significance of this scene by not using complete chords. Triads played on trombones are among the most lushly beautiful sounds that a composer can use. In addition, German-speaking lands in the eighteenth century considered the trombone to be the voice of God. The simple dignity of Austrian church music can be seen in the graveyard scene. But if, when the statue comes to supper, the trombones represent the voice of God, it is his wrath and judgment. The trombones foreshadow not heaven, but hell. Mozart's frequent use of octaves and unisons within the trombone section robs the triads of their completeness, leaving starkness and harshness in place of what would otherwise have been an unfitting beauty.

FRANCE: BEFORE THE REVOLUTION

Tarare

Music: Antonio Salieri
Libretto: Pierre Auguste Caron de Beaumarchais
Premiere: Opéra (Paris), June 8, 1787
Score published by Imbault. Modern edition by Henle (1978)

As noted earlier, Gluck took his Viennese association of trombones with the supernatural to France. The story of the trombone in French opera after Gluck shows the gradual disappearance of this association and the growing use of trombones in other dramatic settings. Among the composers whose works exemplify this trend is Gluck's student Antonio Salieri. *Tarare*, often considered his best opera, was not, initially his idea. French playwright Caron de Beaumarchais had been forced to rewrite his play *Le barbier de Seville* several times. It did not become successful until he edited out most of the philosophical message he wanted to convey. Therefore, he decided to write an operatic libretto, hoping that a musical medium would make his ideas more palatable to the public.[12]

Beaumarchais approached Gluck, who was then (1775) at the height of his popularity in Paris. The composer's well-known opinion that music should be subordinated to the drama probably influenced Beaumarchais's choice. Gluck expressed a definite interest, but by the time Beaumarchais finally finished the libretto, Gluck's health would no longer permit him to compose another opera. He liked the libretto, however, and recommended that Beaumarchais invite Salieri, his student and successor, to compose the music.

Tarare enjoyed great success from the first performance. Under the name *Axur, Re d'Ormus*, with an Italian libretto by Lorenzo da Ponte, the opera was even more successful in Vienna.[13] Unfortunately, I have not been able to see that version.

---

[12] George Lemaitre, *Beaumarchais* (New York: Knopf, 1949), 161.
[13] Alfred Loewenberg, *Annals of Opera, 1597−1940*, 3rd ed., rev. and cor. (Totowa, NJ: Roman and Littlefield, 1978), col. 443.

Summary

Because *Tarare* uses the trombone in more scenes than the other operas so far discussed, it will be necessary to give a much more detailed synopsis. The opera opens with an overture and prologue. The entire cast, presented as unborn spirits, waits to be animated by the Spirit of Fire. The Spirit of Nature, who created them, shows Fire the two largest shades and asks him to choose one as king. He selects Atar, and so Tarare is destined to be a mere soldier. The two spirits then decide to wait about forty years and look in on the outcome.

Act I

After a second and very different overture, the curtain rises on Atar in a jealous rage against Tarare. The soldier has committed the unpardonable crime of being happy, even though the king is miserable. Atar sends Altamort, son of the high priest, to wreck Tarare's cottage and abduct his beautiful wife, Astasie, whom he renames Irza. Having finally made Tarare unhappy, Atar cheerfully grants him leave to seek vengeance. He sends Altamort along, ostensibly to serve him, but actually to make sure that he does not return alive.

Act II

Meanwhile, Arthenée, the high priest, has discovered a military threat against the kingdom. A general must be chosen in a special religious ceremony, named by a young boy in a trance. King and priest conspire to rig the ceremony so that Altamort will become general. Before the ceremony takes place, Calpigi, the head eunuch, tells Tarare the full truth about Atar's treachery. And then, despite the efforts of Atar and Arthenée, the boy names Tarare as general. When a shocked and angry Altamort challenges him to a duel, he coldly accepts.

Act III

The hot-headed and inexperienced Altamort is no match for Tarare. When Atar hears of Altamort's death, the ever-fickle king orders

Calpigi to prepare a feast for "Irza" one day ahead of schedule. Calpigi has already made arrangements with Tarare to steal his wife back and has no time to warn him of the change of plans. Tarare arrives during the feast behind Atar's back and barely has time to hide. When Atar takes Astasie into her chamber to seduce her, Calpigi disguises Tarare as a mute. The faithful Astasie fights off Atar long enough for him to lose interest. Leaving her chamber, Atar sees, but does not recognize Tarare and decides it would be fun to force Astasie to marry the mute.

Act IV

For some reason, when Calpigi informs Astasie of her fate, he neglects to mention who the mute is. She trades clothes with one of the women of the harem. Tarare discovers the switch right away, but has no time to consider what to do next. Atar has changed his mind again and sent soldiers to murder the mute and throw him in the ocean. When the soldiers discover that the mute is their general, they reluctantly arrest him, fearing Atar's vengeance if they let him go.

Act V

Atar gleefully prepares to torture both Tarare and "Irza," but when the couple is finally reunited, they happily face death with utter contentment. As Atar ponders his total inability to make them suffer, his army mounts a coup. Only one way remains for him to make Tarare miserable: he kills himself and names Tarare king. The Spirits of Nature and Fire return, commenting that while fate can determine outer circumstances, character determines the final outcome. King Tarare will rule in wisdom and contentment, greatly loved by his people.

Analysis

Salieri used trombones in seven numbers:

1. The first overture and first scene of the prologue, from the section marked "Pantomine des Vents" until the Spirit of Nature commands the winds to cease.

2. Atar's aria at the close of the first act, in which he gloats about his plan to murder Tarare and seduce the grieving widow.
3. The rigged oracle at the end of the second act. Trombones accompany Arthenée's invocation of the gods. Later, after the young boy lamely explains that the gods inspired him to name Altamort but that Tarare popped out of his mouth, the people clamor for Tarare as the gods' true choice. Trombones reinforce their demand, underlining his name twice.
4. The aria of Urson, captain of the guards, in the third act, in which he describes the duel (which takes place between the acts.) Trombones accompany his description of Altamort's stormy appearance.
5. Tarare's recitative in the third act, in which he describes to Calpigi his narrow escape from Atar's latest attempt to ambush him. (This number takes place after the feast breaks up and before Calpigi provides Tarare with his disguise.)
6. Atar's inventory of his instruments of torture as the curtain rises on the fifth act.
7. The "Choeur funèbre des esclaves" in the fifth act as Tarare and Astasie are being prepared for death, shortly before they recognize each other.

Salieri uses the trombones sparingly in most of these scenes, but with good dramatic effect. Only in the final chorus do the trombones play as many as half the measures. By contrast, the oracle scene lasts 93 measures, of which the trombones play in only 15. Dramatically, these scenes represent some departure from Gluck's practice, in that Salieri uses trombones even when supernatural connotations are absent. He did not break entirely new ground, however; the smell of death and gloom hangs heavily over each scene.

The range (alto, f to b'; tenor e^b to $a^{b'}$, bass E^b to f') is comparable to what Gluck used. And like Gluck, Salieri uses a fairly narrow range in each scene. The E^b in the third trombone part in exceptional and may not have been intended. For the "Choeur funèbre des esclaves", Imbault's engraver indicates that the third trombone should double the third and fourth bassoons. The modern edition includes no critical report and no indication whether the editor consulted part books or manuscript sources. (Therefore, if the Imbault edition omits any trombone parts, the modern edition gives no clue.) In all likelihood, the third trombone played e^b with the cellos rather than E^b with the bassoons. (See Ex. 30.) If so, the third trombone's lowest note is *G*, which is much more typical of the time. The alto trombone part includes passages that Vandenbroek later declared impossible, approaching high notes by leap. (See Ex. 30.)

Example 30. Salieri: *Tarare*, Act V, scene iv, measures 39–47.

The scoring is usually heavy. There are places, however, where the trombones are the only brass instruments heard. When Urson describes Altamort's appearance at the duel, even the strings drop out, leaving only trombones and bassoons. (See Ex. 31.) In Atar's aria at the opening of the fifth act, the wind section includes only oboes, bassoons, and trombones. The funeral chorus is in three parts. The outer sections are accompanied only by a wind band. The brief middle section, a solo by the high priest, is accompanied only by strings and two trombones. Here again, the engraver's decision not to make a separate line for the third trombone raises questions.

There should probably be three trombones here, with the third doubling the cellos.

Rhythmically, the trombone parts are very static. Until the last act, Salieri writes only sustained chords. In two brief passages in Atar's aria, the trombones have repeated notes against sustained notes in the oboes and bassoons. In the funeral chorus, the alto and tenor trombones join the rest of the orchestra (except for the low bassoons and bass trombone) in playing eighth notes and dotted eighth-sixteenth figures.

Example 31. Salieri: *Tarare*, Act III, scene ii, measures 36−40

Text: Son aspect est farouche et sombre comme les spectres de la nuit

Roland

Music: Nicola Piccinni
Libretto: Jean-François Marmontel
Premiere: Opéra (Paris), January 27, 1778
Published by Piccinni; no modern edition

   Roland, the first of Piccinni's operas in French, met with success, although his career in Paris eventually ended in failure. Piccinni selected a libretto by Phillippe Quinault, which had been set earlier by Lully. He used a revised version by Jean-François Marmontel, which reduced Quinault's five acts to three.

   As the opera opens, Angelique is torn between love and pride. She has two suitors. One, Médor, is a poor man of lowly birth. Angelique had found him dying by the side of the road, nursed him back to life, and fallen in love. But she is a queen, and her pride does not permit her to marry beneath her station. Roland, on the other hand, is a great military hero and quite wealthy, but Angelique has no regard for him. Roland does not appear on stage until the middle of the second act. By this time, Angelique has banished Médor, become thoroughly miserable, and decided to take him back. At Roland's first appearance, Angelique makes herself invisible. By the time he actually sees her for the first time in his life, she has found Médor and refuses to consider Roland's claims. Except for Roland, none of the characters introduced in the first two acts appear in the third, in which he reluctantly abandons his dream of winning Angelique, admits ignominious defeat in love, and returns to the service of his king.

Analysis

Piccinni's orchestration was unusually lavish in his Italian period. When he arrived in France, where the orchestra was fuller, he became even more elaborate in his orchestration.[14] In its use of the trombone, *Roland* differs greatly from other pre-Revolutionary operas. It is ahead of its time in requiring only one trombone and in not having any supernatural connotations or any other identifiable affective significance except possibly sadness or sorrow. But it does

---

[14] Dennis Libby and Julian Rushton, "Piccinni, (1) Niccolò," *The New Grove*, vol. 14, 726.

not sink into the dreary dullness of the majority of post-Revolutionary trombone parts.

In the printed score, the trombone appears only in two of Angeliques's arias in the first act. The very opening number uses an orchestra of two oboes, bassoon, two horns, trombone and strings. (The instrumentation of the rest of the opera includes flutes, piccolos, clarinets, trumpets, and timpani.) The trombone never plays while any other instrument is resting. Although its part doubles the second oboe (two octaves lower) at times, it is largely autonomous. The most unusual feature is that it does not always have the longest notes in the texture. In fact, for one brief moment, the trombone has the most active of the wind parts, and this in a fast movement. (See Ex. 32.)

The range (e^b to f) is quite moderate, even by Parisian standards, and well within the limits Vandenbroek later proposed. Rhythmically, the passage just mentioned is probably the most difficult, and it hardly requires the performer to move the slide. The trombone part is thus very easy, but nonetheless rewarding. And since the trombone's note is often needed in order to complete the harmony in its register, its color will be noticed.

The second aria is very similar, using the same orchestra, the same tempo, and even the same key signature, being in the relative minor. The trombone part shows a bit less autonomy, having much in common with the cellos and bassoon. It has several scale passages in eighth note that may be somewhat more difficult than the moving part in the other aria, although there is no point here in which the trombone moves faster than the other parts. Otherwise, the same comments apply.

FRANCE: DURING AND AFTER THE REVOLUTION

Most operas produced during and after the Revolution were intended for one of the smaller theaters and therefore had only one trombone part, invariably bass trombone. (That is, in function. The instrument itself was usually a tenor trombone in B^b.) It merely doubled the bass line, modifying it to omit all embellishment and rhythmic interest. So little did composers trust the trombone, or so it seems, that they changed even octave leaps at cadences. At least as often as not, if the cellos and basses played a dominant above and then below the resolution to the tonic, the trombone merely repeated the

Example 32. Piccinni: *Roland*, Act I, scene i, measures 28—34

Example 32, continued.

las fu-neste A-mour   gloi _____

upper octave. (See Ex. 33). This distrust predates the Revolution. In Vogel's *Demophon* (1788), the bass trombone line is altered to avoid a cadential octave leap down to *F* even though elsewhere the part descends to *C* and thus must be played on a true bass trombone. The trombone was most often in unison with the cellos, but it was sometimes an octave higher. Occasionally it was an octave lower. Wholly independent measures are few and far between.

Example 33. Dalayrac: *Léhéman*, number 5, measures 112–14

While the bulk of post-Revolutionary operas had only one trombone part, those written for the Opéra continued to require three. These are few in number and do not contain nearly as many important works compared with either pre-Revolutionary operas or those composed for the smaller theaters. They do not use all three trombones throughout the opera; some or even most movements use only one or two trombones. Invariably, the bass (i.e. third) trombone is the most important.

Roméo et Juliette

Music: Daniel Steibelt
Libretto: Joseph Ségur
Premiere: Théâtre de la rue Feydeau (Paris), September 10, 1793
Score: Boyer et Nadermann; no modern edition

It is difficult for modern writers to take Daniel Steibelt very seriously. He is best known for introducing tambourine parts into his piano sonatas, for coming out second best in an ill-considered challenge to Beethoven, and for a general lack of moral scruples in his business dealings. *Roméo et Juliette* is the first of several operas he composed, and the only significant one.

Roméo et Juliette was originally written for the Opéra, which declined to produce it. Steibelt revised it for the Théâtre de la rue Feydeau, where it was successfully produced in 1793. The printed score contains three trombone parts, as if the Opéra had mounted the production. The Feydeau probably did not perform it as scored; only one trombonist was on their regular payroll, and hiring extra musicians for larger works seems not to have been the practice in Paris at the time. The upper trombone parts are expendable; they do not strictly double any other part, but their notes are always somewhere in the texture, usually at the unison. Little if anything is lost in leaving them out.

Ségur, the librettist, had special problems in adapting Shakespeare's play as an opera. First, any librettist must cut Shakespeare drastically. Opera moves at a pace so much slower that leaving one of his plays intact would result in an opera both too long and too full of fussy detail and interrupted action to be bearable. Second, eighteenth-century audiences demanded happy endings. Third, 1793 came at the peak of the French government's attempt to expunge all traces of Christianity from French culture. A Catholic friar as a major character in an opera (except, perhaps as a villain or laughing-stock) would have been impossible, or at the very least, inexpedient. Friar Lawrence, therefore, had to be replaced. The resulting libretto bears only the most fleeting and superficial resemblance to Shakespeare's story.

Summary

Act I

The opening monologue, delivered by a character with no equivalent in Shakespeare, and hardly any later relevance in the opera, reveals that Roméo has already killed Théobald and been banished, that Juliette is madly in love with him anyway, and that she plans to meet him on her father's property that night. After Juliette's first aria, Cécile, a young girl who replaces Shakespeare's Nurse, arrives. She has been looking all over for Juliette and is shocked to find her in the very garden where Théobald was murdered, and so late at night. Juliette confesses her love for Roméo and her intention to

Plate 18. Thaleia-Muse of comic Poetry.

Reprinted from *The Trumpet & Trombone in Graphic Arts: 1500–1800* by
Tom L. Naylor © 1979 The Brass Press. Used by permission.

meet him there that night. Cécile leaves, promising continued friendship and imploring Juliette to be careful.

Romeo's first appearance roughly approximates Shakespeare's balcony scene, complete with the discussion between Roméo and Juliette whether the bird they hear is a lark or a nightingale. As soon as Roméo leaves, Cébas, substituting for Friar Lawrence, joins Juliette. Like Cécile, he is surprised to find her still up at that hour. He knows about Roméo, and warns Juliette that Capulet, her father, is on his way to the garden. Capulet, believing that Juliette has not yet gone to bed only because she is mourning Théobald, vows to avenge him and have Roméo executed, then wonders why Juliette turns pale. After she goes to bed, Capulet sings an aria in praise of vengeance and reveals that he has selected Dom Ferdinand (Shakespeare's Paris) to murder Roméo and marry Juliette.

Act II

Cébas tries without success to persuade Capulet to change his mind about rushing Juliette into marriage with Dom Ferdinand. The old man reminds him that his dying wife begged him to marry Juliette to someone who would avenge the deaths of so many Capulets at the hands of the Montaigus. He has chosen Dom Ferdinand. But when Juliette informs him that the name Montaigu is less odious to him than that of Dom Ferdinand is to her, he disowns her.

Juliette vows to kill herself until Cébas tells her of a special potion he learned to make in his native Greece. It will make her appear dead for a while. Then Roméo can rescue her from the tomb and take her away with him. No sooner does Juliette drink the potion than Capulet brings Dom Ferdinand to meet her. In Shakespeare, Juliette is already "dead" by the time her parents and Paris come to awaken her for the wedding, but here, the potion works slowly in front of everyone's eyes. And, of course, Juliette does not miss a note.

Act III

At Juliette's tomb, a chorus of young girls sings a lament, but Cébas chases them away, telling them to sing to Capulet. Roméo, who has received a note from Cébes, sings an aria to Théobald's corpse, declaring that he intends no insult to the dead, but has only come for Juliette. But the note had neglected to mention that Juliette would appear to be dead. When he finds her lifeless body, he begins a great uproar, which Cébas cannot halt.

Capulet and Dom Ferdinand rush on stage from opposite directions, each with a band of armed men. Dom Ferdinand vows to defend the unarmed Roméo from Capulet. Just as it looks like the stage will be littered with corpses in the Shakespearean tradition, Juliette comes out of the tomb, wondering what all the noise is about. The two lovers fall into each other's arms. Everyone forgives everyone else, and they all live happily ever after.

Analysis

Steibelt uses trombones in the overture and nine of fifteen musical numbers:

1. Capulet's aria in praise of vengeance at the end of the first act.
2. A trio with Juliette, Cébas, and Capulet in the second act in which Capulet explains his choice of Dom Ferdinand and disowns Juliette.
3. Juliette's second act aria in which she sings of her hopes and fears as Cébas prepares his potion.
4. The finale of the second act, in which Juliette apparently dies.
5. The chorus of young girls at the beginning of the third act.
6. Roméo's aria to Théobald's corpse and his discovery of Juliette's apparently lifeless body.
7, 8. The confrontation scene with Roméo, Dom Ferdinand, Capulet, and all of the soldiers, at the end of which Juliette leaves the tomb. (This number is divided into two parts in the score, the first ending on a half cadence.)
9. The finale and general rejoicing.

Only the overture uses all three trombones in the printed score. Six scenes require two trombones and three (3, 7, 8 above) use only one, the bass trombone, which is clearly the most important of the three. Not only does it play in three scenes without the others, it plays in more measures than the tenor trombone in the six scenes with two trombones, and in more measures than either of the other trombones in the overture. The alto trombone plays in 71 measures, the tenor 90, and the bass 128 in the 281-measure overture. Even when all three trombones play in the same measure, the bass trombone is often alone on some beats, either anticipating the entrance of the others or continuing through their rests. The tenor trombone occasionally plays alone, but never for more than one measure at a time.

The ranges of the three parts (alto, g to a'; tenor, $f\#$ to $f\#'$; bass, F to b^b) generally fall within Vandenbroek's guidelines, except that every one of the $f\#'$s in the tenor trombone part is approached by leap, which Vandenbroek considered impossible. (See example 34.)

Example 34. Steibelt: *Roméo et Juliette*, Act I, scene x, measures 1–3, 46–49

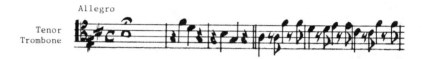

In an overwhelming majority of measures, the bass trombone doubles the cello at the unison, often without rhythmic modification. (That means not that the trombone plays anything rhythmically complex, but that the cello part is usually very plain whenever the trombone plays.) When the trombone and cello are in different octaves, the trombone is somewhat more likely to play the lower than the upper. The avoidance of cadential octaves, so noticeable in so much of French operatic music, is infrequent in *Roméo et Juliette*.

This opera represents a step of sorts in the dramatic emancipation of the trombone. Earlier, the trombone's participation had been largely limited to scenes that offered some combination of supernatural characters, the afterlife, death, or gloom. A composer more traditional is his thinking than Steibelt probably would not have used the trombone until at least the finale of the second act, and very likely not until the opening of the third act, which takes place at the Capulet family mausoleum. At this point, the trombone would have been a fresh timbre, and its long association with the more lugubrious end of opera's emotional palette would have set the scene very effectively. Other wind instruments, and especially other brass instruments, would have largely stayed out of the way.

Here, the trombones, having been used extensively throughout the opera, and being used as part of a brass section instead of by themselves, cannot pack the same emotional punch in Steibelt's hands. To establish a suitably gloomy mood in the mausoleum, Steibelt introduces a gong (or perhaps it is a tuned bell of some sort.)

Just as composers guided by traditional orchestral practice would not have introduced trombones before Juliette's "death," they would not have continued to use them after it became clear that she was still alive. Steibelt's trombone parts continue through the finale. He used his trombones not for any apparent coloristic or affective reasons, but simply because they were available. In this, he seems typical of other post-Revolutionary operatic composers. The way was thus open to using trombones in operas whose plots contained none of the scenes to which they had been limited before. It was also open to finding entirely new situations where the trombone could be used for its color.

By this time (1793), the trombone was a well-known member of the military band. Probably more people heard it in this context than in any other. Not surprisingly, then, Paris saw at least a few operas where the military association is just as strong as supernatural connotations had been earlier.

Léhéman

Music: Nicolas Dalayrac
Libretto: Benoît Joseph Marsollier
Premiere: Opéra Comique (Paris), December 12, 1801
Published by Erard; no modern edition

Léhéman, a rescue opera in three acts, is based on a historical character, Prince Farenc Rákóczi II of Transylvania (Frédéric Ragotzi in the libretto), who led an unsuccessful revolt against Austrian Emperor Leopold I from 1703 to 1711.[15]

Summary

Act I

Frédéric, his captain Léhéman, and his lover Amélina, Léhéman's daughter, have just suffered a military setback. Huddled around a

---

[15] *The New Encyclopaedia Britannica: Micropaedia*, 1975 ed., "Rákóczi II, Farenc."

campfire, outside a tumbled-down hut in a desolate area, they plot their revenge. Over Frédéric's objections, Léhéman sends Amélina away on a perilous spy mission. Upset at being overruled, Frédéric foolishly goes into the hut to put on his uniform. The Austrian army, led by Captain Warner, picks that moment to blunder on stage.

Supposing Léhéman to be an Austrian peasant, Warner asks him if he has seen a young man in a Hungarian uniform. Léhéman says that he has and points out a direction. Warner leads his army in that direction, but leaves two soldiers to stand guard over the hut. Léhéman tricks the guards long enough for Frédéric to get away, but they recognize him as soon as they return.

Fortunately, Warner left two Swiss mercenaries, and not Austrian soldiers. They owe nothing to the emperor, but in an earlier battle, the victorious Léhéman had spared their lives. But if Léhéman's secret is safe, Frédéric's is not; the suspicious Warner divides his unit and captures the Prince. He returns to arrest Léhéman as well. Amélina returns, distraught, to an empty stage.

Act II

Inside the Austrian fortress, Léhéman manages, with great difficulty, to persuade Warner that he and Amélina, who followed everyone else to the castle, are simple peasants, and that Frédéric, merely an ordinary Hungarian soldier, imposed on them. But just as the three rebels and the two Swiss guards begin to breathe easily, an envoy from the emperor arrives and recognizes Frédéric.

Act III

Léhéman's identity is still unknown, but he remains under arrest. Amélina is released. The Swiss guards inform Léhéman that Frédéric will be murdered in his sleep that night. They devise a suitably complicated plot to get Léhéman out of the castle, but fear to help Frédéric, who is too important. At first, Léhéman decides to trade places with Frédéric, but then finds a way for both of them to escape, just in time to surprise and disarm the hired assassins. Meanwhile, Amélina has managed to bring a unit of the Polish army to the castle in order to provide a chorus for the final victory celebration.

Analysis

Léhéman consists of an overture, two entr'actes, and twelve vocal numbers, mostly ensembles, separated by spoken dialogue. Like most post-Revolutionary operas, it uses only one trombone, which joins the overture and eight later numbers. Except for the first entr'acte, one trio, and one aria, these are all choruses. One striking feature of Dalayrac's handling of the trombone here is that it is nearly always associated with the appearance of soldiers. Of the seven vocal numbers with trombone, four involve the Austrian army and one involves the Polish army.

The only two numbers with the trombone and no soldiers are the trio, no. 3, and the aria, no. 10. In both cases, the text takes the form of a prayer. Dalayrac may have intended a reference to the old-fashioned religious connotations. More likely, given the by then well-known association of the trombone with the military band, he may have used it to foreshadow military events. In the first act trio, the situation is more desperate than the rebels realize, because they have no idea that the Austrian army is so close. In the final aria, no. 10, Amélina nervously awaits the arrival of the Polish army, which shortly arrives to sing the chorus no. 11. For some reason, the trombone does not participate in this chorus, the only musical number with soldiers on stage and no trombone. The final chorus, no. 12, does allow the trombone to participate in the general rejoicing.

Basically, the trombone doubles the bass line, either at the unison or an octave higher. Unison doubling occurs in slightly more measures than octave doubling (224 to 209). Some kind of mixture occurs in 87 measures. Only in 41 measures are the trombone and cello parts different enough that the trombone part cannot be analyzed in terms of doubling the cello. Ex. 35 mostly shows a typical relationship between trombone and cello, although it also shows the only moving eighth notes for the trombone in the entire opera. In the penultimate measure of the example, the trombone does not participate in a cadential octave leap. This type of leap is avoided in a similar manner 23 times in *Léhéman*. The trombone plays only two cadential octaves, and both involve longer note values. (See Ex. 36.)

The range of the trombone in *Léhéman*, B to f′, is somewhat higher than that of the typical trombone part written for the smaller theaters. Perhaps for that reason, the percentage of measures in which the trombone is an octave higher than the cello is greater than in other operas that I counted.

More typical is the fact that the trombone part is nearly always

Example 35. Dalayrac. *Léhéman*, number 3, measures 81–95

Example 36. Dalayrac. *Léhéman*, number 3, measures 122–25.

restricted to loud, tutti passages, and that it generally has the longest notes in the texture. This latter point is less typical of *Léhéman* than of the pre-Revolutionary operas, but the difference is not that the later operas have moving parts for trombone, but rather that the trombone frequently has a quarter note and rests in a measure against a sustained note in another part. Except for a few pickups and a very few pairs of eighth notes, the trombone plays nothing shorter than a quarter note. The part presents no technical difficulties to the performer whatsoever.

In less than 30 years, the role of the trombone in French opera changed greatly. Where at first, it had been a rarity, by the end of the century it participated in most operas. Where at first, composers used it only when the action of the opera included supernatural and/or gloomy, deathly elements, by the end of the century it appeared in such a wide variety of dramatic contexts that, for all practical purposes, there was no limit to how and when composers felt free to use it.

The importance of the trombone in operas transcends the theater. Operatic overtures were popular items on concerts. The participation of trombone in concert performances of these pieces paved the way for its eventual inclusion in concertos, symphonies, and other non-theatrical forms.

CHAPTER 7

THE TROMBONE IN THE CONCERT ORCHESTRA

The vast bulk of eighteenth-century music for trombone also requires voices, either in church or in the opera house. The small number of exceptional pieces can be divided into four parts: concertos and other solos with orchestral accompaniment, chamber music, band music, orchestral music. C. Robert Wigness has written about most of the available solo and chamber music.[1] Whatever else needs to be said about it has already been covered in the section on Austrian music in Chapter 3. There may have been dozens of concertos, divertimentos, and chamber works with soloistic parts for trombone written in the Habsburg realms, but I have seen very little beyond that already described by Wigness.

Purely orchestral pieces are few in number and, with very few exceptions, from the 1790s or later. Most of the ones I can identify are French. By purely orchestral pieces, I mean symphonies, concertos, symphonies concertantes, etc. Overtures and excerpts from operas and oratorios, not included in this chapter, were also

---

[1] C. Robert Wigness, *The Soloistic Use of the Trombone in Eighteenth-Century Vienna*, (D.M.A. essay, University of Iowa, 1970; Nashville, Tenn.: Brass Press, 1978).

staples of the concert repertoire. The march from Handel's *Saul* (1738), for example, was a very popular concert number in England, although it appears that eventually the trombone parts were either omitted or played on some other instrument.

Aside from operatic borrowings, it is difficult to tell which concert pieces included trombone parts. Most, of course, did not. In a sample of 131 concertos and symphonies concertantes compiled by David Charlton, only 7, or 5.4 percent, required trombone.[2] Charlton based his study on published sources. Symphonic music was printed for sale to people organizing their own private concerts. Since the forces available to this limited pool of customers varied widely, publishers aimed their products at the least common denominator and did not print the parts for unusual, hard-to-find instruments like the trombone.[3] It is therefore possible that manuscript copies of some of the other pieces in Charlton's sample include trombone parts, although it hardly seems likely that there would be very many. If, however, the practice of having a bass trombonist read from the contrabass part (described by John Marsh) was common on the continent, any piece could potentially have been performed with trombone. See Chapter 2 for the full text.

Beginning in 1789, the orchestra of the *Concert spirituel* included a trombonist on its payroll. After its demise in 1791, it appears that most public concert music was performed in theaters by theater orchestras. Perhaps for this reason, trombone parts in French concert music did not differ significantly from those in theater music.

Jan LaRue and Howard Brofsky[4] have documented the brass players in the various orchestras of Paris, and Ludwig Köchel[5] has listed the musical personnel at the imperial court of Vienna. Aside from these lists, it is difficult to know which other orchestras included trombones and when they were introduced. Adam Carse[6] and

---

[2] David Charlton, *Orchestration and Orchestral Practice in Paris, 1789–1810* (Ph.D. dissertation: King's College, University of Cambridge, 1973), 367.

[3] Ibid., 15.

[4] Jan LaRue and Howard Brofsky, "Parisian Brass Players, 1751–1793" *Brass Quarterly*, 3 (1960), 133–40.

[5] Ludwig Köchel, *Johann Josef Fux, Hofcompositor und Hofkapellmeister der Kaiser Leopold I., Josef I., und Karl VI. von 1698 bis 1740* (Vienna: Alfred Hölder, 1872).

[6] Adam Carse, *The Orchestra in the XVIIIth Century* (Cambridge: Heffer, 1940), 18–27.

Ottmar Schreiber[7] have listed the instrumentation in various orchestras, based on contemporary accounts. That neither list is entirely accurate can be seen from the fact that Carse shows no
trombones in the Opéra until 1790 and Schreiber not until 1810,
even though, as shown in Chapter 4, the trombone was introduced
to that orchestra no later than 1774.

Carse shows three trombones in the royal orchestra of Berlin in
1787. Schreiber mentions them in his list for 1811, but not 1792.
Schreiber also shows three trombones in Frankfurt am Main (1810),
Mainz (1782), and Stockholm (1790).

In all of these orchestras, as well as any others that included
trombones either permanently or only from time to time, the music
with trombone parts must have been nearly all either sacred music
or excerpts from ballets and operas.

The earliest symphony that includes trombone parts appears to be
one in E^b by Franz Beck. Robin Gregory mentions it, unfortunately
without offering any citation or any other detail that would help
locate it.[8] Born and trained in Mannheim, Beck spent some time in
Venice, Naples, and Marseilles before settling permanently in
Bordeaux in 1764. In the late 1750s, at or shortly before the time
Beck moved to Marseilles, Parisian publishers issued about 20 of his
symphonies. He seems to have stopped composing symphonies
shortly after he moved to Bordeaux.[9] It would be well worth dis-
covering Beck's symphonic use of the trombone. Not only is he the
earliest composer so far alleged to have included the trombone in
the symphony orchestra, but he spent his entire career in cities
where I have found no other references to trombone music in his
lifetime.

Another early symphony with trombone parts, by the Salzburg
composer Joseph Krottendorfer, is described on page 141.

---

[7] Ottmar Schreiber, *Orchester und Orchesterpraxis in Deutschland zwischen
1780 und 1850* (Berlin: Junker und Dünnhaupt, 1938), 100–17.

[8] Robin Gregory, *The Trombone: The Instrument and Its Music* (London:
Faber and Faber Ltd., 1973), 127. Barry S. Brook informs me (personal
correspondence, November 19, 1986) that he has found no reference to
Beck's use of the trombone in his extensive research in the history of the
symphony.

[9] Anneliese Downs, "Beck, Franz [François] Ignaz" *The New Grove* vol.
2, 333–4.

The following pieces also include trombone parts:

Auber, Daniel François Esprit. Second Cello Concerto (1804–05).
Beck, Franz. Symphony in E^b Major (c. 1760).
Beethoven, Ludwig van. Fifth Symphony, op. 67 (1804–08, pub. 1809).
Beethoven, Ludwig van. Sixth Symphony, op. 68 (1807–08), pub. 1809).
Cambini, Giuseppe Gioacchino. "La Patriote," Symphonie concertante (1796).
Cramer, Johann Baptist. Fourth Piano Concerto (1807).
Devienne, François. Le Bataille de Jemappes (1792).
Eggert, Joachim. Third Symphony (1807).
Eggert, Joachim. Fifth Symphony (1813--unfinished).
Falbe, Hans Hagerup. Symphony in D Major (c. 1810–12).
Frigel, Pehr. Overture in f Minor (1804).
Haeffner, Johann C. F. Overture in E^b (before 1808).
Haydn, Johann Michael. Symphony in C major (1773--trombone given as alternate instrument to the third horn).
Kreutzer, Rodolphe. Eighteenth Violin Concerto (1810–11).
Krottendorfer, Joseph. Symphony (1768).
Lamare, Jacques Michel. First Piano Concerto.
Lamare, Jacques Michel. Second Piano Concerto.
Lamare, Jacques Michel. Third Piano Concerto (1803–04).
Pleyel, Ignace. Symphonie Concertante, Ben. 113 (prem. 1792, pub. 1794).
Pleyel, Ignace. Symphony in B^b, Ben. 150A (1791?).
Pleyel, Ignace. Symphony in E^b, Ben. 152 (1791?).
Pleyel, Ignace. Symphony in A, Ben. 155 (1791?).
Rode, Pierre. Fist Violin Concerto (1794).
Rode, Pierre. Second Violin Concerto (1795).
Rode, Pierre. Fourth Violin Concerto (1798).
Steibelt, Daniel. Third Piano Concerto (1798).
Steibelt, Daniel. Fifth Piano Concerto (1798).
Struve, Bernhard. Overture in C Minor (1805).
Zimmermann, Anton. Symphony in C Major (c. 1780).

The foregoing list, although probably the longest list of purely orchestral eighteenth-century music with trombone parts ever compiled, may be far from complete. More pieces than have so far been identified must have been written before those of Pleyel and Devienne (1792). Vienna and Salzburg seem the most likely places to look. In the other cities listed earlier where trombones are known to have been in the local orchestras, there was also probably locally written music for them to play.

Of all the pieces listed, only Beethoven's are regularly heard on modern concerts. While some of the others would be welcome at least occasionally on modern programs, most are probably not worth reviving. The same can be said for whatever pieces remain unnoticed in some archive. As scholars sift through more and more obscure manuscripts, some purely orchestral music will be found that calls for trombone, but the proportion of music with trombone parts is never likely to be even as much as that found by Charlton. Considering that his dissertation covers only Paris from 1789 to 1810, a time when the trombone was first becoming common there, the percentage he found must surely be high in comparison with the total orchestral output of the eighteenth century.

IGNACE PLEYEL

Three Symphonies

Ignace Pleyel studied music with Joseph Haydn beginning in about 1772.[10] After spending some years traveling in Italy, he moved to Strasbourg in about 1784 and took a post as assistant kapellmeister at the cathedral. Throughout its history, Strasbourg has changed hands between France and Germany several times. Its cultural life has long been characterized by a mixture of French and German elements. Politically, during Pleyel's lifetime, Strasbourg belonged to France.

Pleyel was promoted to Kapellmeister in 1789, but because of the French Revolution, which began in that year, he could not long enjoy his position there. The Revolution abolished not only the cathedral's religious functions, but also Strasbourg's secular concerts. And so Pleyel accepted the invitation of Wilhelm Cramer to conduct the Professional Concerts in London, where he found himself Haydn's rival.

---

[10] Introductory material on Pleyel is based on Rita Benton, "Pleyel, Ignace Joseph" *The New Grove's Dictionary of Music and Musicians*, ed. Stanley Sadie, 20 vols. (London: Macmillan, 1980), vol. 15, 7.

Regarding the symphonies Pleyel wrote for London, Fétis wrote:

Le succés de la musique de Pleyel fut prodigieux. Il s'était surpassé et s'était montré digne de lutter avec son illustre maître. Les symphonies était au nombre de trois; il s'entrouvait une en *mi* bémol qui a été surtout signalée comme un ouvrage excellent. Malheureusement, le *Professional Concert* fut dissous quelques années après, la bibliothèque dispersée, et les symphonies, dont Pleyel n'avait pas gradé de copies, furent perdus pour toujours.[11]

The success of Pleyel's music was prodigious. He surpassed himself and showed himself worthy to contend with his illustrious master. There were three symphonies; one was in E^b, which was above all pointed out as an excellent work. Unfortunately, the Professional Concerts were dissolved several years later, the library dispersed, and the symphonies, of which Pleyel had not kept copies, were lost forever.

Rita Benton's catalogue of Pleyel's works[12] includes three symphonies that exist in manuscript at the British Library in London: Ben. 150A in B^b major, Ben. 152 in E^b major, and Ben. 155 in A major. (The key of the latter is given in the catalogue as A minor, but only the introduction to the first movement is in minor.) Each of these works exists also in autograph manuscripts at the Bibliothéque Nationale in Paris, Ben. 150A in two autograph manuscripts there. Although the catalogue dates these symphonies 1800?, 1801, and 1803 respectively, Benton later told me that they were probably the same symphonies Fétis had given up for lost.

The description that follows is based on a microfilm of manuscripts numbered (1822), (1826), and (1835) in Benton's catalogue. The other extant manuscripts may differ in detail, but surely not in the general character of the trombone parts. The instrumentation of all three symphonies is the same: flute, two oboes, two bassoons, two horns, two trumpets, trombone, timpani, and strings. The contrabass, and not the cello, is the principal bass instrument; the cello line is blank unless the two parts differ.

---

[11] François Fétis, "Pleyel, Ignace," *Biographie universelle des musiciens et bibliographie général de la musique*, 2d ed. 8 vols. (Paris: Firmin-Didot Frères, 1866–70; facs. ed., Brussels: Editions Culture et Civilization, 1972), vol 7, 75.

[12] Rita Benton, *Ignace Pleyel: a Thematic Catalogue of His Compositions* (New York: Pendragon Press, 1977), 64–66.

Pleyel uses the trombone in all but one of the movements: the second movement of the E^b symphony. The parts are very similar to those in French theater music and band music of the revolutionary period. That is, they double other parts, shorn of all melodic and rhythmic interest, and only during loud passages when all other instruments in the orchestra play as well.

Usually, in French music of the time, the trombone doubles the cello part: strictly if it is simple and in modified form otherwise. In fact, when the cello parts have something as simple as repeated quarter notes, the trombone is very likely to have half notes or whole notes.

In Pleyel's symphonies, such modifications are more common than passages of strict doubling. (See Ex. 37). In fact, the most conspicuous departure from normal French practice is that, when the bass line has any technical difficulty or melodic or thematic significance, the trombone part is often not based on the bass line at all, but rather doubles the timpani, horns, and trumpets. (See Ex. 38).

Example 37. Pleyel: *Symphony in E^b*, Ben. 152, 1st movement, measures 314–29.

Example 37, continued.

Example 38. Pleyel: *Symphony in A*, Ben. 155, 3rd movement, measures 52–70.

With this in mind, some passages where the trombone strictly doubles the bass are surprising. In the rondo of the E^b major symphony, the trombone plays slurred sixteenth notes. (See Ex. 39). In the slow movement of the A major symphony, Pleyel expected his trombonist to execute repeated thirty-second notes. (See Ex. 40). This passage is much more difficult on trombone than the unmodified contrabass part in Ex. 38 would have been. Quick repeated notes, easy enough in the fourth partial (b^b in first position to e in seventh position, although the lowest two notes would never be used in such passages) and above become difficult to play cleanly in the third partial (f to B) and extremely so in the second partial (B^b to E). That Pleyel writes such a figure in the second partial betrays a lack of understanding of the character and capabilities of the instrument.

Example 39. Pleyel: *Symphony in E^b*, Ben. 152, 4th movement, measures 155–60.

Example 40. Pleyel: *Symphony in A*, Ben. 155, 2nd movement, measures 64–68.

Plate 19. von Prenner: The Hearing.

ALT⋅ᴢˢ⋅ LAT⁴ɪ.ᴊɴᴄ.   IOANN IORDAN .PINXIT

Reprinted from *The Trumpet & Trombone in Graphic Arts: 1500–1800* by Tom L. Naylor © 1979 The Brass Press. Used by permission.

The trombone's range in these symphonies extends from E^b to e', prompting question of whether Pleyel intended the symphonies to be played on a bass trombone. Probably not. There are only two E^bs, both in one short passage, which the contrabass cannot play as written, either. Only the cello can play the E^bs, and its line is blank. If a real bass trombone was available to the Professional Concerts, it was probably used. Otherwise, all three symphonies are entirely playable on the tenor trombone.

The trombone's tessitura in these symphonies is approximately B^b to b^b, the first notes a beginning trombonist learns to play and, in the lower half of the octave, nearly the last ones on which he develops a good tone quality. Given the low caliber of trombonists in Paris (and the situation could not have been much if any better in Strasbourg or London), the trombone parts must have sounded very coarse and grating. These symphonies cannot have been widely performed, or Pleyel would have published them. In their own small way, however, they contributed to the bad reputation that the trombone had among many musicians in the early decades of the nineteenth century, which has not entirely gone away: the notion that, as Charles Burney wrote in Abraham Rees's *Cyclopaedia*, "the vibrations of these instruments produce noise, not musical sounds." (See Chapter 2 for the full text.)

JOACHIM EGGERT

Third Symphony

During his short career, Swedish composer Joachim Eggert displayed a powerful and original musical imagination. Poor health prevented him from traveling, and he died at the age of thirty-three. If Stockholm had been as internationally prominent a musical center as Vienna or Paris, Eggert would surely be better known today. His output includes five symphonies, the last of which was left incomplete at his death. Of the completed symphonies, only the third requires trombones. Ironically, it is the least massively scored of his symphonies, lacking the *concertante* instruments and large percussion sections of the others.[13] It also differs from the rest in having only three movements.

---

[13] *The Symphony, 1720–1840*, Barry S. Brook, ed. in chief, Series F, Vol. III, *The Symphony in Sweden*, pt. 2, ed. Bertil van Boer, Jr. (New York: Garland, 1983), xliii.

With the exception of one note, all of the trombone parts are playable on tenor trombones in B^b. Only the third movement appears to require a bass trombone for the third part. In the opening statement of the fugue subject, stated by cellos, basses, bassoons, and the third trombone, the trombone takes the last two notes an octave higher than the other instruments in order to avoid playing D and E^b. It is hard to imagine why any composer would weaken the subject in that way if a true bass trombone had been available. Yet when the allegro section of the fugue begins (with the same instruments), the third trombone part ends on E^b. (See Ex. 41.) It would not surprise me if, in the manuscript sources, the E^b is simply left out. Since the viola begins the countersubject on the same beat, and since this statement, unlike the earlier one, ends with a diminuendo, the absence of the trombone for one note would never be noticed. Yet only a trombonist could look at such a part in context and not quickly assume that the omission was a mere oversight.

Example 41. Eggert: Third Symphony, 3rd movement, measures 1−4, 39−42.

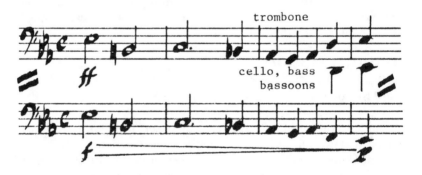

Except for three instances of doubly dotted quarter note and sixteenth in the first trombone part during the introduction to the first movement, the trombones play no note shorter than quarter notes. While shorter notes frequently occur in the string parts, they are much less common in the wind parts. Eggert does not limit the trombones to playing the longest notes in the texture. Nor does he always give all three of them the same rhythms. Throughout the symphony, the trombone parts display great rhythmic independence among themselves. This independence is most notable in the fugue. The trombones do not at all play at the same time until nearly half way through the movement.

The third trombone plays in twice as many measures as the other two, but the effect is not at all the same as that achieved by French operatic composers like Steibelt, who make the bass trombone the most important and write parts of such little significance for the others that they can be omitted entirely. Eggert uses all the trombones to reinforce short passages. They rarely play more than four consecutive measures, although the third trombone plays eleven consecutive measures once and up to eight measures several times.

Also unlike French composers, Eggert uses the trombones at a wide variety of dynamic levels from triple piano to fortissimo. He also calls for various articulations (slurs and staccato) more frequently than French composers. Yet if Eggert had little in common with French practice, he had still less in common with the Austrian practice of continuous doubling and florid soloistic writing. Bertil van Boer writes, "This symphony is far ahead of its time. Certain tone qualities and orchestrational effects would not be out of place even as late as the end of the nineteenth century, and the orchestration is as skillful and innovative as Beethoven's."[14]

LUDWIG VAN BEETHOVEN

Fifth and Sixth Symphonies

Although Beethoven was not the first composer to use trombones in a symphony, he was the earliest composer whose symphonies with trombones entered the standard repertoire. Of all the music listed earlier in this chapter, only Beethoven's had wide influence or more than ephemeral success. He used trombones in three of his nine symphonies: the Fifth, Sixth, and Ninth (opp. 67, 68, 125). Only the Fifth and Sixth, both published in 1809, fall within the chronological limits of this study.

Fifth Symphony

Beethoven reserves the trombones until the last movement. Immediately, he shows an almost French distrust of the trombone's ability to play short notes; in the pickups to the fifth and sixth measures,

---

[14] Ibid., xliv.

only the trombones have rests. The rest of the orchestra plays
dotted-eighth- and sixteenth-note figures (except for the second
violins and violas, who have tremolos.) There is nothing timid or
tentative about the range, however. Beethoven expects the alto
trombonist to sit through the first three movements and then begin
the fourth with an unprepared c''. (See Ex. 42).

Example 42. Beethoven: Fifth Symphony, 4th movement, measures 1−5

The opening sets the pattern for the rest of the movement. Rhythmically and melodically, the trombones play little that is significant enough to bring out, but the alto trombone has a treacherously high range (a^b to f''). The other ranges (c to f' for the tenor and F to c' for the bass) are much more reasonable.

Most of each trombone part can be explained in terms of a modified doubling of the string or woodwind parts, either at the unison or an octave lower. Beethoven uses the trombones either for sustained harmonic filler or for rhythmic punctuation. Every other instrument plays shorter notes than the trombones, although the trombones do not necessarily have the longest note at any given time, as they do in most French music.

It is often written that Beethoven's use of trombones marks the completion of the orchestral brass choir. Such is not the case; Beethoven seldom uses trumpets, horns, and trombones as a unit. The trombones are rhythmically distinct from the other brass. Sometimes no other instrument has comparable rhythmic figures. Often, the trombones' rhythms are more closely related to woodwinds (or, less frequently, those of the strings) than to the trumpets and horns. For example, in measures 7 through 11, the alto and tenor trombones double the clarinets an octave lower, with subtle rhythmic modifications. (The clarinets have half notes instead of dotted quarter notes and eighth rests.) The bass trombone most closely resembles the cellos, basses, and contrabassoon. In measures 12 through 18, the trombones have more in common with the clarinets, bassoons, and low strings than with the rest of the orchestra, although the modifications are more extensive than earlier.

Although most of the trombone parts are mere filler with no real interest of their own, the alto and tenor trombones share one moment of prominence. (See Ex. 43.) On any other instrument, this passage would have been a solo, but not only do the two trombones

Example 43. Beethoven: Fifth Symphony, 4th movement, measures 112–18

play in unison, they are doubled by the bassoons.

Such was Beethoven's influence that the trombone, alone among the ordinary instruments of the orchestra, had no soloistic role in symphonic music until the end of the century. While later composers wrote more thematically significant parts for trombone than Beethoven did, these usually entail either chordal passages for the entire trombone section or melodies for two or more trombones in unison. In fact, Gustav Holst, himself a trombonist, wrote a melody for two unison trombones in *A Somerset Rhapsody* that is far too soft and in a passage too lightly scored to work well as written. It should be played as a solo. But by Holst's day, it was almost dogma that the trombone was not by nature a proper solo instrument.

Sixth Symphony

Although Beethoven used trombones in two movements of his Sixth Symphony, they have an even less important role than in the Fifth Symphony. He wrote parts for only two trombones, alto and tenor, and used them in only 73 measures in the entire symphony, as opposed to 215 measures in the Fifth Symphony. On the original title page, the publisher listed all the instruments in the orchestra; the trombones appear last, after the timpani, almost as if they were an afterthought.

The fourth movement, titled "Gewitter, Sturm" ("Thunder Storm"), begins softly but reaches a furious loudness by measure 21. Beethoven reserves the trombones for the loudest part of the storm, which begins at measure 106. The trombones add nothing but volume for 13 measures, then cease playing for the rest of the movement as the storm subsides. For the first nine of these, they simply double the timpani part, the tenor trombone an octave higher and the alto two octaves higher. For the last four measures, they do not double any other instrument, but they continue to play whole notes in octaves very loudly until their last measure, when they play only a quarter note, marked *piano*, on the downbeat. Rhythmically, the trombones are identical with most of the other wind instruments; only the piccolo and bassoons ever play anything different.

The trombones play in a little less than a quarter of the fifth movement, entitled "Hirtengesang: Frohe, dankbare Gefühle nach dem Sturm" ("Shepherd's Song: Thanksgiving after the Storm"). Here again, they play only during loud, tutti passages. Beethoven does not limit them, in this movement, to octaves; the spacing varies from thirds to double octaves.

The trombones often double the clarinets, trumpets, or horns, shorn of all melodic and rhythmic interest, but they do not always double anything. Rhythmically, they nearly always have the longest notes in the texture. In no case do they ever play a moving part against another instrument's longer note. The trombones also omit all of the eighth-note pickups that are so common in the other instruments. (See Ex. 44.)

Example 44. Beethoven: Sixth Symphony, 5th movement, measures 219—24

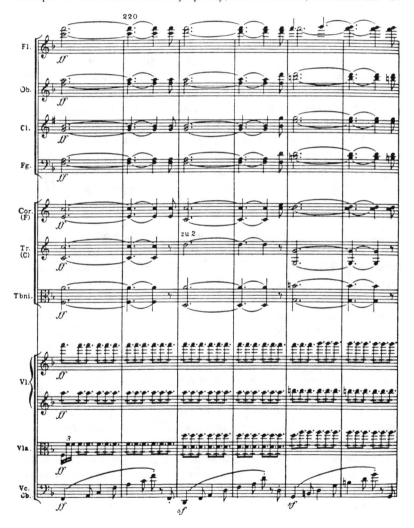

In French music, the extreme rhythmic simplicity of the trombone parts was one sign among several that composers did not understand the trombone's capabilities and that trombonists there were not very proficient. In Vienna, the high point of trombone virtuosity seems to have been reached in the 1760's, when Wagenseil and Albrechtsberger wrote their concertos. Nothing comparable in terms of trombone solos exists between Albrechtsberger's concerto, written in 1769, and Beethoven's symphonies, premiered 40 years later. Possibly a deterioration in the quality of Viennese trombonists occurred during that time, but surely not enough to account for the utter lack of rhythmic complexity in Beethoven's trombone parts.

For one thing, Beethoven demanded a strong high register, to f'' in the Fifth Symphony. The range of the Sixth Symphony (f' to d'' for the alto trombone and c to g' for the tenor) is more reasonable, but the alto trombone part is still very high and would present severe problems of endurance if it were any longer or if the 60 measures in the last movement were not broken up with long rests. Also, Viennese trombonists were still expected to double the voices in religious choral music, and some passages, even in Beethoven's own music, include very intricate rhythms and florid passagework. Therefore, no incompetence on the part of trombonists available to Beethoven can account for the lack of intrinsic interest in his trombone parts.

Three possible explanations remain. First, the style of trombone playing exemplified by Austrian religious music was, by Beethoven's time, very old-fashioned. The French style, for all of its shortcomings, represented the vanguard; Beethoven was hardly a conservative. As shown in Chapter 5, his handling of the trombone in his oratorio most closely resembles the Handel/Haydn tradition; the Ninth Symphony and *Missa solemnis* show a combination of the French and "English" styles. Second, Beethoven sought performance opportunities for his works outside Vienna, but everywhere else in Europe, expert trombonists were in short supply. The Fifth and Sixth Symphonies were published in Leipzig, where it had been possible to perform Mozart's *Requiem* with the trombone parts only recently. (See the section on Germany in Chapter 3). More challenging and important trombone parts would have cut into potential sales and performance. As it is, the hardest parts can simply be left out with little of no harm to the total impact of the work. Third, Beethoven seems not to have been much interested in the trombone. In his "Drei Equali für vier Posaunen" (WoO 30, 1812), each movement is shorter, less carefully marked in terms of dynamics and articulation than the one before, almost as if Beethoven were in a hurry to finish a commission he did not much care about.

For whatever reason, Beethoven exploited only the least interesting of the trombone's capabilities. His immediate followers hardly explored any additional possibilities, leaving it to Mahler and later generations to discover what the trombone could add to a symphony orchestra.

CHAPTER 8

THE TROMBONE IN MILITARY MUSIC

Although wind and percussion instruments had been the backbone of military music for centuries, it was only in the late eighteenth century that the band attained its modern form and function. As shown in Chapter 4, that happened rather suddenly in France at the start of the Revolution. The most important military music with trombone parts is all French. The few pieces written outside of France that I have identified are all mentioned in Chapter 3. I have not seen any of these, so this chapter is necessarily limited to French music.

Nearly all of the best Revolutionary band music was written between 1789 and 1794. After the end of the Reign of Terror, a desire for calm and stability replaced Revolutionary zeal. The government continued to sponsor festivals, and some new music, including a few significant pieces, was composed for them. The impulse that led to the earlier festivals, however, had largely run out of steam.

Music for the festivals has attracted considerable scholarly attention, most recently from band directors seeking early music to use for program balance. David Whitwell has cataloged 158 pieces written for the various festivals.[1] ("W" numbers used in this chapter refer to

---

[1] David Whitwell, *Band Music of the French Revolution* (Tutzing: Hans Schneider, 1979), 101–202.

285

this catalog.) In addition, there were dozens of arrangements of popular tunes for military band, some of which require trombones.

Both Sherwood Dudley[2] and David P. Swanzy[3] construct full scores of several works in their dissertations. David Charlton provides one more score in his dissertation. In all, the following pieces are available for examination from these sources:

W. 13   Frédéric Blasius, "Ouverture"
W. 25   Charles Simon Catel, "Ouverture in C"
W. 26   Charles Simon Catel, "Ouverture in F"
W. 28   Charles Simon Catel, "Simphonie militaire"
W. 73   François Joseph Gossec, "Marche lugubre
W. 81   François Joseph Gossec, "Chant de 14 juillet"
W. 107 Louis Emanuel Jadin, "Symphonie"
W. 108 Louis Emanuel Jadin, "Ouverture"
W. 113 Rodolphe Kruetzer, "Ouverture: Journée de Marathon"
W. 128 Xavier Lefèvre, "Marche militaire"
W. 129 Xavier Lefèvre, "Pas de manoeuvre"
W. 142 Etienne Méhul, "Ouverture"

Of these twelve pieces, four (W. 13, 26, 73, 81) require three trombones. The rest include parts only for bass trombone. Some of these are available in modern editions, as is Gossec's "Symphonie in C" (W. 71), which is not included in the dissertations. It requires three trombones.

Although this repertoire includes several very interesting pieces, well worthy of modern performance, it includes no masterpieces. The occasions for which this music was written demanded that it be loud, simple in structure, and, relative to contemporary symphonic music, short. It had to appeal to a large audience of unsophisticated people and stir them to patriotic fervor. In addition, several of the pieces were composed, copied, engraved, and printed on extremely short notice.[4] Very little, if any, of the band music counts among the composers' best works. Given the need for melodic, rhythmic,

---

[2] Walter Sherwood Dudley, *Orchestration in the "Musique d'harmonie" of the French Revolution* 2 vols. (Ph.D. dissertation: University of California, Berkeley, 1968).

[3] David P. Swanzy, *The Wind Ensemble and Its Music During the French Revolution, (1789–1795)* Ph.D. dissertation: Michigan State University, 1966).

[4] Whitwell, 88.

and structural simplicity, only the aspects of harmony and orchestration gave the composers any scope to display special compositional skill or inspiration.

HARMONY

Swanzy has examined harmonic aspects of band music in detail. He reports that in shorter works, even the harmony shows little imagination. Most chords are tonic or dominant, with even the subdominant occurring only rarely.[5] More extended works use a more varied harmonic palette. All diatonic triads and seventh chords appear, along with such standard chromatic devices as secondary dominants and augmented sixth chords. Modulations to the dominant and the relative and parallel major or minor are frequent. Catel, Louis Jadin, and Méhul, at least, successfully used chromatic modulation.[6] Most often, the music modulates directly back to the tonic with no intermediate modulations.

Although most of the chord progressions are standard ones (down a fifth, down a third, up a second), Swanzy points out several nonstandard ones.[7] He does not say whether they sound bold and imaginative or merely inept. Among the standard nonharmonic tones, pedal points and suspensions appear so regularly that they become an important stylistic trait for the entire repertoire.

Composers presumably used the same harmonic devices in their band music that they used for anything else they wrote. There is, however, one significant difference between band music and other repertoires: only three of the pieces in Whitwell's catalog, all by Lesueur, are in sharp keys. This fact can probably be explained on the basis of the orchestration, for if the harmony of band music is commonplace, the orchestration is wholly without precedent.

ORCHESTRATION

In the orchestra, the violin is the primary melody instrument and the cello is the primary bass instrument. Stringed instruments are

---

[5] Swanzy, 108.
[6] Ibid., 114.
[7] Ibid., 115.

Plate 20. Engelbrecht: Trumpets, Kettledrums and Trombones.

happiest in sharp keys. Therefore, sharp keys are more useful to orchestral composers.[8] Since the bands had no string choir, other instruments had to fulfill the functions of the violin and cello. In traditional bands, it was the oboe and the bassoon. In the Revolutionary bands, however, oboes took a back seat to the more flexible and brilliant clarinets.

The early clarinet could not be played well in all keys because of fingering difficulties, and so became the earliest of the transposing woodwind instruments. Clarinets in A, B^b, B, C, and D became standard late in the eighteenth century. Most composers preferred the B^b clarinet as a solo instrument and considered the higher ones tonally less pleasing than the lower ones.[9] The French in particular cherished the tonal variety inherent in using various clarinets to the extent that they resisted adopting a new design that allowed one clarinet to play in all keys when it became available early in the nineteenth century. They liked to use A clarinets for pastoral music, B^b clarinets for pathetic and majestic music, and C clarinets for lively and brilliant music.[10] Since music for the festivals was supposed to be majestic and brilliant, but hardly pastoral, it would have made no sense to write band music in sharp keys, which would have been awkward for the most appropriate clarinets.

Dudley points out that, since clarinets were the principal melody instruments of the French band, other instruments in the same register (flute and oboe) were relegated to the status of secondary doubling instruments when they were used at all.[11] The piccolo likewise was a secondary doubling instrument and, largely because of its brilliance and carrying power, was used more frequently than the flute and oboe.

The bassoon was the primary bass instrument, seconded by the serpent and bass trombone. Of these latter two instruments, the serpent was the more important. It frequently doubled the bassoon parts exactly. When both bassoons were playing countermelodies in the tenor register, the serpent took over the bass line. Occasionally, its part was a simplification of the bassoon part.

---

[8] Cecil Forsyth, *Orchestration* (London: Macmillan, 1914), 380.

[9] F. Geoffrey Rendall, *The Clarinet: Some Notes upon Its History and Construction*, 3rd ed., revised with additional material by Philip Bate (London: Benn; New York: Norton, 1971), 119.

[10] Ibid., 90.

[11] Dudley, passim.

The bass trombone joined the bassoons and serpent mainly in heavily scored, very loud passages. In fact, only rarely does the trombone play while any other instrument is resting for more than a measure at a time. Like the serpent, the bass trombone essentially doubled the bassoons, but it was more likely than the serpent to have a modified part. The trombone never strictly doubled the bassoon part at the same time the serpent had a modified part. On these occasions, the trombone usually doubled the serpent. In Catel's "Ouverture in C," in fact, the trombone part is actually a simplification of the serpent's simplification of the bassoon part. (See Ex. 45.) In Jadin's "Ouverture," the trombone and serpent briefly double the second bassoon antiphonally. (See Ex. 50.) Jadin and Méhul write some passages in which the trombone part is independent of the bassoon and serpent. (See Ex. 46, 47, 48.)

Example 45. Catel: *Ouverture in C*, measures 55–61

The bass trombone was clearly the most important of the trombones. Of the twelve pieces examined for this book, only four include parts for alto and tenor trombones. With the exception of Gossec's "Chant de 14 juillet" (W. 81), the bass trombone plays in more measures than the others. There are only two measures, both in Blasius's "Ouverture," in which the alto and tenor trombones play without the bass trombone. (See Ex. 49.) When all three trombones play together, they nearly always play the same rhythm. Only in Gossec's "Marche lugubre" is there any deviation. (See Ex. 50.)

Alto and tenor merely provide harmonic filler. Their parts have no melodic or thematic significance. Although they are not bound by the overtone series and can play all diatonic and chromatic notes in all keys, their parts were less important than those of the other

Example 46. L. E. Jadin: *Ouverture*, measures 108–17

Example 47. Méhul: *Ouverture*, measures 9–14

Example 48. Méhul: *Ouverture*, measures 119−22

Example 49. Blasius: *Ouverture*, measures 100−05

Example 50. Gossec. *Marche lugubre*, measures 35–43

harmonic filler instruments, the trumpets and horns. Parts for alto and tenor trombone cannot be described as easily as can bass trombone parts. Their notes can always be found somewhere in the texture, either at the unison on one or two octaves higher, but the lines often do not follow any other part long enough to be analyzed in terms of doubling. They are not always autonomous, however. Ex. 51 shows how the alto and tenor trombones double flute parts in Catel's "Ouverture in F."

Example 51. Catel: *Ouverture in F*, measures 30–41.

The foregoing comments do not apply to the alto and tenor trombone parts of Gossec's "Chant du 14 juillet." In this piece, the only one of dozens of Revolutionary choral pieces available for examination, the trombone parts are closely associated with the choral parts, often doubling them strictly.

RANGE AND RHYTHM

The ranges of these pieces are, with two exceptions, well within the limits recommended by Vandenbroek: g-$b^{b'}$ (c'') for alto trombone, G-f' (g') for tenor trombone, and F-g' for bass trombone. (See Chapter 2 for the complete text.) Kreutzer, however, wrote E for the bass trombone, and Jadin required D in his symphony. (See Ex. 52.)

Example 52. L. E. Jadin: *Simphonie*, measures 104–08

Jadin's D is especially noteworthy. A B^b or A trombone without a trigger, which had not yet been invented, cannot produce D except as a false tone (bending G down a fourth). This technique, although described by Praetorius nearly two centuries earlier,[12] seems to be far beyond anything that could reasonably be expected of Parisian trombonists. The slur only makes the passage more difficult. On the other hand, the true bass trombone (most likely in E^b, or F) appears to have been rare in Paris at this time. Only a small handful of works require it.

Relative to the other parts, the trombone's note values in military music are long. Only two pieces, Gossec's "Marche lugubre" and Jadin's "Symphonie," require anything quicker than pairs of eighth notes; both contain dotted-eighth- and sixteenth note figures. The two pieces are not comparable in terms of difficulty; Gossec's piece is marked Largo while Jadin's is fast.

---

[12] Nicholas Bessaraboff, *Ancient European Musical Instruments* (Boston: Harvard University Press, 1941), 186.

Jadin's "Ouverture" uses trombones in a dynamic range from forte to quadruple forte. Most other composers content themselves with an upper limit of fortissimo. Soft passages for trombone are rare, occurring in only five of the twelve pieces: Catel's "Symphonie militaire," Gossec's "Marche lugubre" and "Chant de 14 juillet," Kreutzer's "Ouverture," and Méhul's "Ouverture." The other pieces all include soft passages, but the trombone does not participate in them. It is nearly always the first instrument to drop out whenever the composers wanted to lighten the texture. The trombones play in only about half of the measures in each piece: less, on the whole, than any other instrument except the virtually useless buccin and tuba curva, pseudo-archaic instruments used more for show than for anything they could do musically.

Considering that the trombones seemed most valued for making a loud noise, it is ironic that no trombone partbooks were made for the big outdoor festival concert given July 14, 1794 at the Tuileries, even though the program included at least one piece, Gossec's "Ronde nationale" (W. 85) that included trombone parts. Charlton, calling attention to the small number of trombones and trombonists available in Paris at the time, speculates that they were omitted from this festival on the grounds that their limited tone could not possibly make any kind of impression among the large forces engaged for the occasion.[13]

Dudley speculates that the trombone's association with the church hindered its acceptance into the orchestra and limited its use in the band.[14] Since there is no evidence that trombones were ever used either extensively or exclusively in French church music, as they were in Austria for most of the century, this explanation is unlikely. It is true however, that trombone parts in eighteenth-century France were seldom either technically challenging or musically significant. The important fact is that the French developed a taste for trombones at this time. As Chapter 4 has shown, the popularity of trombones followed Napoleon's armies all over Europe. The fanfares of the cavalry bands featured the most spectacular sonority since the time of Giovanni Gabrieli. But it is in the music of the *orchestre*

---

[13] David Charlton, *Orchestration and Orchestral Practice in Paris, 1789−1810* (Ph.D. dissertation: King's College, University of Cambridge, 1973), 141−42, 153.

[14] Dudley, vol. 1, 99.

d'harmonie that composers first exploited the musical possibilities of
the trombone in a large wind ensemble, however tentatively. Very
likely, the band music of the French Revolution provided the im-
petus for the explosion of trombone parts in both operatic and
symphonic orchestras, not only in France, but all over Europe as
well.

AUTHORS CITED IN ZEDLER'S GROSSES VOLLSTANDIGES UNIVERSAL-LEXICON

One of the longest documents reproduced in Chapter 2, a series of articles from Zedler's *Grosses vollständiges Universal-Lexicon*, cites the greatest number of sources and authors, but it also includes some of the least practical information for the modern scholar. Because the articles themselves are of such limited use, most readers of this book would probably not find much interest in a detailed listing of the sources, but thoroughness dictates that such a listing be made available. The list that follows is in the order that the sources or authors occur in the articles.

Only the first source cited is primarily about music. *Digt- sang- en speel-konst soo der ouden, als bysonder der Hebreen*, by Salomon van Til (1644–1713), was published in Dordregt in 1692. German translations were published at Frankfurt and Leipzig in 1706 and again in 1719.

Of the numerous editions of Eustathius's commentary on Homer, the one most accessible to Zedler's author was probably the one published in Basle in 1559–60. The edition issued in Florence between 1730 and 1735 probably appeared too late to have been of use. Eustathius, Archbishop of Thessalonica, lived at the end of the twelfth century.

I have not been able to identify Gräfe's *Conc. in Hos.* It is evidently a commentary on the book of Hosea and was probably available to the encyclopedia's readers. I have also been unable to identify Amelius. Elsewhere in Zedler's encyclopedia, there are biographies of Georgius Amelius, a sixteenth-century jurist, his son Martinus Amelius, also a jurist, and Petrus Amelius, Bishop of Urbino in the fourteenth century. The Amelius cited in the articles on the trombone is not necessarily any of these men.

The "old scholastics" Suarez and Thyräus are Spanish theologian Francisco Suarez (1548–1617) and, probably, Hermann Thiräus, a German Jesuit who lived in Rome. The author of the articles seems to have learned of their dispute not from reading any of their writings, but from Adami, probably Johann Samuel Adami (1638–1713), who sometimes wrote under the pseudonym Misander. According to his biography in Zedler, he wrote *Deliciæ Evangelico-Emblematicæ*, which includes more than 2,000 emblems, only some of which the article enumerates.

Johann Heinrich Weyhenmeyer (1637–1706), a noted Lutheran preacher, wrote prolifically. His biography in Zedler includes a list of 31 books, most of which appear to be compilations of his sermons. The two cited in the articles on the trombone are *Fest-Posaune* (Ulm, 1691; Nürnberg, 1698) and *Evangelischer Buß- Gnaden- Lehr- und Trost-Prediger* (Ulm, 1716).

John Lightfoot (1602–1675) was an English rabbinical scholar. A Latin edition of his best-known work, *Horae Hebraicae Talmudicae* was published in Leipzig (1675–79).

Finally, Saint John Chrysostom, one of the early church fathers of the fourth century, was Archbishop of Constantinople. Theophylacticus may be the late eleventh-century Greek Orthodox Archbishop of Ochrida.

MUSICAL EXAMPLES IN FROHLICH'S "POSAUNENSCHULE"

The four volumes of Joseph Fröhlich's *Vollständige theoretisch-pracktische Musikschule* are of similar size (about 11 × 14 inches), but not of similar appearance. The fourth volume, for example, is set in Roman type and has large, clear, readable musical examples. The third volume is engraved in italics and has small, cramped, barely legible musical examples. Unfortunately, the "Posaunenschule" is in the third volume. The tiny size of some of the characters and inking so light that the staff lines sometimes disappear makes some of the examples difficult to read even in the original size. Reduced to the size of this volume, they become indeciperable in places.

The pages that follow reproduce the musical notation, captions, and slide positions in a readable size. Because the recopying requires two or three pages for each of the plates reproduced here (8, 10, 11, 12), no attempt has been made to preserve the original layout. That, at least, should be clear enough in the plates printed in the text.

As was the case with the text of this treatise, the number of errors that the engraver made is truly astounding. I have attempted to copy all of his mistakes accurately without adding any of my own. Captions, note names, etc., however, have been translated into English.

David M. Guion

Plate 8. Example K: Slide Positions.

1st position in B♭

2nd position in A

3rd position in A♭

4th position in G

5th position in F#

6th position in F

7th position in E

Plate 8. Examples L, M.

302 David M. Guion

Plate 10. Examples O–T.

Plate 10. Example V: "Various useful scales in major and minor"--Major.

Plate 10. Example V (concluded)--Minor.

Plate 11. Tenor Trombone Slide Positions.

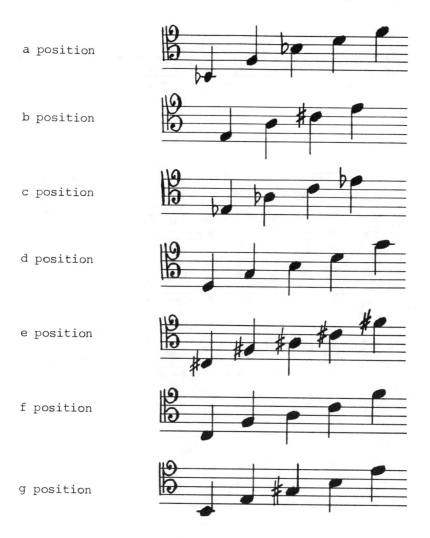

David M. Guion

Plate 11. Tenor Scales.

(N.B. The first of each pair is on top in the original.)

Plate 11. Tenor Scales (concluded).

Plate 12. Alto Trombone Slide Positions.

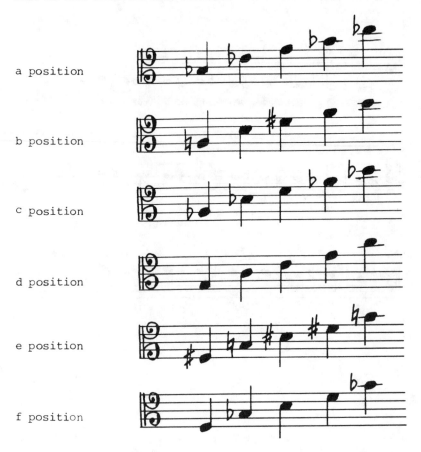

a position

b position

c position

d position

e position

f position

Plate 12. Alto Scales.

Plate 12. Alto Scales (concluded)

BIBLIOGRAPHY

I. Primary sources.

Albrechtsberger, Johann Georg. *Answeisung zur Composition*, 3d ed. Leipzig: Breitkopf und Härtel, 1821.

Almanach musical (1781). facs. ed. Paris: Minkoff, n.d.

Apuleius. *The Transformation of Lucius, Otherwise Known as the Golden Ass*, trans. Robert Graves. New York: Farar, Straus & Young, 1951.

Bach, Johann Sebastian. *Neue Ausgabe sämtliche Werke*. 8 series. Kassel: Bärenreiter, 1954-.

Beethoven, Ludwig van. *Ludwig van Beethovens Werke*. 25 series. Leipzig: Breitkopf & Härtel, 1864–90.

Bonanni, Filippo. *Gabinetto armonico*. Rome: Giorgio Placho, 1722.

——. *The Showcase of Musical Instruments*, introduction and captions by Frank Ll. Harrison and Joan Rimmer. New York: Dover, 1964.

Brossard, Sébastien de. *Dictionnaire de musique*. Paris: Christoph Ballard, 1703.

Burney, Charles. *An Account of the Musical Performances in Westminster Abbey and the Pantheon, May 26th, 27th, 29th; and June the 3rd, and 5th, 1784. In Commemoration of Handel*. London: T. Payne, 1785.

——. *An Eighteenth-Century Musical Tour in Central Europe and the Netherlands; Being Dr. Charles Burney's Account of His Musical Experiences*. ed. Percy Scholes. London: Oxford University Press, 1959.

——. *The Present State of Music in France and Italy*. London: Becket et al., 1773; facs. ed. New York: Broude Bros., 1969.

——. *The Present State of Music in Germany, the Netherlands and United*

Provinces. 2d ed., cor. London: T. Becket, 1775; facs. ed. New York: Broude Bros., 1969.

Chambers, Ephraim. *Cyclopaedia: or An Universal Dictionary of Arts and Sciences.* 2 vols. London: Knapton, 1728; 5th ed. London: printed for D. Midwinter, et al., 1741.

Cyclopaedia, ed. Abraham Rees, 39 vols. London: Longman, et al, 1802−20.

Eisel, Johann Philipp. *Musicus autodidactos, oder der sich selbst informirende Musicus.* Erfurt: Johann Michael Funcken, 1738.

Encyclopaedia Britannica 3 vols. Edinburgh: Bell and Macfarquhar, 1771.

Encyclopédie, ou Dictionnaire raisonné des sciences, des arts et des métiers. 35 vols. Paris: Briason et al., 1751−80.

Francoeur, Louis Joseph. *Traité général des voix et des instruments d'orchestre,* new ed. by Alexandre Choron. Paris: Aux adresses ordinaires de musique, 1813.

Fröhlich, Joseph. *Vollständige theoretisch-pracktishce Musikschule für alle beym Orchester gebrauchliche wichtigere Instrumente.* 4 vols. Bonn: Simrock, [1811].

Fux, Johann Joseph. *Samtliche Werke.* 8 series. Kassel: Bärenreiter, 1959-.

[Gardeton, César]. *Bibliographie de la France et de l'étranger, ou Répertoire général systematique de tous les traités et oeuvres de musique vocale et instrumentale.* Paris: Niogret, 1822.

Gerber, Ernst Ludwig. *Historisch-biographisces Lexikon der Tonkünstler.* 2 vols. Leipzig: J. G. I. Breitkopf, 1790−92.

——. *Neues historisch-biographisches Lexikon der Tonkünstler,* 4 vols. Leipzig: A. Kühnel, 1812−13.

Gluck, Christoph Willibald. *Sämtliche Werke.* 6 series. Kassel: Bärenreiter, 1951-.

Gossec, François. "Notice sur l'introduction des cors, des clarinettes et des trombones dans les orchestres français, extraite des manuscrits autographes de Gossec." *Revue musicale* 5 (1829), 217−23. [According to François Fétis, the publisher and editor, the notice was written in about 1810.]

Grassineau, James. *A Musical Dictionary.* London: J. Wilcox, 1740.

Halle, Johann Samuel. *Werkstätte der heutigen Kunst.* 4 vols. Brandenburg: J. W. Halle, 1761−65.

Händel, Georg Friedrich. *Hallische Händel-Ausgabe.* 5 series. Kassel: Bärenreiter, 1955-.

Haydn, Franz Joseph. *Werke.* 34 Series. Munich: G. Henle. 1958-.

Koch, Heinrich Christoph. *Musikalisches Lexikon.* Frankfurt am Main: August Hermann dem jüngern, 1802.

La Borde, Jean Benjamin de. *Essai sur la musique ancienne et moderne.* 4 vols. Paris: Ph.-D. Pierres, 1780.

Luther, Martin. *Die gantze Heilige Schrifft Deudsch,* ed. Friedrich Kur. Munich: Rogner & Bernhard, 1972.

Majer, Joseph Friedrich Bernhard Caspar. *Museum musicum theoretico practicum*. Halle: G. M. Majer, 1732; facs. ed. Kassel: Bärenreiter, 1954.
——. *Neu-eröffneter theoretischer Musik Saal*. Nürnberg: Krehmer, 1741.
Musik Saal. Nürnberg: Krehmer, 1741.
Marsh, John. *Hints to Young Composers of Instrumental Music*. London: Clementi, Banger, Hyde, Collard & Davis, c. 1807; reprinted with an introduction by Charles Cudworth in *The Galpin Society Journal* 18 (1965), 57–71.
Marpurg, Friedrich Wilhelm. *Historisch-kritische Beyträge zur Aufnahme der Musik*. 5 vols. Berlin: G. A. Lange. 1754–78.
Martini, Giovanni Battista. *Storia della musica*. 3 vols. Bologna: Lelio dalla Volpe, 1757 [i.e. 1761].
Mattheson, Johann. *Das beschützte Orchestre*. Hamburg: Schillerische Buchhandlung, 1717.
——. *Das neu-eröffnete Orchestre*. Hamburg: The Author, 1713.
Mersenne, Marin. *Harmonie universelle: The Books on Instruments*. trans. Roger E. Chapman. The Hague: Martinus Nijhoff, 1957.
Mozart, Wolfgang Amadeus. *Briefe Wolfgang Amadeus Mozarts*. 2 vols. ed. Erich Müller von Asow. Berlin: Alfred Metzner Verlag, 1942.
[——]. *The Letters of Mozart & His Family*. trans. and ed. Emily Anderson. 3 vols. London: Macmillan, 1938.
——. *Neue Ausgabe sämtlicher Werke*. 10 series. Kassel: Bärenreiter, 1955-.
Niedt, Friedrich Erhard. *Musicalischer Handleitung. Anderer Theil: Von der Variation des General-Basses*. 2d ed., ed. Johann Mattheson, Hamburg: Schiller, 1717; facs. ed., n.p.: Frits Knuf, 1976.
Praetorius, Michael. *Syntagma musicum. Tomus secundus: De organographia*. Wolfenbüttel: Holwein, 1619.
Rousseau, Jean-Jacques. "A M. D'Alembert" (1758). *Œuvres complètes de J. J. Rousseau*. 25 vols. ed. V. D. Musset-Pathay. Paris: P. Dupont, 1824. vol. 2, 9–193.
Schubart, Christian Friedrich Daniel. *Ideen zu einer Aesthetik der Tonkunst*. ed. Ludwig Schubart. Vienna: J. V. Degen, 1806.
Speer, Daniel. *Grundrichtiger kurtz- leicht- und nöthiger Unterricht der musikalischen Kunst*. Ulm: Kühnen, 1687.
——. *Grundrichtiger kurtz- leicht- und nöthiger jetzt wol-vermehrter Unterricht der musikalisches Kunst oder vierfaches musikalischen Kleeblatt*. Ulm: Kühnen, 1697.
[Stößel, Johann Christoph, and Stößel, Johann David]. *Kurtzgefaßtes musicalisches Lexicon*. Chemnitz: Johann Christoph und Johann David Stößel, 1737.
Table analytique et raisonnée des matieres contenues dans les XXXIII volumes in-folio du Dictionnaire raisonné des sciences, des arts et des métiers et dans son supplément. Paris: Panckoucke et al, 1780.
Tans'ur William. *The Elements of Musick Display'd*. London: Stanley Crowder, 1767.

Vandenbroek, Othon. *Traité général de tous les instrumens à vent à l'usage des compositeurs*. Paris: Louis Marchand, 1794?

Verschuere-Reynvaan, J[oos]. *Muzijkaal Kunst-Woordenboek*. Amsterdam: Wouter Brave, 1795.

Walther, Johann Gottfried. *Musikalisches Lexikon, oder musikalische Bibliothek*. Leipzig: Deer, 1732; facs. ed. Kassel: Bärenreiter, 1953.

Zarlino, Gioseffo. *Sopplimenti musicali*. Venice: Fr. de' Franceschi, Sanese, 1588.

Zedler, Johann Heinrich. *Grosses vollständiges Universal-Lexicon*, 64 vols. Leipzig: Zedler, 1732−50.

II. Secondary sources.

Abraham, Gerald. "Union of Soviet Socialist Republics, §IX, 1, ii." *The New Grove* (q.v.) vol. 19, 381−82.

Adler, Guido. *Musikalische Werke der Kaiser Ferdinand III., Leopold I. und Joseph I.*. 2 vols. Vienna: Artaria, [1892−93].

Anderson, John Drummond. *Brass Scoring Techniques in the Symphonies of Mozart, Beethoven, and Brahms*. Ph.D. dissertation: George Peabody College for Teachers, 1960.

Anderson, Stephen C. "The Soloistic Use of the Alto and Tenor Trombones in the Choral Music of Franz Ignaz Tuma." *Journal of the International Trombone Association* 14 (Summer 1986), 48−53.

Antonicek, Theophil. "Ziani, Marc'Antonio." *The New Grove* (q.v.) vol. 20, 673−75.

Arnold, Denis. "Orchestras in Eighteenth-Century Venice." *The Galpin Society Journal* 19 (1966), 3−19.

Austin, Raymond. "The Moravian Trombone Choir." *The Instrumentalist*, December 1967, pp. 38−39.

Bach, Johann Sebastian. *Cantata No. 4: "Christ lag in Todesbanden"*. ed. Gerhard Herz. New York: Norton, 1967.

Badura-Skoda, Eva. "Reutter, (Johann Adam Joseph Karl Georg (von) (ii)." *The New Grove* (q.v.) vol. 15, 772−74.

Baines, Anthony. *Brass Instruments: Their History and Development*. New York: Scribner, 1978.

——. "James Talbot's Manuscript (Christ Church Library Music MS 1187) I. Wind Instruments." *The Galpin Society Journal* 1 (1948), 9−26.

——. "Trombone." *Grove's Dictionary of Music and Musicians* 5th ed., ed. Eric Blom, 9 vols. London: Macmillan, 1954, vol. 8, 552−59.

——. "Trombone." *The New Grove* (q.v.) vol. 19, 163−70.

——. "Trombone." *The New Oxford Companion to Music*. 2 vols. gen. ed. Denis Arnold. Oxford: Oxford University Press. 1983. vol. 2, 1851−55.

Banning, Helmut. *Johann Friedrich Doles, Leben und Werke.* Leipzig: Kistner & Siegel, 1939.

Bate, Philip. *The Trumpet and Trombone: An Outline of Their History. Development, and Construction.* 2d ed. London: Benn; New York: Norton: 1978.

"Beethoven's Use of Trombones." *The Musical Times* 45 (1904), 444.

Benton, Rita. *Ignace Pleyel: a Thematic Catalogue of His Compositions.* New York: Pendragon Press, 1977.

——. "Pleyel (i). (1) Ignace Joseph [Ignaz Josef] Pleyel." *The New Grove* (q.v.) vol. 15, 6–10.

Berlioz, Hector. *Gluck & His Operas, with an Account of Their Relation to Musical Art.* [ca. 1860] trans. Edwin Evans. London: Reeves, ca. 1914.

Bessaraboff, Nicholas. *Ancient European Musical Instruments.* Boston: Harvard University Press, 1941.

Blandford, Walter Fielding Holloway. "Handel's Horn and Trombone Parts." *The Musical Times* 80 (1939), 697ff, 746–7, 794; 81 (1940), 223.

Blom, Eric. "Vandenbroek, Othon." *The New Grove* (q.v.) 19, 519–20.

Brofsky, Howard. "Martini, Padre Giovanni Battista." *The New Grove* (q.v.) vol. 11, 723–25.

Brook, Barry S. *La symphonie française dans la second moitié du XVIIIe siècle.* 3 vols. Paris: Institute de musicologie de l'Université de Paris, 1962.

——. and Kafka, Barbara S. "Widerkehr [Wiederkehr, Viderkehr], Jacques (-Christian-Michel)." *The New Grove* (q.v.) vol. 20, 395.

Buelow, George J. "Majer, Johann Friedrich Bernhard Caspar." *The New Grove* (q.v.) vol. 11, 542–43.

——. "Mattheson, Johann." Ibid. vol. 11, 832–36.

——. "Niedt, Friedrich Erhard." Ibid. vol. 13, 222.

Carse, Adam. "Brass Instruments in the Orchestra." *Music & Letters* 3 (1922), 378–82.

——. *The History of Orchestration.* New York: Dutton, 1925.

——. *Musical Wind Instruments.* London: Macmillan, 1939; reprinted. New York: Da Capo Press, 1965.

Carse, Adam. *The Orchestra in the XVIIIth Century.* Cambridge: Heffer, 1940.

Charlton, David. *Orchestration and Orchestral Practice in Paris, 1789–1810.* Ph.D. dissertation: King's College, University of Cambridge, 1973.

Coover, James B. "Dictionaries and Encyclopedias of Music." *The New Grove* (q.v.) vol. 5, 430–59.

——. *Music Lexicography.* 3d ed., rev. and enlarged. Carlisle, Penn.: Carlisle Books, 1971.

Coerne, Louis Adolphe. *The Evolution of Modern Orchestration.* New York: Macmillan, 1908.

Cucuel, Georges. *Etudes sur un orchestre au 18me siècle*. Paris: Fischbacher, 1913.

Downs, Anneliese. "Beck, Franz [François] Ignaz." *The New Grove* (q.v.) vol. 2, 333–4.

Duckles, Vincent. *Music Reference and Research Materials*. 3d ed. New York: Free Press, 1974.

Dudley, Walter Sherwood. *Orchestration in the Musique d'harmonie of the French Revolution*. 2 vols. Ph.D. dissertation: University of California, Berkeley, 1968.

Dufrane, Louis. *Gossec: sa vie, ses oeuvres*. Paris: Fischbacher, 1929.

Eitner, Robert. *Biographisch-bibliographisches Quellen-Lexikon der Musiker und Musikgelehrten der christlichen Zeitrechnung bis zur Mitte des neunzehnten Jahrhunderts*. 11 vols. Leipzig: Breitkopf & Härtel, 1898–1904; facs ed. Graz: Akademische Druck, 1959.

Farmer, Henry George. *Memoirs of the Royal Artillery Band*. London: Boosey & Co., 1904.

——. *The Rise & Development of Military Music*. London: W. Reeves, [forward 1912].

Federhofer, Helmut. "Unbekannte Kirchenmusik von Johann Joseph Fux." *Kirchenmusikalisches Jahrbuch* 43 (1959), 113–54.

——, and Friedrich W. Reidel. "Quellenkundliche Beiträge zur Johann Joseph Fux-Forschung." *Archiv für Musikwissenschaft* 21 (1964), 111–40.

Fétis, François. *Biographie universelle des musiciens et bibliographie générale de la musique*. 2d ed. 8 vols. Paris: Firmin-Didot Frères, 1866–70; facs. ed., Brussels: Editions Culture et Civilization, 1972.

Fiske, Roger. *English Theatre Music in the Eighteenth Century*. London: Oxford University Press, 1973.

Forsyth, Cecil. *Orchestration*. London: Macmillan, 1914.

Freeman, Robert N. *Franz Schneider (1737–1812): A Thematic Catalogue of His Works*. New York: Pendragon, 1979.

Galpin, Francis William. "The Sackbut, Its Evolution and History." *Proceedings of the Royal Musical Association* 33 (1906–07), 2–25.

Gregory, Robin. *The Trombone: The Instrument and Its Music*. London: Faber and Faber, Ltd., 1973.

Grimm, Jacob and Wilhelm. *Deutsches Wörterbuch*. 16 vols. Leipzig: S. Hirzel, 1854–1960.

Guion, David M. "French Military Music and the Rebirth of the Trombone." *Journal of Band Research* 21 (Spring 1986), 31–35.

——. "The Instrumentation of Operas Published in France in the 18th Century." *Journal of Musicological Research* 4 (1982), 134–41.

——. "The Pitch of Baroque Trombones." *Journal of the International Trombone Association* 8 (1980), 24–28.

——. "The Seven Positions: Joseph Fröhlich's New Trombone Method." *Journal of the International Trombone Association* 14 (Spring 1986), 50–53.

Hailparn, Lydia. "Haydn: The Seven Last Words. A New Look at an Old Masterpiece." *The Music Review* 34 (1973), 1–21.

Hall, Harry H. "Early Sounds of Moravian Brass Music in America: A Cultural Note from Colonial Georgia." *Brass Quarterly* 7 (1964), 115–23.

———. *The Moravian Wind Ensemble: Distinctive Chapter in America's Music*. Ph.D. dissertation: George Peabody College for Teachers, 1967.

Heartz, Daniel. "*Orfeo ed Euridice*: Some Criticisms, Revisions, and Stage Realizations During Gluck's Lifetime." *Chigiana* 29–30 (n.s. 9–10) 1972–73), 383–94.

———. "Rousseau, Jean-Jacques." *The New Grove* (q.v.), vol. 16, 270–73.

Herbert, Trevor. *The Trombone in Britain before 1800*. Ph.D. dissertation; Open University, 1984.

Herrmann, Hildegard. *Thematisches Verzeichnis der Werke von Joseph Eybler*. Munich: Katzbichler, 1976.

Hind, Harold C. "The British Wind Band: A Brief Survey of Its Rise and Progress During Three Centuries." *Music Book* 7 (1952), 183–94.

———. "Military Band." *Grove's Dictionary of Music and Musicians*. 5th ed., ed. Eric Blom, 9 vols. London: Macmillan, 1954, vol. 5, 766–73.

Hoboken, Anthony van. *Joseph Haydn Thematisches-bibliographisches Werkverzeichnis*. Mainz: Schott, 1971.

Howey, Henry Eugene. *A Comprehensive Performance Project in Trombone Literature with an Essay Consisting of a Translation of Daniel Speer's "Vierfaches musikalisches Kleeblatt."* D. M. A. Essay: University of Iowa, 1971.

Jahn, Fritz. "Die Nürnberger Trompeten- und Posaunenmacher im 16. Jahrhundert." *Archiv für Musikwissenschaft* 7 (1925), 23–52.

Kade, Otto. *Die Musikalien-Sammlung des Grossherzoglich Mecklinburg-Schweriner Fürstenhauses aus den letzten zwei Jahrhunderten*. 2 vols. Wismar: Hinstorff'sche Hofbuchhandlung, 1893.

Kinsky, Georg. *Das Werk Beethovens: thematisches-bibliographisches Verzeichnis seiner sämtlichen vollendeten Kompositionen*. Munich: Henle, 1955.

Klafsky, Anton M. "Michael Haydn als Kirchenkomponist." *Studien zur Musikwissenschaft*. Beihefte der Denkmäler der Tonkunst in Oesterreich. vol. 3. ed. Guido Adler. Leipzig: Breitkopf & Härtel, 1915, 1–23.

———. "Thematischer Katalog der Kirchenmusik von Michael Haydn." *Denkmäler der Tonkunst in Oesterreich*, vol. 62. Vienna: Universal-Edition, 1925, v-xiii.

Klinka, Theodore. *The Choral Works of Franz Ignaz Tuma, with a Practical Edition of Selected Choral Works*. Ph.D. dissertation: University of Iowa, 1975.

Köchel, Ludwig Ritter von. *Chronologisch-thematisches Verzeichnis sämtlicher Tonwerke Wolfgang Amadeus Mozarts*. 6th ed., ed. Franz Giegling, Alexander Weinman, and Gerd Sievers. Wiesbaden: Breitkopf & Härtel, 1964.

———. *Johann Josef Fux, Hofcompositor und Hofkapellmeister der Kaiser Leopold I., Josef I, und Karl VI. von 1698 bis 1740*. Vienna: Alfred Hölder, 1872.

———, *Die Kaiserliche Hofmusikkapelle in Wien von 1543 bis 1867*. Vienna:

Beck'sche Universitätsbuchhandlung, 1869; facs. ed. Hildesheim: G.
    Olms, 1976.
Kurtz, Saul James. *A Study and Catalogue of Ensemble Music for
    Woodwinds Alone or with Brass from ca. 1700 to ca. 1825*. Ph.D.
    dissertation: University of Iowa, 1971.
Lajarte, Théodore de. "Introduction du trombone dans l'orchestre de
    l'Opéra." *La chronique musicale* 6 (Oct.–Dec. 1874), 75–79.
Landon, H. C. Robbins. *Haydn: Chronicle and Works*, Vol. 4. *Haydn: The
    Years of "The Creation," 1796–1800*. London: Thames and Hudson,
    1977.
Langwill, Lyndesay G. *An Index of Musical Wind-Instrument Makers*. 5th
    ed. Edinburgh: Langwill, 1977.
———. "Two Rare Eighteenth-Century London Directories." *Music &
    Letters* 30 (1949), 37–43.
La Rue, Jan, and Brofsky, Howard. "Parisian Brass Players, 1751–1793."
    Brass Quarterly 3 (1960), 133–40.
Lavoix, Henry. *Histoire d'instrumentation depuis le seizième siècle jusqu'á
    nos jours*. Paris: Firmin-Didot, 1878.
Leaman, Jerome. Notes to "Music of the Moravian Trombone Choir." Los
    Angeles: Crystal Records, 1976.
———. "The Trombone Choir of the Moravian Church." *Moravian Music
    Foundation Bulletin* 20 (1975), 2–7; reprinted *Journal of the International
    Trombone Association* 5 (1977), 44–48.
Lemaitre, George. *Beaumarchais*. New York: Knopf, 1949.
Libby, Dennis, and Rushton, Julian. "Piccinni, (1) Niccolò [Nicola]
    (Marcello Antonio Giacomo) Piccinni [Piccini]." *The New Grove* (q.v.)
    vol. 14, 723–28.
Liess, Andreas. *Johann Joseph Fux: ein steirischer Meister des Barock*.
    Vienna: Doblinger, 1948.
Loewenberg, Alfred. *Annals of Opera, 1597–1940*. 3d ed., revised and
    corrected. Totowa, N.J.: Rowman and Littlefield, 1978.
MacDonald, Robert James. *François-Joseph Gossec and French
    Instrumental Music in the Second Half of the Eighteenth Century*. 3 vols.
    Ph.D. dissertation: University of Michigan, 1968.
Mansfield, Orlando A. "Some Anomalies in Orchestral Accompaniments to
    Church Music." *The Musical Quarterly* 2 (1916). 208.
Marcuse, Sibyl. *A Survey of Musical Instruments*. New York: Harper &
    Row, 1975.
Maurer, Joseph A. "The Moravian Trombone Choir." *The Historical
    Review of Berks County* 20 (Oct.–Dec. 1954), 2–8.
McGowan, Margaret M. and Dobbins, Frank, "Louis XIV." *The New
    Grove* (q.v.) vol. 11, 254.
Merritt, Frederick. "La Borde [Laborde], Jean Benjamin (-François de,"
    The New Grove (q.v.) vol. 10, 342–43.

Miller, Robert Melvin. *The Concerto and Related Works for Low Brass: A Catalogue of Compositions from c. 1700 to the Present*. Ph.D. dissertation: Washington University, 1974.

Miller, Thomas Andrew. *An Investigation of Johann Sebastian Bach's Cantata 118 "O Jesu Christ meins* [sic] *Lebens Licht"*. D. M. A. Essay: University of Missouri, Kansas City, 1971, 1971.

Monter, Em. Mathieu de. "La musique et la société française aux XVIII^c siècle." *Revue et gazette musicale de Paris* 31 (1864) 329—30, 339—40, 348—49, 363—64, 370—71, 404—06, 411—12.

Montgomery, Jim, "The Use of the Trombone by G. F. Handel." *Journal of the International Trombone Association* 13 (July 1985), 32—34.

Mozart, Leopold. "Concerto für Trombone oder Viola und Orchester." Klavierauszug, ed. Alexander Weinmann. Zürich: Eulenberg, 1977.

Naylor, Tom. L. *The Trumpet & Trombone in Graphic Arts, 1500—1800*. Nashville, Tenn.: The Brass Press, 1979.

The New Encyclopaedia Britannica. 1975 ed.
   Micropaedia: "Grosses vollständiges Universal-Lexikon." "Rakóczi II, Farenc."
   Macropaedia: "France, History of: IV. France, 1717—1789" by Patrice Louis-Réné Higonnet and Albert M. Soubel.

The New Grove Dictionary of Music and Musicians. ed. Stanley Sadie, 20 vols. London: Macmillan, 1980.

Olleson, Edward. "Church Music and Oratorio." *The New Oxford History of Music* vol. 7 *The Age of Enlightenment, 1745—1790*. ed. Egon Wellesz and Frederick Sternfeld. London: Oxford University Press, 1973, 228—335.

Ossenkop, David. "Schubart, Christian Friedrich Daniel." *The New Grove* (q.v.) vol. 16, 750—51.

Panoff, Peter. *Militärmusik im Geschichte und Gegenwart*. Berlin: Karl Siegismund, 1938.

Perger, Lothar Herbert. "Thematisches Verzeichnis der Instrumentalwerke von Michael Haydn." *Denkmäler der Tonkunst in Oesterreich* vol. 29. Vienna: Artaria; Leipzig: Breitkopf & Härtel, 1907, xv-xxix.

Pfohl, Bernard J. *The Salem Band*. Winston-Salem, N. C.: Winston Printing Co., 1953.

Pierce, Terry. "The Trombone in the Eighteenth Century." *Journal of the International Trombone Association* 8 (1980), 6—10.

Pierre, Constant. *B. Sarrette et les origines du Conservatoire Nationale de Musique et de Déclamation. Paris: Delalain Prères, 1895*.

———. *Le Conservatoire Nationale de Musique et de Déclamation: documents historiques et administratifs, recueillis ou reconstitués*. Paris: Imprimérie nationale, 1900.

———. *Historie du Concert Spirituel: 1725—1790*. Paris! Société Française de Musicologie, 1975.

——. *Les Hymnes et chansons de la Révolution. Apercu général et catalogue avec notices historiques, analytiques et bibliographies*. Paris: Imprimérie nationale, 1904.

Pro'homme, Jacques-Gabriel. "Austro-German Musicians in France." *The Musical Quarterly* 15 (1929), 171–93.

Rasmussen, Mary. "Two Early Nineteenth-Century Trombone Virtuosi: Carl Traugott Queisser and Friedrich August Belcke." *Brass Quarterly* 5 (1961), 3–17.

Rendall, F. Geoffrey. *The Clarinet: Some Notes upon Its History and Construction* Ed ed., revised with additional material by Philip Bate. London: Benn; New York: Norton, 1971.

Répertoire international des sources musicales. series A: *Einzeldrucke vor 1800*. 9 vols., ed. Karlheinz Schlager and Otto Albrecht. Kassel: Bärenreiter, 1971–81.

Richardson, E. "Handel's Horn and Trombone Parts." *The Musical Times* 81 (1940), 180. [Letter in reply to Blandford's article, q.v.]

Riedinger, Lothar. "Karl von Dittersdorf als Opernkomponist." *Studien zur Musikwissenschaft: Beihefte der Denkmäler der Tonkunst in Oesterreich*. vol. 2. Leipzig: Breitkopf & Härtel; Vienna: Artaria, 1914, 212–349.

Riley, Maurice W. "A Tentative Bibliography of Early Wind Instrument Tutors." *Journal of Research in Music Education* 6 (1958), 3–24.

Roberts, Rosemary. "Speer, Daniel." *The New Grove* (q.v.) vol. 17, 821–23.

Robinson, Bradford. "Doles, Johann Friedrich." *The New Grove* (q.v.) vol. 5, 526–27.

Robinson, Michael F. "The 1774 S. Carlo Version of Gluck's *Orfeo*." *Chigiana* 29–30 (n.s. 9–10) (1972–73), 395–405.

Sartori, Claudio. *Bibliografia della musica strumentale stampata in Italia fino al 1700*. 2 vols. Florence: Olschki, 1952, 1968.

Schaefer, Jay Dee. "The Use of the Trombone in the 18th Century." *The Instrumentalist*, April 1968, pp. 51–53; May 1968, pp 100–02; June 1968, pp. 61–63.

Schering, Arnold. "Die Leipziger Ratsmusik von 1650 bis 1775." *Archiv für Musikwissenschaft* 3 (1921), 17–53.

Schmieder, Wolfgang. *Thematisch-systematisches Verzeichnis der musikalischen Werke von Johann Sebastian Bach. Bach-Werke-Verzeichnis (BWV)*. Leipzig: Breitkopf & Härtel, 1950.

Scholes, Percy. *The Great Dr. Burney*. 2 vols. London: Oxford University Press, 1948.

——. "Trombone Family." *The Oxford Companion to Music*. 10th ed., ed. John Owen Ward. London: Oxford University Press, 1970, 1044–47.

Schreiber, Ottmar. *Orchester und Orchesterpraxis in Deutschland zwischen 1780 und 1850*. Berlin: Junker und Dünnhaupt, 1938.

Schwarz, Boris. *French Instrumental Music between the Revolutions (1789 to 1830)*. Ph.D. dissertation: Columbia University, 1950.

Sehnal, Jiří. "Das Musikinventar des Olmützer Bischof Leopold Egk aus dem Jahre 1760 als Quelle vorklassischer Instrumentalmusik." *Archiv für Musikwissenschaft* 29 (1972), 285–317.

Senn, Walter. "Zum vorliegenden Band." *Neue Mozart Ausgabe.* Serie I: *Geistliche Gesangwerke*, Werkgruppe 1: *Messen und Requiem*, Abteilung I: Messen, Band 1. Kassel: Bärenreiter, 1968.

Selfridge-Field, Eleanor. *Venetian Instrumental Music from Gabrieli to Vivaldi.* New York: Praeger, 1975.

Sluchin, Benny. "The Trombone in the Sacred Works of W. A. Mozart." *Brass Bulletin* no. 46 (1984), 31–35.

Somfai, László. "Albrechtsberger-Eigenschriften in der National-bibliothek Szechenyi, Budapest." *Studia musicologica* 1 (1961), 175–202; 4 (1963), 179–90; 9 (1967), 191–220.

Soyer, M. A. "De l'orchestration militaire et de son histoire." *Encyclopédie de la musique et dictionnaire du Conservatoire.* pt. 2: *Technique--Esthétique-Pédagogie.* Vol 4 *Orchestration--Musique liturgique des différents cults.* Ed. Albert Lavignac and Lionel de la Laurencie. Paris: Delagrave, 1929, 2135–2214.

Steinmetz, Paul. "German Church Music." *The New Oxford History of Music* vol. 5: *Opera and Church Music.* ed. Anthony Lewis and Nigel Fortune. London: Oxford University Press, 1975, 557–775.

Stieger, Franz. *Opern Lexikon.* 11 vols. Tutzing: Hans Schneider, 1975–83.

Swanzy, David P. *The Wind Ensemble and Its Music During the French Revolution (1789–1795).* Ph.D. dissertation: Michigan State University, 1966.

The Symphony, 1720–1840. Barry S. Brook, ed. in chief. Series F, Vol. III: *The Symphony in Sweden*, pt. 2. ed. Bertil van Boer, Jr. New York: Garland, 1983.

Temperley, Nicholas. "Tans'ur, William." *The New Grove* (q.v.) vol. 18, 566–67.

Terry, Charles Sanford. *Bach's Orchestra.* London: Oxford University Press, 1932.

Thomas, T. Donley. "Michael Haydn's 'Trombone' Symphony." *Brass Quarterly* 6 (1962), 3–8.

Tyson, Alan. "The 1803 Version of Beethoven's *Christus am Oelberge.*" *The Musical Quarterly* 56 (1970), 551–84.

Wattenbarger, James Albert. *The Turmmusik of Johann Pezel.* Ph.D. dissertation: Northwestern University, 1957.

Weiner, Howard. "The Trombone: Changing Times, Changing Slide Positions." *Brass Bulletin* no. 36 (1981), 52–63.

Whitwell, David. *Band Music of the French Revolution.* Tutzing: Hans Schneider, 1979.

——. "Early Brass Manuscripts in Vienna." *The Instrumentalist*, December 1970, pp. 36–37.

Wigness, C. Robert. *The Soloistic Use of the Trombone in Eighteenth-*

Century Vienna. D.M.A. Essay, University of Iowa, 1970; Nashville, Tenn.: Brass Press, 1978.

Williams, Jeffrey Price. *The Trombone in German and Austrian Concerted Church Music*. D.M.A. Essay: North Texas State University, 1974.

Wörthmüller, Willi. "Die Nürnberger Trompeten- und Posaunenmacher des 17. und 18. Jahrhunderts." *Mitteilungen des Vereins für Geschichte der Stadt Nürnberg* 46 (1955), 372–480.

Young, Percy M. *The Concert Tradition from the Middle Ages to the Twentieth Century*. London: Routledge and Kegan Paul, 1965.

Young, Robert. *Analytical Concordance to the Bible*. 22d American ed., rev. William B. Stevenson. Grand Rapids, Mich.: Eerdmans, [1951].

GENERAL INDEX

INDEX OF MUSIC WITH TROMBONE PARTS

329

61,922